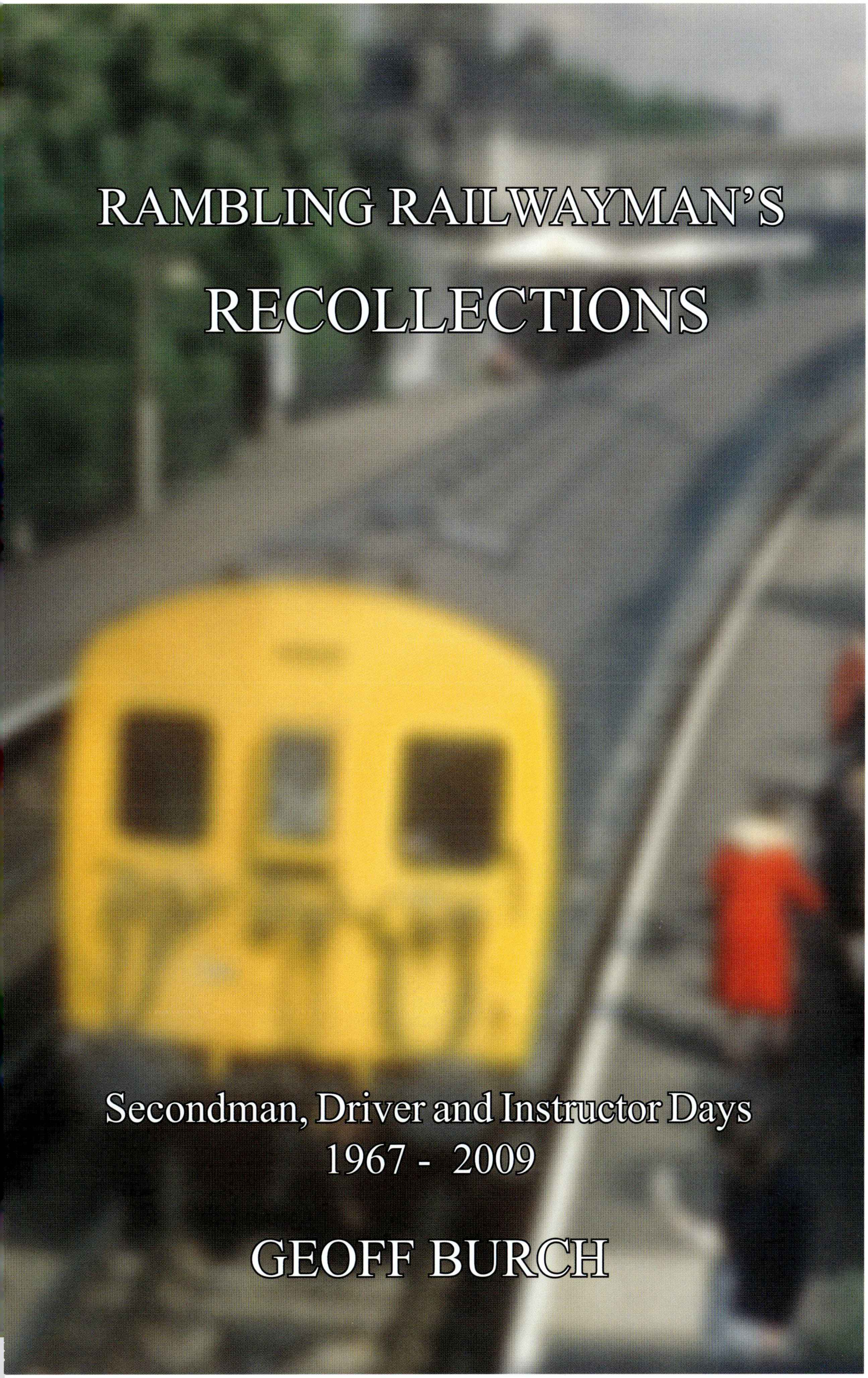

RAMBLING RAILWAYMAN'S RECOLLECTIONS

Secondman, Driver and Instructor Days
1967 - 2009

GEOFF BURCH

Acknowledgements

Again I'm eternally grateful to the many people that have assisted me in the creation of this book as without their help, it would never have been possible.

In particular, I'd like to thank my old work chums: David Timothy, Pat Kinsella, Alex 'Mac' McClymont, Chris Lemon, Ian Verrinder, Brian Cook, Mick Oakley and Fred Johnson for their invaluable help and for also re-living some of the experiences we had together in those days.

As well as those mentioned above, I'd also like to thank everyone below for their help and generosity in allowing me to use images from their splendid photographic collections, namely:

Nick Catford, Charlie Hampshire, John Scrace, David Rose, Alex McClymont, Alan Edwards, Steve West, Ian Docwra, Mike Morant, Jeffrey Lloyd, Gordon Edgar, Hugh Llewellyn, Ernie Brack, Julie Hogben, Bob Hind, Steve Poole, Pete Beyer, Andy Gibb, George Woods, David Hird Kevin Lane, Alec Swain, Jack Hills, David Hayes, Stacey Harris, Michael Thorne, David Ingham, Stuart Ray, Pat Kinsella, Nick Waite, Tony Watson, Adrian Nicholls, Adrian Pink, Kevin Cooke, Martin Loader, Timothy Saunders, David Mant, Tony Watson, Martin Addison, Damon Hart-Davis, Hassocks 5489, Chris Lemon, Matthew Taylor, Tony Callaghan, Michael Thorne, David Timothy, Ben Brooksbank, Network Rail, Edgepedia, Ivor the Driver, Eduard Marmet, Gary Blyth, Brian Cook, Janderk1968, SWT & Island Line Trains, Mike Knell, David Christie, Richard Sulzmann, John Simpkins, Leigh Darnton and Richard S Greenwood MBE.

I'd also like to thank David Hey for all his help and encouragement and Marc Sellis for allowing me to use extracts from SWTs training material.

Also a special thanks to David Timothy, Brian Cook and Pat Kinsella whom I gave the unenviable task of proof reading the final draft of this book.

Finally, I would like to thank my wife Pauline for putting up with my trials and tribulations over the years of being a railwayman working shift work.

After his retirement, my old regular Driver Stan Harms sent us a Christmas card in which was written "Pauline, you withstand your life's burden with magnificent fortitude."

Below: Class 33/1 No. 33118 in charge of the 10.45 Waterloo to Salisbury, and on to Exeter as semi-fast, near Pirbright Junction comprising two 4TC units on 4th April 1984.

Photo: Gordon Edgar.

Contents

Page No.

Secondman Days at Woking MT	*1*
Passed Secondman Days at Woking MT	*29*
Driving Days at Effingham Junction	*67*
Driving Days at Woking MT	*83*
Instructor Days at OTC South Side Waterloo	*149*
Surrey Police Days	*213*
Trainer Days at South West Trains	*227*
Epilogue	*287*

Published by Geoff Burch

Printed by Craddocks Print Solutions
Great George Street, Godalming, Surrey GU7 1EE

ISBN: 978-0-9567967-6-9

Above: 2HAL 2651 leaves Woking with a Guildford - Waterloo stopping service in the late 1960s.

Photo: Les Mills - Phyllis Mills Collection.

Below: Woking in Winter.

Photo: The Author's Collection.

Front Cover: 4BUF 'Nelson' 3077 forms the front part of a Reading and Guildford - Waterloo service at Ascot on 5th December 1970 - Class 159/1 'Sprinter' 159104 leaves Waterloo with a Salisbury service in July 2008 - Class 73/2 electro-diesel 73235 Cab Controls - Route Learning Assessment - Hampton Court Junction. Photos: Gordon Edgar and the Author's Collection,

Rear Cover - Above: 4COR and 4BUF 'Nelson' units 3123 and 3081 leave Guildford with a Portsmouth - Waterloo fast service on 18th July 1970 - Photo: Gordon Edgar. Below: Driver Neil Larby during Class 73 Training between Poole and Eastleigh - 2007. Photo: the Author's Collection.

About the Author

I was born in Guildford on 5th March 1946 and was educated at Worplesdon Primary School and Northmead Secondary School for Boys. Starting work at the tender age of 15 as an Engine Cleaner at Guildford Motive Power Depot on the 4th April 1961, I graduated to become a Fireman on the 9th April 1962.

During my career as a Fireman from 1962 - 1967, I was fortunate enough to have been given the opportunity to fire to an incredible variety of Drivers and Southern steam locomotives ranging from Drummond M7 tank engines to Bulleid's Merchant Navy Class Pacifics. I was also a fireman on one of the last locomotives to leave Guildford Motive Power Depot when it closed on Sunday 9th July 1967.

The following day, I transferred to Woking Mixed Traction Depot as a Secondman and after successfully passing the Driver's Rules, EMUT and Diesel Locomotive Traction Driving examinations in 1969, I remained at Woking as a Passed Secondman.

However, in order to progress to Driver status, I applied for a Driver vacancy at Effingham Junction and moved there on the 11th December 1972.

Utilising an 8b move, I then moved back to Woking as a Driver in January 1974 and attended the Training School at Waterloo for a Class 47 course.

I remained at Woking Mixed Traction Depot until 1987 when I was selected to become an Acting Instructor at the Operations Training Centre, Waterloo, making this a permanent position in October 1988.

In August 1989, I was promoted to Senior Instructor (Mixed Traction) and held that post until 1994. On the advice of the Adam Smith Institute, under John Major's Conservative government's Railways Act 1993, British Rail (BR) was split up and privatised so I decided to take voluntary severance after a railway career spanning 33 years.

My next 'Career' was with Surrey Police working in their new Computer Based Training Department and in the following 11 years held the posts of Training Officer, Computer Trainer, Communications Trainer, Assessor / Evaluator, Quality Officer, Data Manager, and finally, Business Development Analyst.

I still kept in contact with my railway colleagues and in 2004, I was 'persuaded' to re-join the railway industry as an Operations Trainer at the South West Trains Operations Training Centre at Basingstoke.

The following year I took on the role of Assistant Operations & Safety Training Manager and then in 2008, I was appointed as their Training Design Manager, finishing my railway career in February 2009.

As well as keeping busy writing books and conducting talks / presentations about my railway life, I continue with my passion for photography and amongst other work, perform photographic duties for Network Rail and Stagecoach South Western Trains Limited.

Foreword by Ian Verrinder - Eurostar Operations Standards Manager.

I joined the railway in 1980; the days of Margaret Thatcher, the Falkland Islands war and national strikes. Although I didn't realise it at the time, this was a railway still coming to terms with the end of steam. I joined the 'line of promotion', as those in the driving fraternity called it, straight from school, aged 16. The men I came in contact with were largely ex-steam men and they were immensely proud of it. My outlook, and those of my generation, was diesel. The steam men tolerated the diesel age but their memories were tied to coal and water.

Looking back on the first ten years of my railway career, I now appreciate what a fantastic upbringing it was. I experienced a wide variety of people; the good, the bad and downright ugly! The humour of the mess room gave me a back catalogue of comic material, sayings and anecdotes that have stood me in good stead ever since. I listened to some genuinely thoughtful and intelligent discussions from men with no academic qualifications, yet who, to my mind, had more about them than many of the managers that I subsequently met later on in my career. This was also a time when a youngster could receive a thorough grounding in practical railway work. We worked with diesel and third rail electric locomotives on freight, ballast and passenger trains. Braking was by vacuum or air; and the air brake sometimes included the dreaded (by some people) triple valves! Then there was the coupling locomotives in multiple, loose shunting and the very occasional steam heat boiler to contend with.

Geoff Burch was one of the drivers with whom I rubbed shoulders in the formative years of my railway career. He was, in railway terms, 18 years my senior and this made him one of the 'steam men'. I being one of the 'second men', was not exactly at the top table of the depot. Nevertheless, men like Geoff always treated the younger 'second men' with friendliness. Life long friendships developed, which survive to this day. As the years went by, the men I grew up with gradually went their separate ways; Geoff to the training school (and I to follow some years later), others moved depots and many just retired. Inexorably, that peculiar mix of ex-steam men and young 'second men' just faded away; never again to play cards around the mess room table or to work 'spoil' trains to Farnham tip.

When Geoff decided to write a book about his railway reminiscences, it was always going to centre on his first love; 'the steam'. A second book followed, such was the interest from enthusiasts and the wealth of material available to him. Both books have proved popular and deservedly so. Nevertheless, I always felt there was another important chapter to be written and I pestered him to write it; this book represents the culmination of this idea. It covers the period from the end of steam, through the 'blue' diesel era to privatisation and beyond. The array of previously unpublished photographs alone should make the book a 'must have'. Yet it is the description of a time that has now passed, which will endear it to railwaymen and enthusiasts alike. The post-steam period is often neglected in favour of the more aesthetically pleasing era that preceded it. Personally, I'm glad Geoff has produced a book that is able to redress this imbalance.

Above: Eurostar Operations Standards Manager Ian Verrinder stands alongside Class 373 3223 before leaving Brussels for London Waterloo.

Photo: The Author's Collection.

Introduction

Monday 10th July 1967 brought on a whole new meaning to my railway career. Instead of travelling to Guildford, I had to make my way to Woking where most of the men at Guildford had also transferred. While we were still at Guildford, the Woking Motormen's mess room was only the bottom area of the building; the upstairs hadn't been extended into the mess room until it was decided that Guildford steam men were going to be moved en-bloc to Woking.

There were conflicting reports leading up to closure of Guildford shed including those from the A.S.L.E & F. union about the move; some reports were to the effect that we were all going to be made redundant and would have to apply for positions throughout the industry. After a meeting in the old Labour club at Guildford, the impression was that the union wasn't too sure about what was happening and cared even less to be honest.

Anyway, the Woking drivers' mess room was extended ready for our arrival. The original mess room had a locked up timber cupboard containing cups, plates and cutlery; the door being secured by an 'S key' lock. There was a lot of animosity between the original motormen and the mixed traction men, some of which was understandable because some of our number would deliberately annoy them; flashing their payslips showing earnings nearly twice as much as motormen.

Originally, the lockers provided were standing directly on the floor and when 'Hovermop' (as Alex McClymont christened Frank Mitchell) swilled his mop round the floor, the dirty water would slosh inside the doors of the bottom lockers.

A plinth was later placed under the lockers to keep them about 3 inches off the floor.

There wasn't a television until later, just a radio on the small windowsill on the top deck. Pat Kinsella remembers a Reading driver, threatening to throw it down the stairs during one altercation!

Some of the Running Foremen at that time were: Charlie Cook, Derek Hayter, Harry Harvey, Arthur Vodden, Frank Warren and Frank Chudley. There were also a number of Acting Running Foremen namely Bernie Gray, Doug Stent, Roy Vigars, Vic Pratt, Ray Beeson, John Berriman and John Carter. Non-clerical staff: Claude Johns and Steve Burke.

Although I was still classed as a fireman, (later to be renamed secondman), the duties performed were of an entirely different nature to the sweat and grime of the footplate. I still had another two years before I was eligible to take my driving exams so had to be content to ride as secondman on a variety of mixed-traction duties and learn my apprenticeship so to speak.

Most of the drivers that had transferred to Woking had already learnt the relevant traction types, the main freight and ballast work being performed by Type 3 'Crompton' 1550hp diesel-electric locomotives and the JA & JB type 1600-600hp electro-diesel locomotives. Other duties involved riding secondman on the 350hp diesel-electric shunter at Woking Up & Down Yards, Brush Type 4 diesel-electric locomotives, HB electro-diesel locomotives and on various EMU duties allocated to the depot.

I begin my story at Woking MT on Monday 10th July 1967........

Above: 'Hovermop' Frank Mitchell.

Photo: Steve West Collection.

Above: Non-clerical Timekeeper Claude Johns '64519'.

Photo: Alex McClymont.

Monday 10th July 1967 had arrived and I made my way to Woking where I was going to start on my new career. My mode of transport at that time was a 500cc 'Tiger 100' motorcycle that I'd bought earlier that year from Pascall's Cycle & Motorcyles, Woodbridge Road, Guildford.

Above: 500cc Triumph Tiger 100 - The Author's mode of transport in 1968.

Photo: The Author's Collection.

As mentioned in my introduction, the type of work that I would be doing would be completely different from what I'd been used to, although I had already acted as a secondman on a number of running turns before the end of steam, so had a good idea of what was expected of me.

All of the freight and ballast work would now be worked by diesel traction and at that time, quite a number of goods yards were still in operation. We also had several passenger turns; some over the Reading - Redhill line which were quite enjoyable.

The depot also had a number of stone train turns from Woking Yard to either Three Bridges Yard, Tonbridge Yard or sometimes New Cross Gate Yard. We also worked the stone train empties to Salisbury and as before in the steam days, I never tired of working to this location.

I kept a diary of notable experiences that happened at work but unfortunately, some diaries (including that of 1967) were lost during my moving house in 1969, so my experiences will have to start from January 1968.

On 4th January, I had a Waterloo Depot 'On Loan' job. It entailed going 'pass' from Woking to Wimbledon and I met my Driver (Clive Groome) at Wimbledon West Yard. I'd seen Clive around at Nine Elms and Waterloo during my earlier days on the steam and we exchanged pleasantries and climbed aboard our 'steed' for the day, a 350hp shunting diesel. After making up our train, we proceeded into Wimbledon station and worked the train round the single line to Merton Abbey where we took a diversion to the Lines Brothers' Tri-ang toy factory. We left some wagons and then travelled at slow speed to the very end of the siding which at one time connected to the main line at Tooting Junction.

Clive then suggested that it was time for a break so after shutting down the diesel engine and securing the loco, we then visited a pub for a pint followed by some fish and chips and because we had some time on our hands, visited the local ABC Cinema to see a rather risqué film (in those days) called 'Seventeen'. We then took the 350hp diesel back to Wimbledon West Yard and I made my way back to Woking.

Below: Tooting with the disused Merton Abbey branch platform on the right (1968). The stop block is exactly the place where we left the 350hp shunter.

Photo: Nick Catford Collection.

Above: A 4EPB unit heads towards Tooting station in 1968 - the old platforms can be seen in the foreground.

Below: A view looking west showing the old platforms and what remains of the sidings in 1974.

Photos: Nick Catford Collection.

Some of the other duties performed in January 1968. Entries in my 1968 diary and typical work was as follows:

Saturday 6th

Signed on at 10.24 and worked with Drivers Eddie Green and Ted Harper working a freight from Aldershot Yard - Redhill Yard and return light engine to Woking.

Monday 8th

Changed turns with Peter Butter and worked a stone train from Woking Yard to New Cross Gate and return with Driver Ted Sharp.

Tuesday, Wednesday, Thursday 9th, 10th & 11th

07.50 Spare

Monday 15th

04.00 Spare

Went Malcolm Peto's turn with Driver Pat Kinsella - Guildford - Wokingham freight.

Tuesday 16th

02.00 Spare

Went with Driver Doug Stent, pass by taxi to Sunbury and relieve Waterloo men on site. Once work was completed, work a ballast train to Woking Yard.

Wednesday, Thursday 17th & 18th

02.00 Spare (went in overnight). Worked a freight to Basingstoke with Driver Doug Stent.

Friday 19th

02.00 Spare (went in overnight). Pass by taxi to Horsley with Driver Allen Gaff. Return Ballast train to Woking Yard when work completed.

Saturday 20th

02.00 Spare (went in overnight). Worked 05.20 Vans to Farnham with Driver Terry Butwell.

Sunday 21st

Booked on 05.00. Pass by taxi to Guildford with Driver Eddie Wells and relieved another Woking crew on a Ballast. On completion work the train to Feltham and home pass.

Monday 22nd Booked on 07:00 Pass to Eastleigh with Driver Bill Brain and work a banana train to Feltham Yard and home pass.

Tuesday, Wednesday, Thursday 23rd, 24th & 25th

08.00 Spare.

Friday 26th Rest Day Off

Saturday 27th Signed on 08.00 and worked a stone train to Three Bridges and return empties with Driver Bernie Gray.

Monday 29th

08.00 Spare. Went with Driver Jimmy Luff light engine to Feltham for repairs and back light engine.

Tuesday 30th, Wednesday 31st

Signed on at 08.57. Pass to Farnham and work a test train to Alton with Driver John Berriman on the first day and Driver Jim Parker on the second day. This was a prototype of locomotives that had originally been an electric locomotive only (HA Class). They had been stripped of their booster and fitted with an auxiliary Paxman diesel engine so the locomotive could be used in non-electrified areas. They would primarily be used for boat train workings between Waterloo and Southampton Docks and also Weymouth Quay.

Below: HB Class E6102 with the test train at Alton on the 31st January 1968. On the platform next to the loco are Instructor Terry Smith and Divisional Inspector Bill Neal and a CM&EE technician is in the cab.
Rebuilt at Crewe from original Class HA locomotives, they were numbered E6101-E6110. Later, they were renumbered as Class 74 (74001-74010) under the TOPS system.

Photo: The Author's Collection.

Secondman Days - Woking MT

And so the months went by and the turns were as much the same as the ones I've listed in January. Exceptions were working boat trains from Waterloo to Southampton Docks with Driver Charlie Hampshire on 9th April and Driver Bernie Gray on 19th April. On both of these days, the trains being hauled by 1550hp Type 3 'Crompton' locomotives.

However, one week in May 1968 was quite notable. The turn of duty entailed signing on at 22. 24 and going pass to Guildford and then working a van train to Reading. After our break at Reading, we would then walk down to Reading West Yard and wait for the 'Tavi' (a train from Tavistock that arrived around 04.00) and work the train to Feltham Yard and then home pass. On the Monday, my driver was Ted Wells and for the rest of the week (except for Thursday when Driver Ben Ringer was booked the turn) my Driver was Len Boxall. On arrival at Reading and after being relieved, we'd have our PN break in the railway canteen which was open all night. Len and I spoke to the chef during the week and asked him if it would be possible for him to supply us with steak and chips on the Friday night and this he duly did!

Above: Charlie Hampshire in charge of a 1550hp Type 3 'Crompton'.

Photo: Charlie Hampshire Collection.

Below: Type 3 1550hp 'Crompton' 33037 at platform 9 at Reading on 5th December 1985.

Photo: David Hird.

By this time, I had exchanged my 35mm Ilford Sportsman camera for a Practica 1b SLR (single lens reflex) with a 50mm 2.8 Tessar lens which gave me the added flexibility of changing to a telephoto lens when necessary.

I'd also bought a 70-200mm zoom lens and remember taking it with me one day when working a stone train to Three Bridges Yard with Driver Lew Wooldridge and taking photographs of the planes coming into Gatwick Airport as we were standing under the flightpath. Another photograph I took that day was of the cottages that border the limestone cliffs on the approach to Betchworth (following page).

On the 2nd June 1968, I went on a flight myself from Fairoaks airport, Chobham in an Auster light-aircraft and it was then that I took the photo of Guildford Loco that featured in my first book (also featured again on the following page).

Left: Mirror image of the Author testing the Practica 1b.

Below: BEA Airtours De Haviland DH.106 Comet 4B Registration G-ARJK on a landing approach at Gatwick Airport on 2nd February 1968.

Photos: Author's Collection.

Above: The cottages below the chalk cliffs at Betchworth in February 1968. Photo taken from the cab whilst working a stone train from Woking Yard to Three Bridges on 2nd February 1968.

Below: Guildford Loco - Photo taken from an Auster light-aircraft on 2nd June 1968.

Photos: Author's Collection.

Tuesday 4th June

My driver, Charlie Hampshire and I booked on at 21.55 and took a 'Crompton' light engine to Buriton Sidings (just outside Buriton tunnel) where we picked up an engineer's train. The object of the exercise was for us to place the train in Buriton tunnel while the workmen re-pointed the brickwork with a specially-nozzled cement gun. After placing the train in the tunnel, we then unhooked the loco and dropped back outside the tunnel portal, otherwise the fumes from the diesel engine exhaust would have suffocated the workmen. In the morning when the work was completed, we picked up the train, placed it back in Buriton Siding and then took the loco back light engine to Woking and berth.

Tuesday 11th June

The following week I was booked early turn - well you couldn't get much earlier - 02.30 on the Monday going pass by taxi to Feltham, relieving on-site on a ballast train and working back to Woking Yard.

Wednesday 12th June

Booked on 02.30 Spare and ended up going to Basingstoke with Driver Pat Kinsella on the 'juice'.

The rest of the week I booked on at 01.20 to work a stone train from Woking Yard to Tonbridge and back with the empties with Driver Denis Copus. As mentioned in my first book, it was always a pleasure to be booked with Denis no matter what time of day or night.

The following weeks it seemed that all I was doing was

working a very early turn or very late turn; usually going by taxi to various locations to relieve other crews on ballast trains.

Wednesday 24th July

Driver Charlie Hampshire and I booked on at 03.00 and made our way by taxi to Petersfield where we relieved a Woking crew within an occupied possession between Petersfield and Buriton tunnel. A ballast cleaner was working on the adjacent track and after the wagons of our train had been loaded, we then worked the train to Basingstoke via Havant and Netley. I was doing the driving and on approaching Havant's home signal, the signal suddenly went back to danger. So as not to give the guard a 'rough shunt', I had the presence of mind to 'buffer the train up' with the straight air brake before using the emergency brake to stop the train. With so much weight in the train, it was impossible to stop before meeting the converging line from Brighton and ended up near to the signal box. The signalman then appeared to apologise profusely admitting that he'd placed the home signal to danger too early, which was a bit of a relief!

In August, I had another week of very early turns with Driver Ben Ringer. Booking on at 00.25 we worked a van train to Clapham Junction, went light to Feltham Yard, worked a freight to Eastleigh Yard and home pass.

Top: Driver Charlie Hampshire in Woking Mess Room.

Above: Driver Fred 'Ben' Ringer in Woking Mess Room.

Left: Driver Denis Copus at Woking - a legend and an absolute pleasure to be in his company.

Photos: Alex 'Mac' McClymont.

Above: Four types of motive power at Guildford in 1968.

From left to right: On platform 5, the rear unit of a Portsmouth - Waterloo express formed of 4COR 3126. On platform 4 displaying a 73 headcode and forming the front part of a Waterloo - Portsmouth & Southsea stopping service is 2BIL 2086.

On platform 3, 2BIL 2152 forms the rear part of a stopping service from Guildford to Waterloo via Woking and finally on platform 2 displaying headcode 55, an unidentified 1550hp type 3 'Crompton' leaves with a parcels train to Redhill.

Photo: John Scrace.

Secondman Days - Woking MT

On Sunday 11th August 1968, Driver Ben Ringer and I booked on at 00.25 and went pass to Waterloo by taxi and then worked the 03.40 paper train to Woking. I didn't bother going to bed when I got home and instead went to Brands Hatch with some friends to see the 'Hutchinson 100' motorcycle racing (where they race round the circuit in reverse). My hero, Mike 'The Bike' Hailwood dominated the main races and I took my Practica SLR along loaded with some fast speed Anscochrome film to capture the action. When I got home having not slept for 30 hours, I slept like a log!

Below: The start of the 'Hutchinson 100' International race where the competitors race around Brands Hatch short circuit in reverse!

Bottom: Mike 'The Bike' Hailwood riding the Honda Six plays 'cat and mouse' with rival Phil Read.

Photos: The Author's Collection.

Above: This photo of 1600/600hp electro-diesel E6013 was taken at Guildford Up Yard Carriage Sidings and was crewed by Driver Mick Sparrow and fireman Allen Mansbridge. The collector shoes are down on the conductor (juice) rail and the crew are waiting to work a freight from Guildford Up Yard to Feltham Yard.

The 600hp diesel engine would be used in non-electrified areas (or in yards or sidings) and once regaining the main line, the conductor shoes would be lowered onto the conductor rail and electric power employed. Six prototypes (JA) of this class were originally built in 1962 with slight differences and were painted green.

They were a tremendous success and a further 43 locomotives were built numbered E6007-E6039 (JB) painted blue.
In the background, several 2BIL units are also berthed in the Up Yard Carriage Siding awaiting duties on the evening rush hour service to Ascot.

Photo: Alex 'Mac' McClymont.

A couple of weeks later, I was booked along with Driver Vic Pratt, signing on at 20.43 and working a double trip from Guildford Yard to Feltham and return. We were booked together all week. The duty was usually worked by a JB Type 1600/600 hp electro-diesel locomotive. Vic was pretty conversant with the controls of this type of locomotive but other drivers that I'd been with didn't have a clue how to work the locomotive, especially on electric power. Some wouldn't even shut the diesel engine down for fear of not being able to re-start it and would perform the whole trip to Feltham and return using diesel power only. They were also in constant fear of knocking the collector shoes off when going into a non-electrified siding and to save embarrassment, some drivers would rather let you do the driving instead!

The following week, in September, I was again booked along with Vic Pratt; this time on an early turn, booking on at 00.25 and working a freight from Woking to Feltham and return freight to Aldershot.

Aldershot at that time was still handling a huge amount of freight traffic. Apart from the busy goods yard, it handled quite a lot of MOD traffic from Aldershot Government Sidings.

Above: The complex electric / diesel controller arrangement of a JB type (Class 73) electro-diesel locomotive.

Photo: Courtesy of South West Trains.

Secondman Days - Woking MT

Heavy rain began to fall on the night of Saturday 14th September 1968, continuing unabated the next day. Guildford was the worst hit place, as water began seeping into homes and premises beside the River Wey near the town centre.

By the Monday (16th September), murky flood water had reached six feet in places, pouring into more homes, businesses and shops (such as Plummers in Millbrook), into St Nicolas Church and the Yvonne Arnaud Theatre, causing thousands of pounds worth of damage.

Roads were blocked in and out of the town and a number of stricken householders had to be rescued by boat.

The store Plummers was badly hit. Opened only a year before, flood water filled the whole of the basement, while the ground floor was flooded to a height of three feet. Guildford fire brigade pumped out five million gallons of water from the basement. Much stock was ruined, including everything in the food hall.

Alderman R. M. Hardy, who owned a men's outfitters in Friary Street, estimated that he had lost £10,000 of stock – and he was not insured against floods. He was soon selling flood-damaged goods, with shirts being offered at five shillings each.

Nearly £15,000 damage had been done at Court Bros furnishing store on the corner of Millbrook and the High Street. The manager had boated in through a broken window to see furniture and crockery floating about, wallpaper peeling off, rolls of wet carpet and everything covered in a layer of silt.

When water began to lap round the vestry door of St Nicolas Church near the Town Bridge, the rector, the Rev. W. Goddard, and helpers, moved vestments onto the high altar. However, when it was realised that the water was getting higher, valuable items, including a 17th Century chalice, were taken out to a boat moored by the churchyard wall and ferried to safety. The rector described witnessing a small tidal wave going down the nave.

Early on the Monday morning, staff at the Yvonne Arnaud Theatre were able to move scenery from the stage to safety. Then the waters rose and completely covered the stage and about 100 seats in the auditorium. It receded the next day, but much damage had been done.

Above Top: Walnut Tree Close.

Middle: The High Street Bridge.

Left: The arch in Friary St.

Above: River Wey looking towards Plummers and floating coffee table!

Text reproduced with kind permission from David Rose.

Photos: Alan Edwards Collection.

At Billings, the printers, in Walnut Tree Close, all its bound stock, flat sheets and printed white paper had to be thrown out. By the Wednesday afternoon, the pile of rubbish outside had grown to about 20 yards long by 10 feet wide.

There was no shortage of willing volunteers who helped with the clear-up operation. These included girls from the Women's Royal Army Corps Camp at Stoughton, the Red Cross, the Women's Royal Voluntary Service and local scouts and guides. The town clerk, Herbert Weller, said that the first task was to clean and dry the 150 flooded homes.

Supt. J. M. Packham of Guildford police said that the floods became an emergency on the Sunday when it was found that within a short time the main roads to London would be blocked. These included the A3 at Send, the A321 at Worplesdon and the A320 at Jacobs Well. Traffic converged at the AA roundabout at the top of Stoke Park, and although there was floodwater there, the road was passable, but it was very congested.

The police had several calls to evacuate people from houses along the River Wey. They were rescued in police and army inflatable dinghies and taken to Sandfield Terrace Drill Hall, where at one time, 250 people were accommodated.

At his home in Guildford, amateur meteorologist Dennis Mullen recorded 3.75 inches of rain on the Sunday. A water board spokesman said that statistically the scale of the flood could only happen once in 1,000 years.

A fund was set up to help those who had suffered and the mayor urged people who had not been affected to contribute.

The High Street was closed to through traffic on the Sunday night and the Monday, when the flood water was at its highest. However, it was strange to see people still pressing the button on the pedestrian crossings and waiting until the sign indicated it was safe to cross!

The manager of the Yvonne Arnaud Theatre, Gordon Marshall, claimed he was the only person held up in a rowing boat by the pedestrian crossing in Millbrook!

On Monday 16th September, I was booked the double Feltham turn signing on at 20.30 with Driver Bob Stuckey on the first trip and Driver Arthur Streatfield on the second. As we went round Addlestone Junction towards Addlestone, in the gloom you could only make out the signal box as all the surrounding fields resembled a lake as the nearby River Wey at Cox's Lock had broken its banks.

Above Top: The bus station resembling a boating lake.

Middle: Moons & Sons, Timber Merchants.

Above: Walnut Tree Close and the New-Line Railway Bridge.

Text reproduced with kind permission from David Rose.

Photos: Alan Edwards Collection.

Secondman Days - Woking MT

My Triumph motorcycle had become rather unreliable in recent months and to top it all, on the 30th September, I ran out of petrol on the A3 at Hurtmore and had to push my bike to the garage at Milford. This was what, I think, brought on the onset of a back injury which would culminate in having to go into hospital for traction the following summer.

In December, I was again booked the double Feltham freight turn but this time with Driver Bill Brain. As mentioned in my first book, Bill was one of those people that lived life to the full and loved his curry, beer, smoking his 'roll ups' and the ladies and the hotter the better (the curry that is)! When we returned from Feltham to Guildford Yard on the first trip, Bill would go and get a curry from the Indian takeaway in Guildford Park Road and stink the cab out as he ate the curry on the way to Feltham!

In late February 1969, I received a letter from my Depot Master (Arthur Coe) that I would have to attend Southern House at Croydon for a medical exam and on passing this would be taking my Driver's Rules exam (as I would be 23 years of age on 5th March). I'd been studying hard with the help of work colleagues several nights a week as I didn't want to fail the exam.

I passed my medical without any problems and on the 2nd April, I was booked to attend the main office at Woking for my Rules & Regulations exam. This was conducted by Inspector Fred Smith. The exam lasted most of the day with Fred asking me Rules questions such as the eleven propelling moves and the thirteen exceptions for passing a signal at danger. After lunch, the protection rules were also covered. Around 4pm, Fred informed me that I'd passed my Rules exam and would be booked to attend a Traction Course at a later date.

On 28th April, I was booked a three-week course at Waterloo South-Side training School to learn Southern Electric Units. All the Southern Units were covered, from 2BIL, 2HAL, 4SUB, and 4COR Portsmouth Express, and Brighton Express, which were Westinghouse brake only units that were built in 1936 & 1946. More modern stock were also covered such as the 4EPB, 2HAP, 4BEP, 4CEP and 4VEP units that were built in 1951, 1957 and 1963 respectively. Even the MLV single-car units that could run on battery power in non-electrified sidings were covered on this course (not that I ever got to drive one until later on in my railway career).

There were four trainees on the course, two from Waterloo; Alan Cook and Ian Turner plus Colin Wells and myself from Woking. The course was very enjoyable; some of the lessons and practical work being covered by Bob Phillips and various instructors from different areas of the Southern Region. I remember going to New Cross Gate to do our Static Instruction including Preparation & Disposal and paddling up procedures with Derek Gane. I knew Derek well as I'd fired to him on occasions when he came to Guildford Loco from Salisbury to obtain promotion as a Driver. On another occasion, I remember us all meeting Jack Gardner at Sevenoaks.

Prior to the start of the two-day exam, on the 14th May, my companion from Woking, Colin Wells went sick, which meant that I had to undertake the exam on my own, my examiner being Bob Phillips.

As Bob wasn't a South Western man, the exam was conducted on the Central Division and on the second day, 15th May, I remember working my final train from Coulsdon North to Victoria where Bob informed me that I'd passed my driving exam and duly handed me my E.P. key! A very memorable event in my railway career.

Above Top: Coulsdon North station.

Photo: Ian Docwra.

Above Left: British Railways 1950 Rule Book. The Rule book would have to be amended periodically and the amendments stuck into the relevant pages with glue or Sellotape.

Below: E.P. keys from left to right: Effingham Junction EP Key, EP Key No. 7145 given to me by Traction Instructor Bob Phillips on the 15th May 1969 to mark that I'd passed my EMU Traction exam and a brass EP key with my initials specially engineered by Charlie Hampshire on a lathe that I'd given him as a gift.

Scans: The Author's Collection.

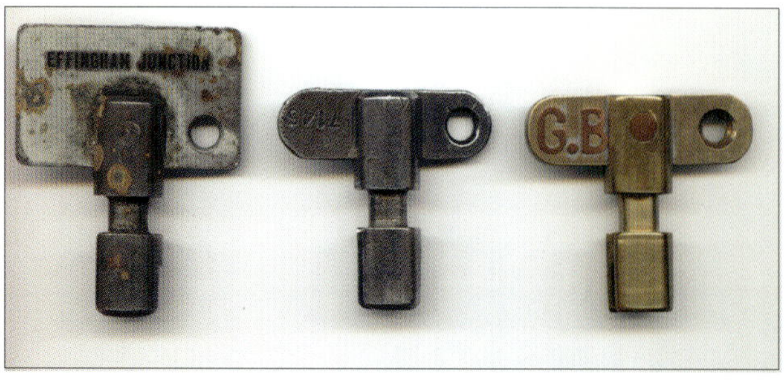

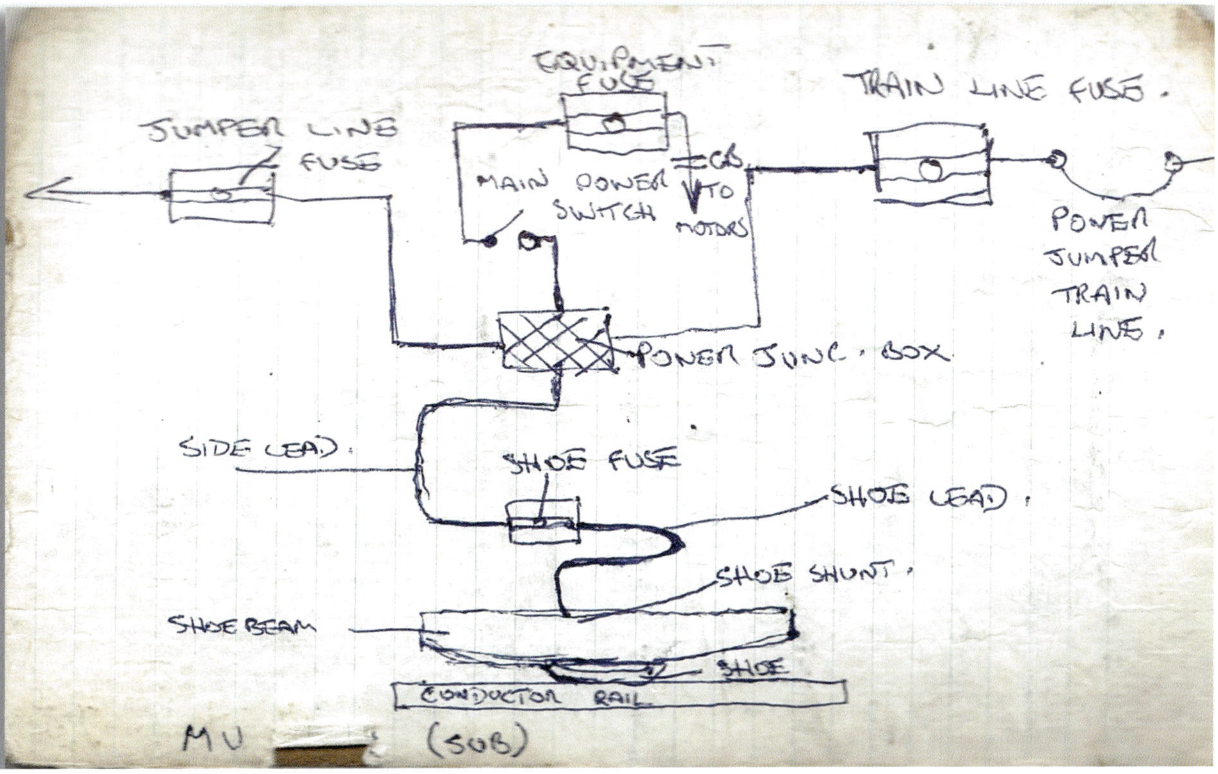

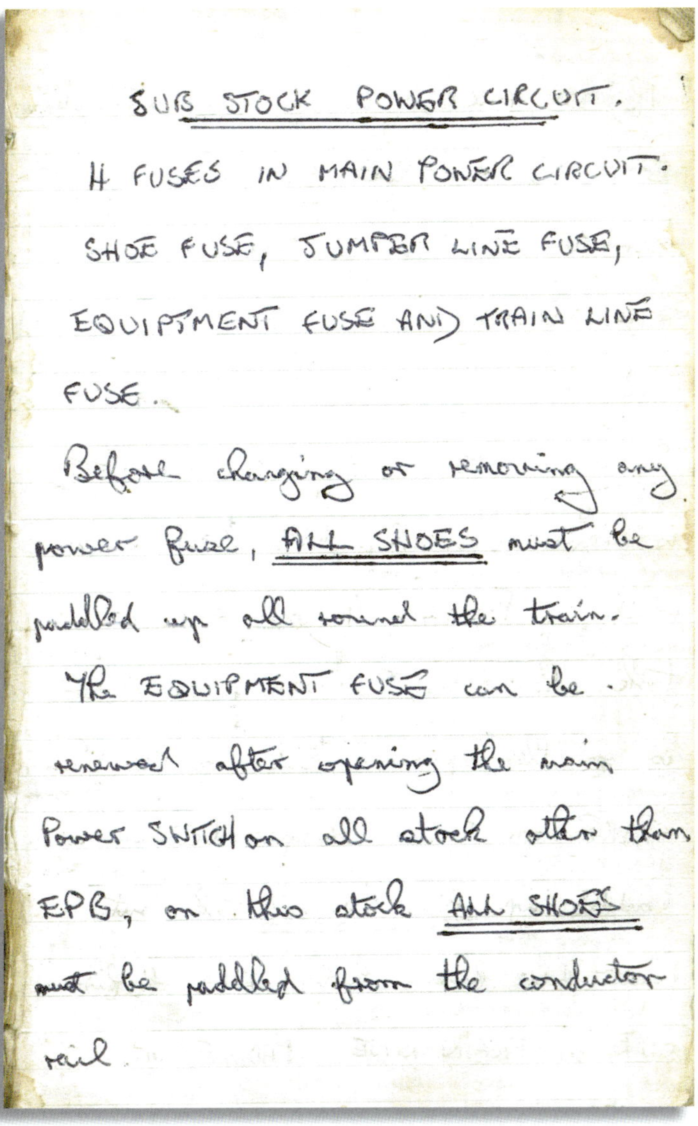
SUB STOCK POWER CIRCUIT.

4 FUSES IN MAIN POWER CIRCUIT.

SHOE FUSE, JUMPER LINE FUSE, EQUIPMENT FUSE AND TRAIN LINE FUSE.

Before changing or removing any power fuse, ALL SHOES must be paddled up all round the train.

The EQUIPMENT FUSE can be renewed after opening the main Power SWITCH on all stock other than EPB, on this stock ALL SHOES must be paddled from the conductor rail.

Above: Extract from my original 1969 EMU notebook showing the 750 volt conductor rail supply to a 4SUB Unit with the Jumper, Equipment and Train Line fuse configuration (JET).

Left: SUB Stock Power Circuit instructions for changing any of the Power fuses.

Below: Copper Strip Fuse.

Photo: Author's Collection.

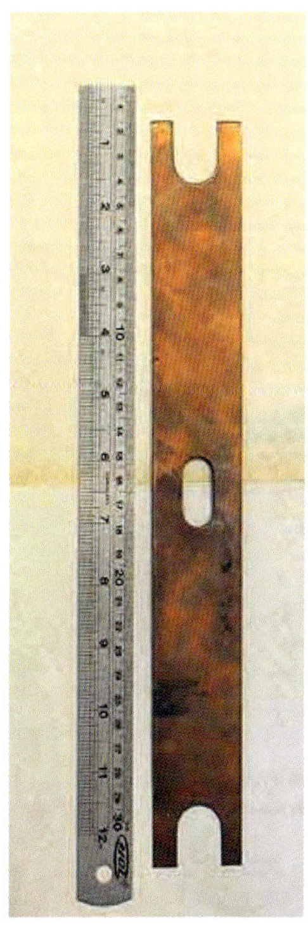

The 1936 type unit collected its power from the third rail via shoes attached to a shoebeam arrangement and the train's equipment and motors could be isolated from the third rail by several methods depending on the severity of the reason: i.e. fire on the train, power earth fault etc. If an emergency occurred and it was of vital importance to get the current switched off immediately, a short circuiting bar could be utilised to create a short circuit between the conductor rail and running rail and the effect of this would be that the line breakers in the control room that was supplying the current, would trip.

As long as the short circuiting bar was kept in place, the current could not be returned, as it would immediately trip the line breaker as soon as the control room operator tried to replace it. After two attempts of replacing the line breakers, the control room operator would then need to ascertain the cause of the short circuit before trying to replace the switch. Another option would be to ask for a current isolation. This could be done via an Electrification telephone or a signal-post telephone (via the signalman). The person asking for the isolation was the only person that could obtain permission to restore the current.

The traction motors were situated beneath each driving cab on a 4-car unit and beneath one cab on a 2-car unit and could be isolated if necessary by operating a pole switch using the Master Switch key. The train's power line was also protected by copper strip fuses (shown on previous page) and these would not only protect the equipment but could be removed to isolate the equipment (or unit) from the conductor rail supply. In order to remove or replace these fuses, a number of wooden paddles would be utilised. The wooden paddles, placed under the shoes, acted as an insulator to allow the driver to remove and replace the fuses. It was important to remember that ALL shoes must be 'paddled up' and this was especially important when dealing with units in multiple because a train line jumper existed between units which allowed the current to go to both unit's equipment even if there was only one shoe on the conductor rail. The driver would walk round the unit on both sides to ensure ALL shoes were paddled up because in certain areas, the conductor rail might exist on both sides of the line.

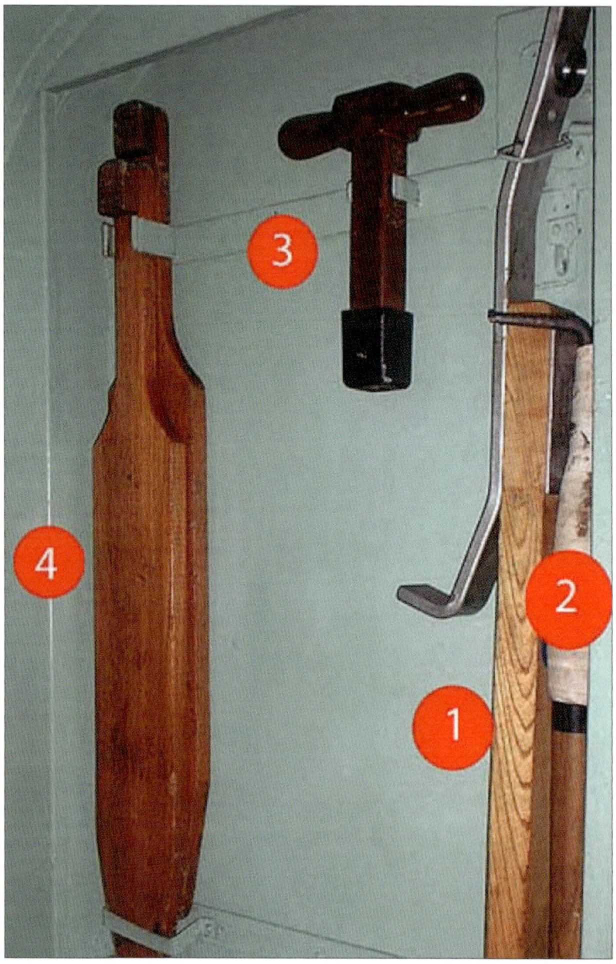

Above: In the cab of VEP stock - 1. Short Circuiting Bar 2. Hook Switch Pole 3. Box Spanner 4. Wooden Paddles.

Photo: David Timothy.

Below: A trainee Driver firmly applies the short circuiting bar and causes an immediate short circuit between the conductor rail and the running rail.

Photo: Steve West.

The 4SUB (and 2BIL, 2HAL, 4COR Portsmouth Express) units had a Westinghouse air-brake, (subsequent stock built in 1951, 1957 and 1963 possessed a combined Westinghouse and electro-pneumatic brake). Each 4-car unit had a set of 'keys' (brake valve & Master Switch) which were connected to each other by a length of cord (right). When changing ends (at a terminus for instance), it would be necessary to take the keys with you to drive from the other end (unless working an 8-car). The purpose of the keys being connected with cord was that it wouldn't then be possible to accidentally leave a brake valve open in another cab. Brake tests were carried out before departure or when coupling to another portion of train so as to test the brake continuity. A DSD test was also carried out whenever a new cab was used.

The Westinghouse brake was an excellent brake system but had to be used with caution because although it was possible to partially apply the brake, it was not possible to partially release it. Once the brake handle was moved to the release position, all brakes were completely released throughout the train. I thoroughly enjoyed my time driving the SUB units and as time went on, I mastered the art of using the Westinghouse brake and preferred to use it even on stock that possessed the EP brake as I found it more challenging.

In 2011, Bob Hunt, a good friend of mine and fellow fireman at Guildford, gave me a SUB Controller which he'd acquired some years ago from Selhurst depot. Another two friends of mine had acquired one each at the same time and had cleaned them up as 'railwayana' exhibits. I'm pleased to say that the one I possess is also in fine fettle and considering it was created in the same year as I was born, is in better nick than myself!

Interestingly, two recent SWT trainee drivers looked at it and thought it was an instrument to tap out Morse code! How far technology has come during the last 60-70 years!

Above and Right: Cleaned up and gleaming as it probably was when it came out of Eastleigh works in 1946, this SUB Controller takes pride of place in my dining room.

Photos: The Author's Collection.

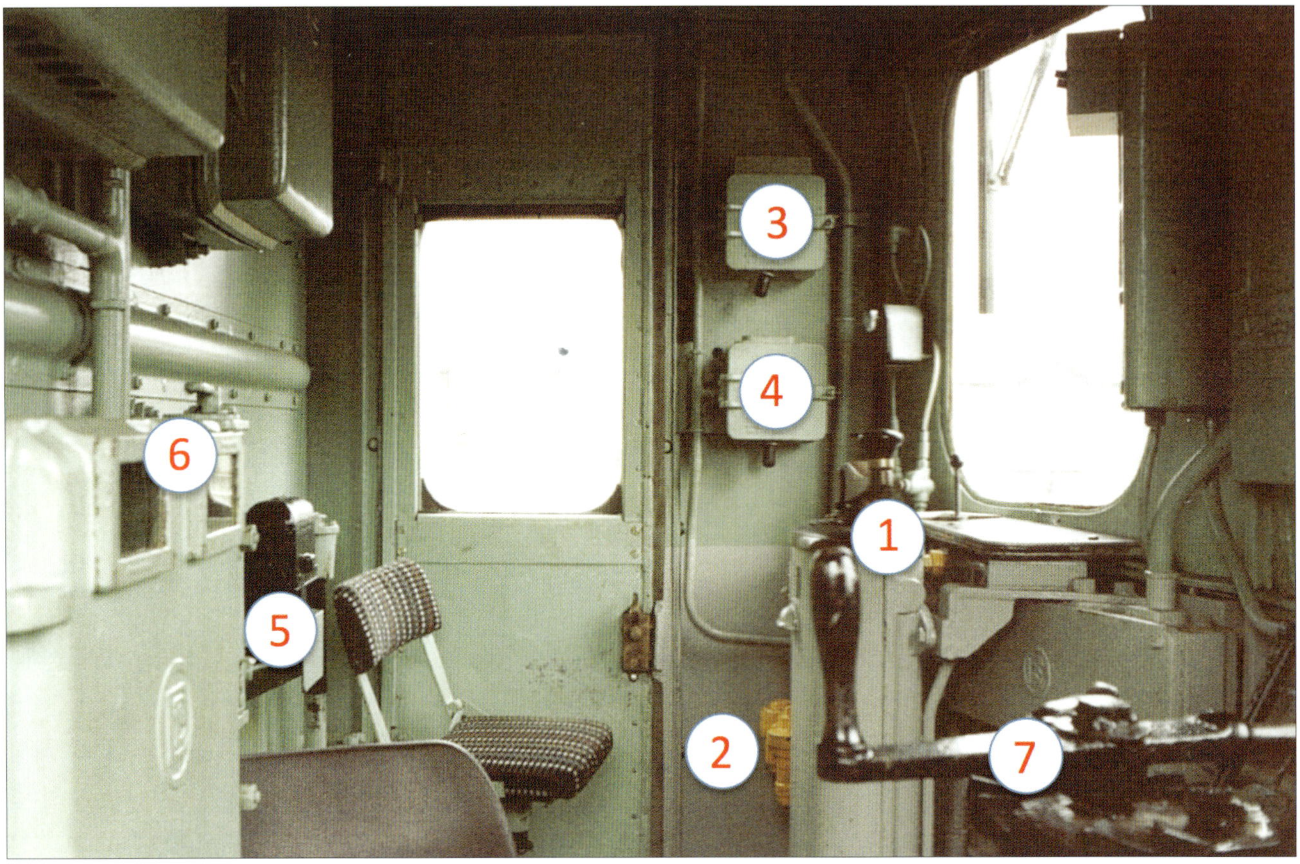

Above: Cab of 4SUB showing basic controls: 1. Deadman, 2. Brake Valve, 3. Control Switch, 4. Control Trip & Set Switch, 5. Compressor Governor, 6. Seven-point Cut-Out Switch, 8. Handbrake.

Photo: Chris Lemon.

Below: Cab of EPB Unit showing basic controls: 1. Power Controller, 2. Combined Master & Reverser Switch, 3. Five Position Brake Valve, 4. AWS (Automatic Warning System), 5. Loudaphone Communication, 6. Handbrake.

Photo: Ian Docwra.

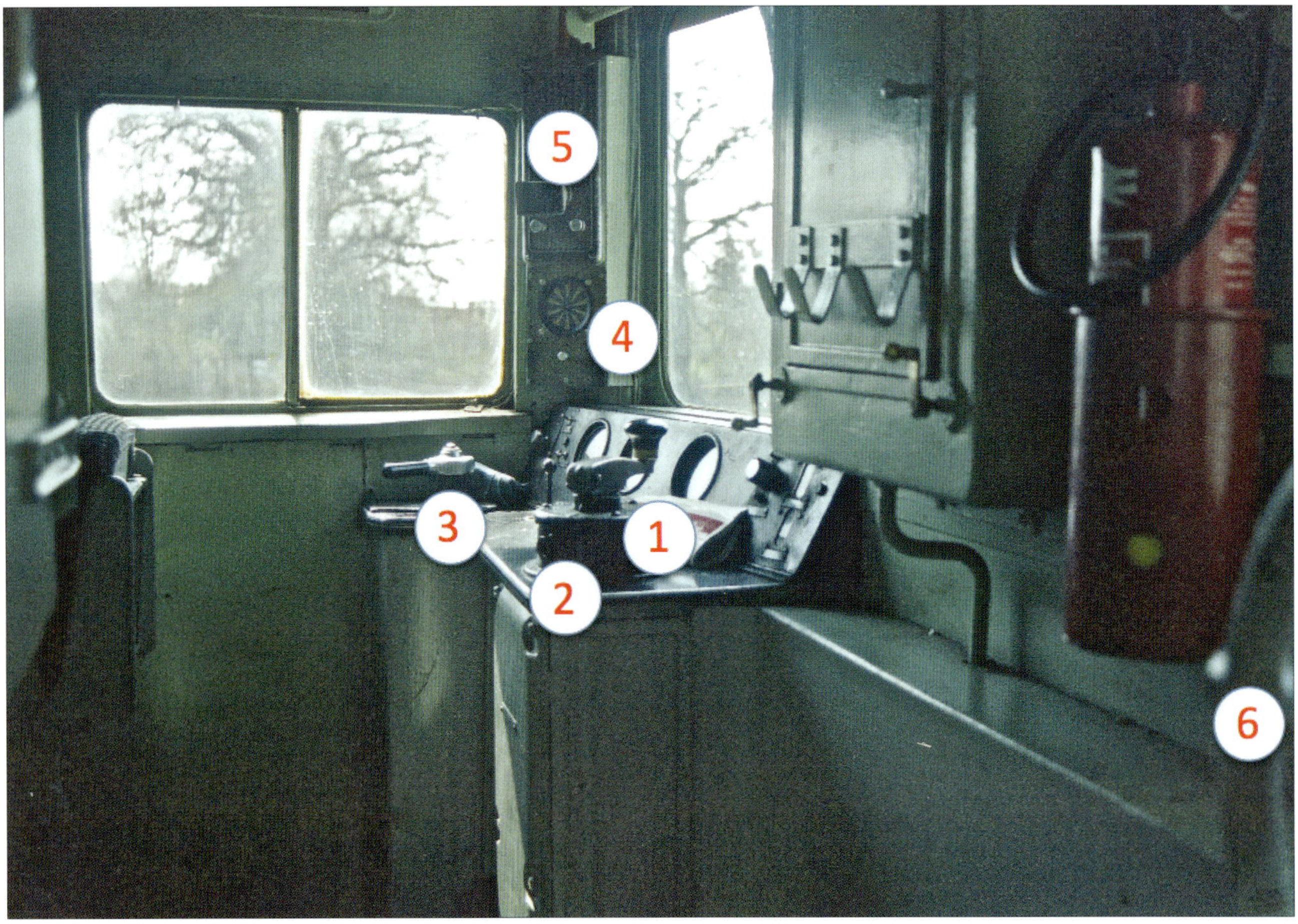

The Equipment Box (right) contained: 1. Control & Brake Keys (with connecting cord); 2. Detonators; 3. Red Flags; 4 & 5. Spare Fuses of various amperages. The box was secured by an 'S' Key (below).

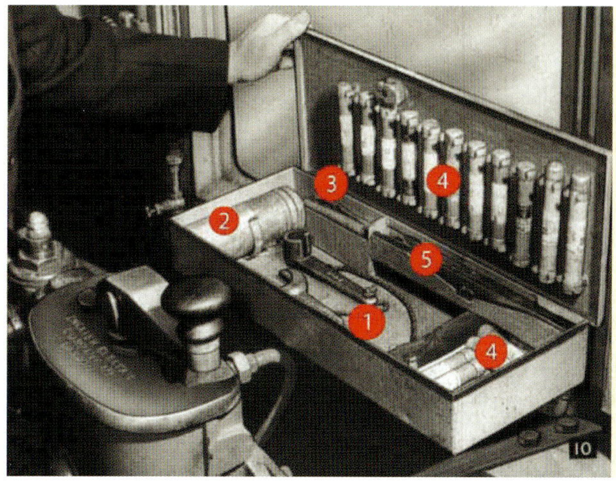

Opposite Page: Cab controls were very basic - a brake handle and power controller (the latter having to be held down by hand pressure all the time that the train was moving). If the pressure on the controller was released for any reason i.e. the driver becoming incapacitated or falling asleep, the 'deadman' would operate cutting off power to the traction motors and instantly applying the emergency brake.

Creature comforts weren't apparent either; a small swivel seat was fixed on a bracket on the inside of the driver's door and in a lot of cases, drivers stood up most of the time as the seats were quite uncomfortable. There were no other seats and if you had anyone else ride with you in the cab, they had to stand. On SUB units, the only instrument gauge present was a duplex main reservoir air /train pipe pressure gauge.

There were no luxuries of a speedometer, line indicator, brake cylinder gauge, AWS or headlight. The headcode was displayed using metal stencils (held within a metal frame); this was fixed in front of a white background - the background being lit during darkness. Changing the headcode stencil frame was normally carried out by opening the hinged-window on the non-driver's side (please see following page).

The voltage of the units was between 600-750v, so extra care was required when operating the 'bakelite-handled' knife switches (right) or when changing fuses that were contained in the switch and fuse cupboard. If handled with care, the high voltage knife switches were not dangerous and drivers were always taught to keep their other hand in their pocket and NOT to be holding onto any other metal parts whilst performing this task.

The reason being thus: electricity will find its quickest path to earth and should you accidentally touch a high voltage switch, and be touching metal framing etc. the path of electricity would flow across the heart area and could cause a cardiac arrest. Therefore, if you weren't touching anything metal with your other hand, the path of electricity would probably not occur as your shoes or boots would act as an insulator. I always remember my instructor saying - 'If you touch that lad, you'll end up picking your nose with your elbow!'

To avoid causing an arc when opening the Main Auxiliary (2-way) knife switch, it was important to remember that an arc would only be created when an electrical current was under load - i.e. The compressor or heating working. The policy of the '2-way' knife switch being 'first in - last out' was the important motto to learn.

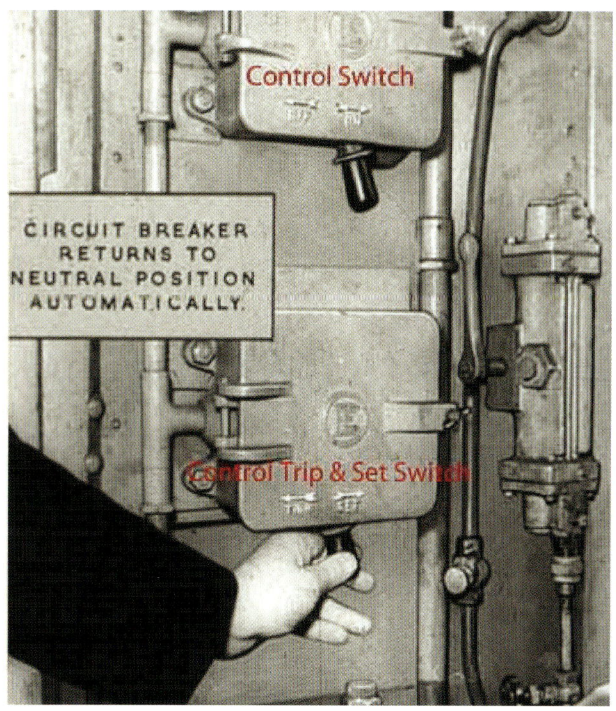

(Right) The Trip & Set Control switch was used to re-set traction motor overloads but was quite often unofficially used for a completely different purpose. When moving the switch to the 'set' position, an arc or large spark would be created. Drivers would use this spark to ignite a folded strip of newspaper to light their cigarettes!

Above: The Driver of 4SUB 4738 has opened the hinged window and is lifting the catch to insert the headcode stencil frame into position.

Photo: Steve West Collection.

Above: Driver Dave Jackson from Staines in the cab of a 4SUB.

Photo: Steve West Collection.

Below: 4SUB 4657 leaves Staines with a Windsor - Waterloo stopping service.

Photo: David Hird.

Secondman Days - Woking MT

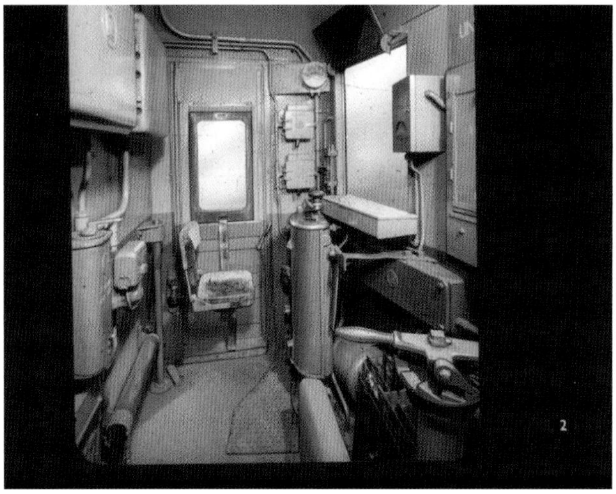

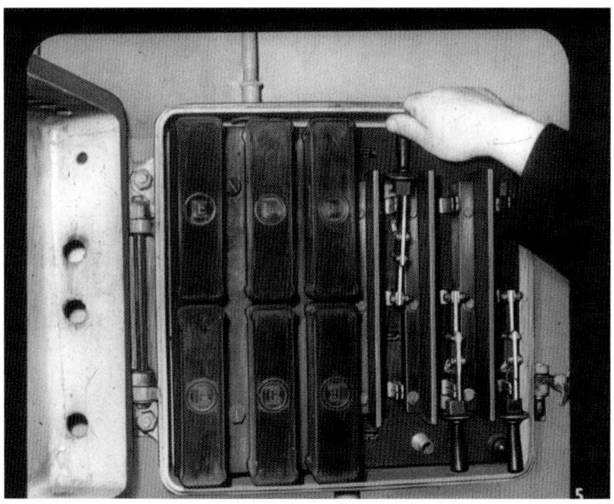

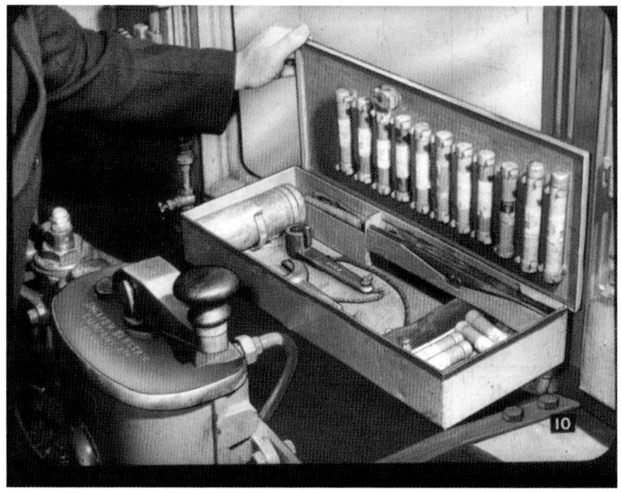

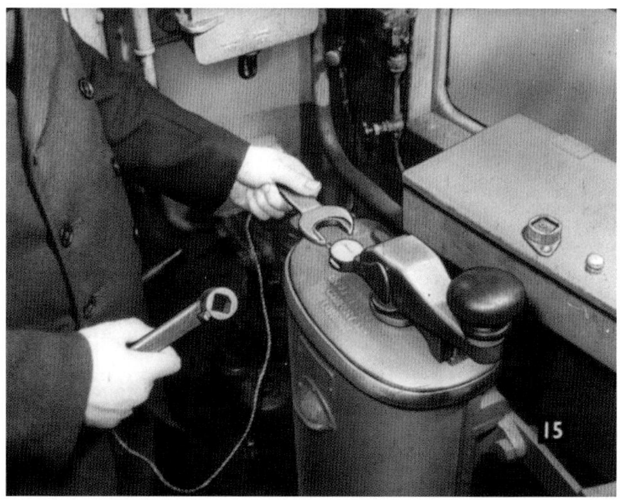

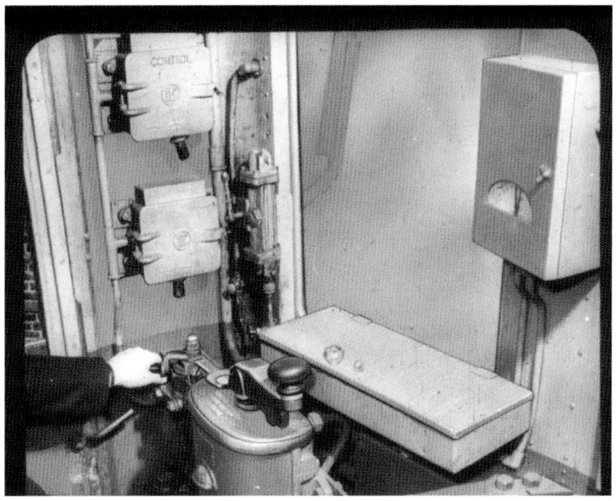

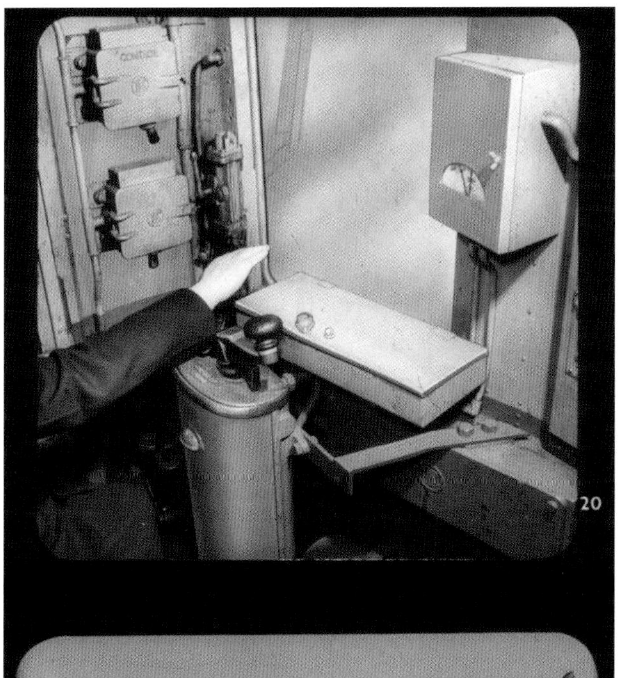

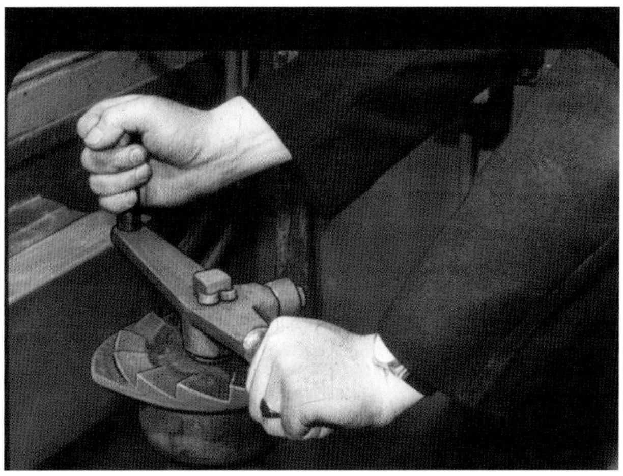

Previous Frames of film strip:

Driver's Preparation of 4SUB Unit.

The knife switches in the Electrical Cupboard all carried a high voltage supply 600 to 750volts so special care was needed when operating the switches. The '2-way' Switch was always 'first in last out' and if operated in this sequence was completely safe. Should this method of operation not be followed, an arc would be created when removing the switch under load (coach heating, lighting, etc).

Frame 10 shows the equipment box containing spare fuses, red flags and detonators. A set of keys for the controller and brake valve (attached to each other with a length of cord) are also shown. The box was secured by an 'S' key.

Some of the frames show the brake test procedure undertaken by the guard and driver.

Photos: The Author's Collection.

Secondman Days - Woking MT

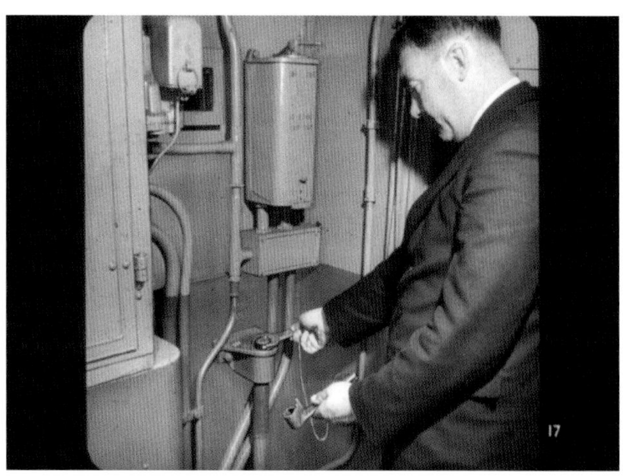

Previous Frames of film strip:

Driver's Preparation of 4COR Portsmouth Express Unit 3117.

The first frame shows a Waterloo - Portsmouth Express headed by 4COR 3129 exiting St Catherine's Tunnel towards Shalford Junction.
The following frames show the relevant preparation procedures carried out by the Driver utilising the special keys belonging to each 4-car unit.
The Portsmouth Express stock had a Motor-Generator which was energised by inserting an extra metal key into a key-switch box situated in the cab behind the driver's head. Some of the frames show the brake test procedure undertaken by the guard and driver.

Photos: The Author's Collection.

Above: 4COR 3107 heads a Waterloo - Portsmouth Express service at Guildford in 1962. The Portsmouth Express stock were nicknamed 'Nelsons' because of the route indicator on the non-driver's side resembling a patch over one eye.

Photo: Les Mills Collection.

Below: Outside the 'Gentlemens' toilet on No. 2 Platform at Guildford circa 1967. DEMU 1204 is berthed in the dock probably suffering from a radiator water leak. An assortment of mopeds and motorcycles belonging to various drivers & guards including Woking Driver Charlie Hampshire's 650cc Triumph Thruxton Bonneville! The Guildford Motormen's room is pictured adjacent to the DEMU and Charlie and I used to leave our motorcycle helmets there on occasion much to the disgust of some of the Guildford motormen.

Photo: Jeffrey Lloyd Collection.

Above: A 12-car train comprised of Portsmouth Express stock passes through Clandon with a Waterloo - Portsmouth Harbour service diverted via the 'New Line' because of engineering works in 1966.

Photo: Bob Hind Collection.

Below: Ex-works Bulleid 4SUB 4364 about to stop at Raynes Park station in the early 1960s. The 62 headcode denotes that this was a Waterloo (W) to Waterloo (M) service via Teddington. The headcode was revised to [32] at a later date.

Photos Mike Morant Collection.

Above: Brand new 2EPB 5759 at Wimbledon with the usual '2' headcode for the Wimbledon - West Croydon service.

Photo: Mike Morant Collection.

Below: 2HAL 2623 forming a local service from Ascot approaches Guildford on 18th July 1970. Guildford University is under construction in the background.

Photo: Gordon Edgar.

I was now passed for driving duties and although already conversant with a lot of the local routes, I still had to learn all the routes in the London area so that I would be eligible to work any of the EMU turns allocated to the depot. Waterloo Main to Waterloo Windsor Side via Kingston (Round the World), Waterloo - Chessington, Waterloo Windsor Side to Waterloo Windsor Side via Brentford (Round the Loop). The Guildford to Waterloo via Cobham (New Line) and the Guildford to Portsmouth Harbour direct line would also have to be learnt.

I was also still being booked secondman duties during this time; mainly working very early or late afternoon turns.

Unfortunately, during June 1969, my back took a turn for the worst and in July I was diagnosed with having a prolapsed inverted disc which would need hospital treatment. On Wednesday 16th July, I was admitted to the Rowley Bristow orthopaedic hospital at Pyrford where I was put on 'traction' (which was a bit different to the term 'Traction' that I'd been used to! A 10lb weight was strapped to my left leg with a pulley attachment and that's how I spent the next three weeks. Not pleasant I can assure you – especially as the sun was shining outside. However, the staff did wheel some of us patients out to enjoy the rays on the last week I was there.

The other unfortunate thing about it was that the moon landings were being televised and the only television was a black/white set right up the other end of the ward, so I missed it all!

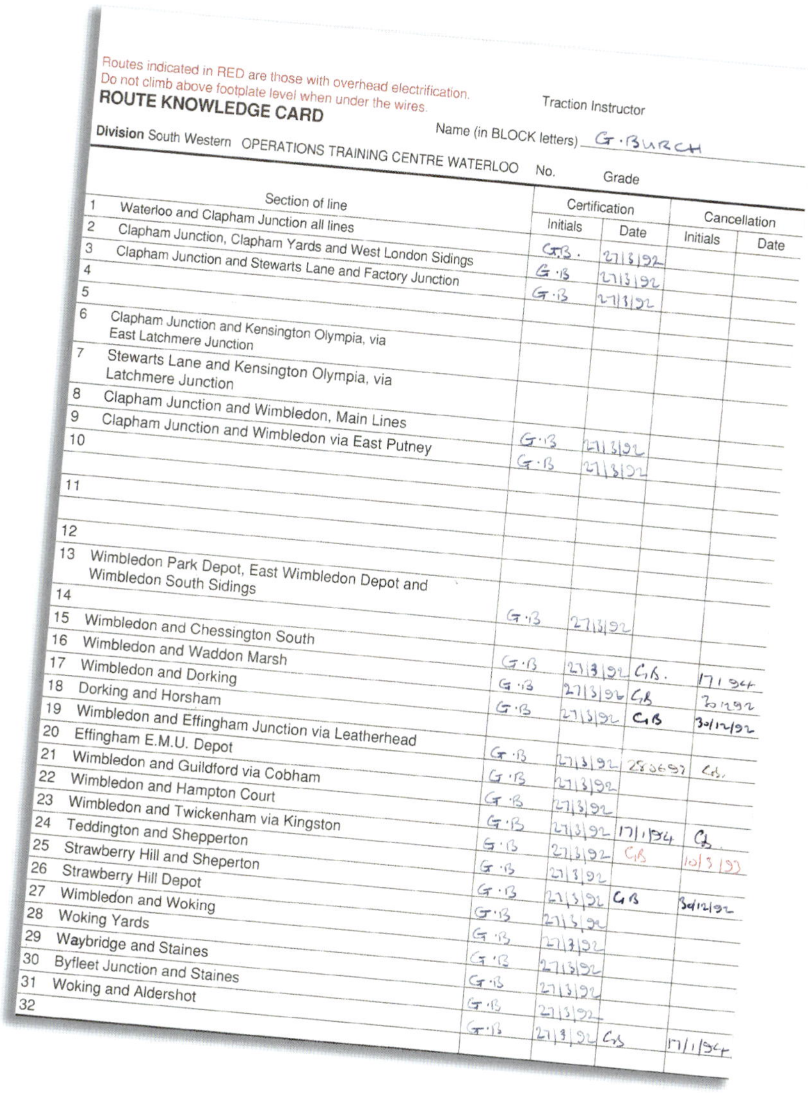

Routes indicated in RED are those with overhead electrification.
Do not climb above footplate level when under the wires.

ROUTE KNOWLEDGE CARD

Traction Instructor

Name (in BLOCK letters) G.BURCH

Division South Western OPERATIONS TRAINING CENTRE WATERLOO No. Grade

	Section of line	Certification		Cancellation	
		Initials	Date	Initials	Date
1	Waterloo and Clapham Junction all lines	G.B.	27/3/92		
2	Clapham Junction, Clapham Yards and West London Sidings	G.B	27/3/92		
3	Clapham Junction and Stewarts Lane and Factory Junction	G.B	27/3/92		
4					
5					
6	Clapham Junction and Kensington Olympia, via East Latchmere Junction				
7	Stewarts Lane and Kensington Olympia, via Latchmere Junction				
8	Clapham Junction and Wimbledon, Main Lines	G.B	27/3/92		
9	Clapham Junction and Wimbledon via East Putney	G.B	27/3/92		
10					
11					
12					
13	Wimbledon Park Depot, East Wimbledon Depot and Wimbledon South Sidings				
14					
15	Wimbledon and Chessington South	G.B	27/3/92		
16	Wimbledon and Waddon Marsh	G.B	27/3/92	G.B.	17/1/94
17	Wimbledon and Dorking	G.B	27/3/92	G.B	30/12/92
18	Dorking and Horsham	G.B	27/3/92	G.B	30/12/92
19	Wimbledon and Effingham Junction via Leatherhead				
20	Effingham E.M.U. Depot	G.B	27/3/92	28/6/97	G.B.
21	Wimbledon and Guildford via Cobham	G.B	27/3/92		
22	Wimbledon and Hampton Court	G.B	27/3/92		
23	Wimbledon and Twickenham via Kingston	G.B	27/3/92	17/1/94	G.B.
24	Teddington and Shepperton	G.B	27/3/92	G.B	10/3/93
25	Strawberry Hill and Sheperton	G.B	27/3/92		
26	Strawberry Hill Depot	G.B	27/3/92	G.B	30/12/92
27	Wimbledon and Woking	G.B	27/3/92		
28	Woking Yards	G.B	27/3/92		
29	Waybridge and Staines	G.B	27/3/92		
30	Byfleet Junction and Staines	G.B	27/3/92		
31	Woking and Aldershot	G.B	27/3/92		
32		G.B	27/3/92	G.B	17/1/94

Above: A copy of one of the Route Knowledge Cards that a Driver would need to sign to authenticate their route knowledge over a particular route.

Drivers were also booked route refresher days should they not have been over the route recently. A Driver would need to confirm their knowledge of the route every twelve months and initial the card if cancellation was necessary.

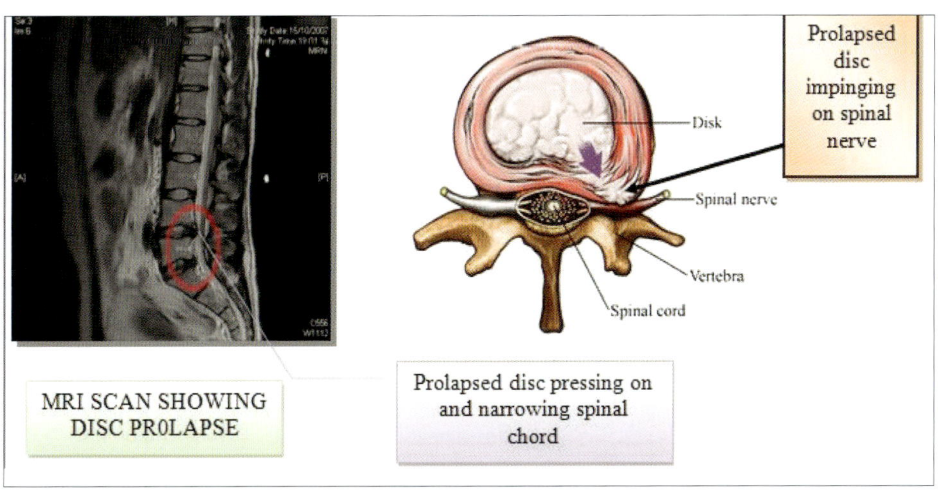

Above: Prolapsed disc showing the possible reasons for back pain and sciatica.

I was discharged from hospital on 5th August and had to wear a corset which was coloured a delicate shade of pink which *"didn't really suit me at all darrrling!"* as Strictly Come Dancing judge Craig Revel-Horwood might say. I spent a further month off recuperating and was booked light duties for a while when I returned to work.

I decided that the Triumph Tiger 100 motorcycle would also have to go and cycled to and from work from then on, this of course being good exercise for my back injury.

Passed Secondman Days - Woking MT

My first driving turn was of course on 'the juice' as it was the only type of traction that I was eligible to drive.

The turn was on Sunday 7th September 1969 and I was booked Special 26 & 27.

It involved signing on at 08.11 and working the 08.31 passenger service to Waterloo arriving there at 08.56. The unit I had was 2HAP 6011. I then went 'pass' (passenger) to Portsmouth & Southsea on the 09.23 service and when I got there, was booked A/O (as ordered) and have my meal break.

Special 27 involved relieving and working the 14.24 passenger service from Portsmouth & Southsea High Level to Waterloo arriving there at 16.10. The train consisted of three 4-car Portsmouth Express Units 4COR 3102, 4GRI 3087 and 4COR 3158. I remember quite clearly Pauline, (my then fiancée and wife to be), meeting me at Guildford station when I ran in with my train from Portsmouth and chatting whilst awaiting departure for Waterloo.

I was then booked home passenger on the 16.23 from Waterloo to Woking, booking off at Woking at 17.25.

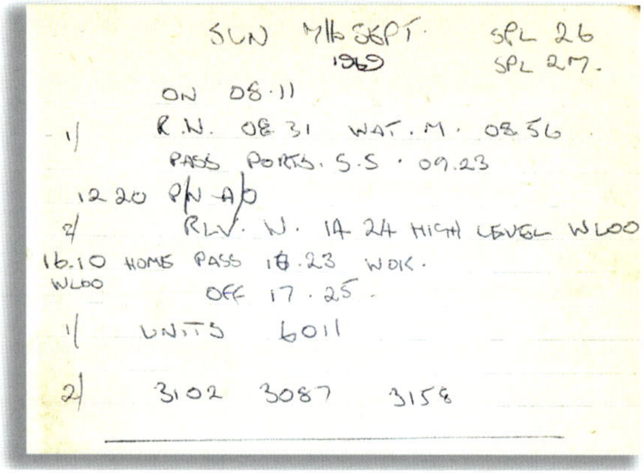
SUN 7th SEPT 1969 SPL 26 SPL 27.
ON 08.11
1/ R.N. 08.31 WAT. M. 08.56
PASS PORTS. S.S. 09.23
12 20 P/N A/O
2/ RLV. W. 14 24 HIGH LEVEL WLOO
16.10 WLOO HOME PASS 16.23 WOK.
OFF 17.25.
1/ UNITS 6011
2/ 3102 3087 3158

Above: The workings of my first driving turn on Sunday 7th September 1969.

Photo: The Author's Collection.

Left: 2HAP 6011 - the very first unit that I worked as a driver.
This photo was taken near Beaulieu Road on 24th August 1982 and the train formed the 07.58 Lymington Pier to Eastleigh service. This was a once a day through service from Lymington to Southampton and Eastleigh, the hourly branch train terminating at Brockenhurst for the rest of the day.

Photo: John Dedman.

Below: The second train I worked on my first day's driving was formed of 4COR 3102, 4GRI 3087 and 4COR 3158. Portsmouth & Southsea High Level to Waterloo on Sunday 7th September 1969.

Photo: Hugh Llewellyn.

Above: 4GRI 3087 (which was the middle unit of my train on my first day's driving) is shown here on 6th February 1971 at Littlehampton on a rail tour which marked the end of service for 4GRI EMU's introduced in 1937/38 for the Portsmouth/Bognor electrification. These were originally identified as 4RES units but were re-classified following conversion by BR during the 1950's. Alongside is 2BIL 2112.

Below: 4GRI 3087 at Portsmouth Harbour station the same day. At the other end of the train was 4GRI 3086. On this leg of the journey, it left Portsmouth Harbour and ran to London Victoria via Havant- Petersfield - Guildford - Effingham Junction - Leatherhead - Epsom - Sutton - West Croydon - Selhurst - Streatham Common - Balham - Clapham Junction - Stewarts Lane - London Victoria.

Photos: Ernie Brack.

Above: Guildford Down Yard is virtually devoid of goods traffic with only a few box wagons and loaded stone hoppers in attendance. The cliff face that was at the rear of the loco can still be seen in the background, the multi-storey car park that exists today is yet to be built.

Above: A 12-car Portsmouth to Waterloo fast service leaves Guildford for Waterloo on 18th July 1970. Comprised of 4COR 3161, 4BUF 3073 and 4COR 3150. This train is not dissimilar to the one that I worked on my first day as a driver ten months earlier.

Photo: Gordon Edgar.

Above: A 4COR + 4BUF make up the stock for this Portsmouth semi-fast to Waterloo as it passes Wimbledon 'C' box.

Photo: Mike Morant Collection.

Below: A Waterloo to Reading stopping service comprising 2HAL and 2BIL units 2612, 2693, 2694 and 2012 at Longcross Halt on 2nd May 1970.

Photo: Gordon Edgar.

On Monday 6th October 1969, I was booked to attend Waterloo South-Side Training School for 1550hp Crompton training. This course was of a six-week duration and for company, Bill Tickner, another Woking Driver attended with me. There were six of us on the course in total, the other Drivers being from Stewarts Lane, Gillingham, Norwood and Waterloo.

The course was taken by several instructors and on static days we would normally go to Stewarts Lane and on practical handling days, we went all over the Southern – even as far as Hastings where we'd work back up to Tonbridge with a freight train. Needless to say, the instructor that we had that day lived at Tonbridge!

I remember that on one of the practical handling weeks we worked a passenger service from Bournemouth to Reading via Basingstoke and unfortunately on the Friday, one of our group (who was riding in the train on part of the journey) decided to buy and drink some alcohol from the buffet car! This resulted in a long wait at Reading for him to sober up before we were all allowed to go home.

There were three variants of 'Cromptons'. Most were of the same design, classed KA (later classed 33/0).

Eighteen of the class were classed KB and fitted with a modified 'Push-Pull' Westcode apparatus which made them fully compatible with the JB type 1600/600hp electro-diesels and any other EMU stock fitted with a 27-way control jumper. These locomotives were painted blue with full yellow ends.

With the advent of TOPS, they were grouped, instead, into Class 33/1 being numbered in the range 33101–33119.

Ten of the locomotives were built with narrower bodies so they could work through the narrow tunnels situated on the Tonbridge to Hastings line. This led to their nickname 'Slim Jims' and were later classed 33/2.

The locomotive had a maximum speed limit of 85mph (if the class of train permitted) and were restricted to 65mph light loco.

I was fortunate to have already been working on this type of loco as a secondman (even before steam traction had finished) and because of this apprenticeship, found it quite easy to pass the course.

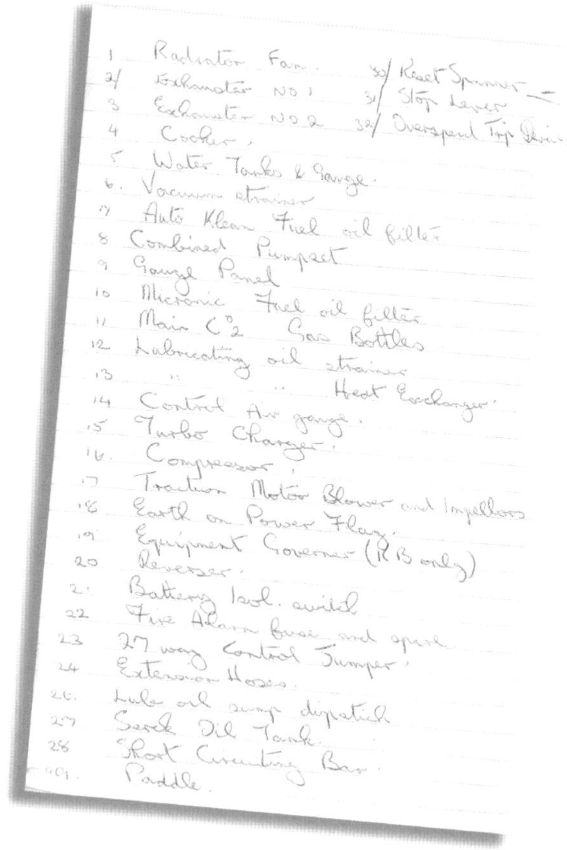

Above & Below: Extracts from the Author's 1550hp 'Crompton' course notebook showing a copy of the drawing that was intricately drawn on the blackboard (in various colour shades) by Wally Ward (our course instructor for the day). We would then copy this into our notebooks (my effort of reproduction is not so intricate)! It's no wonder the course lasted six weeks!

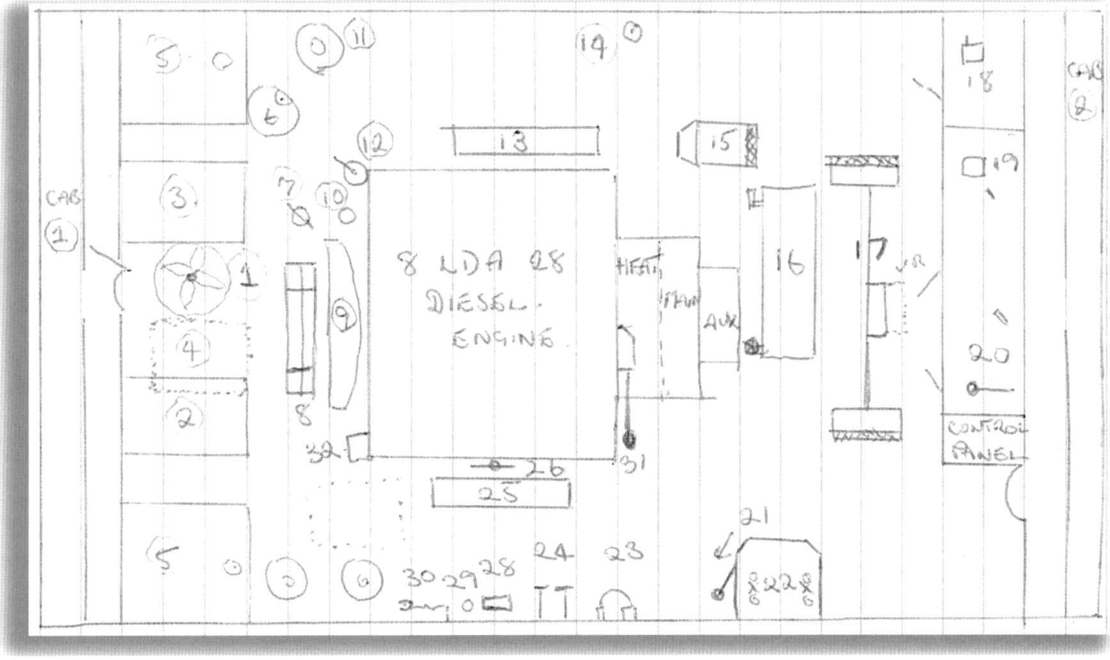

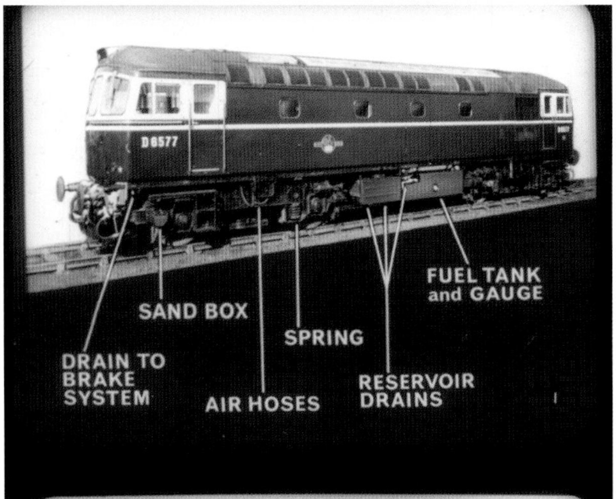

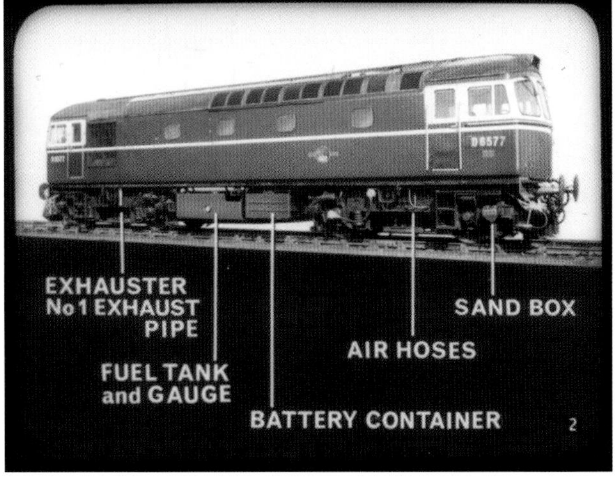

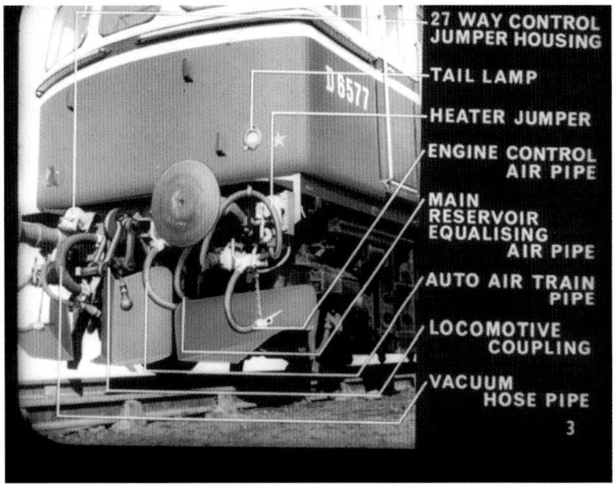

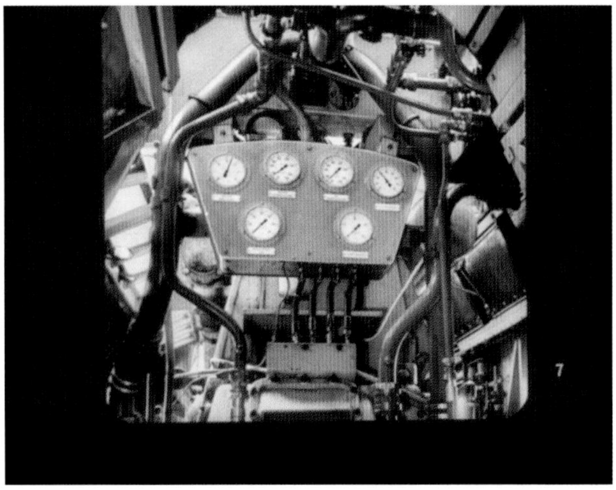

Above and Left: The 1550hp Type 3 'Crompton' diesel-electric locomotive, interior and exterior equipment. Once the fuel racks were given time to prime, the generator was used as a starter motor to start the engine.
The diesel engine then turned the generator to produce electrical current via a voltage regulator to the traction motors.
Two other generators were also utilised; one to provide train heating (when necessary) and an auxiliary generator to provide a 110volt current supply for battery charging and control purposes.
Note also that each locomotive had to carry paraffin tail lamps to place on the rear of a locomotive when running light locomotive. At that time, red route indicator blinds (or electric tail lamps) were not then recognised as a safe indication.

Photos: The Author's Collection.

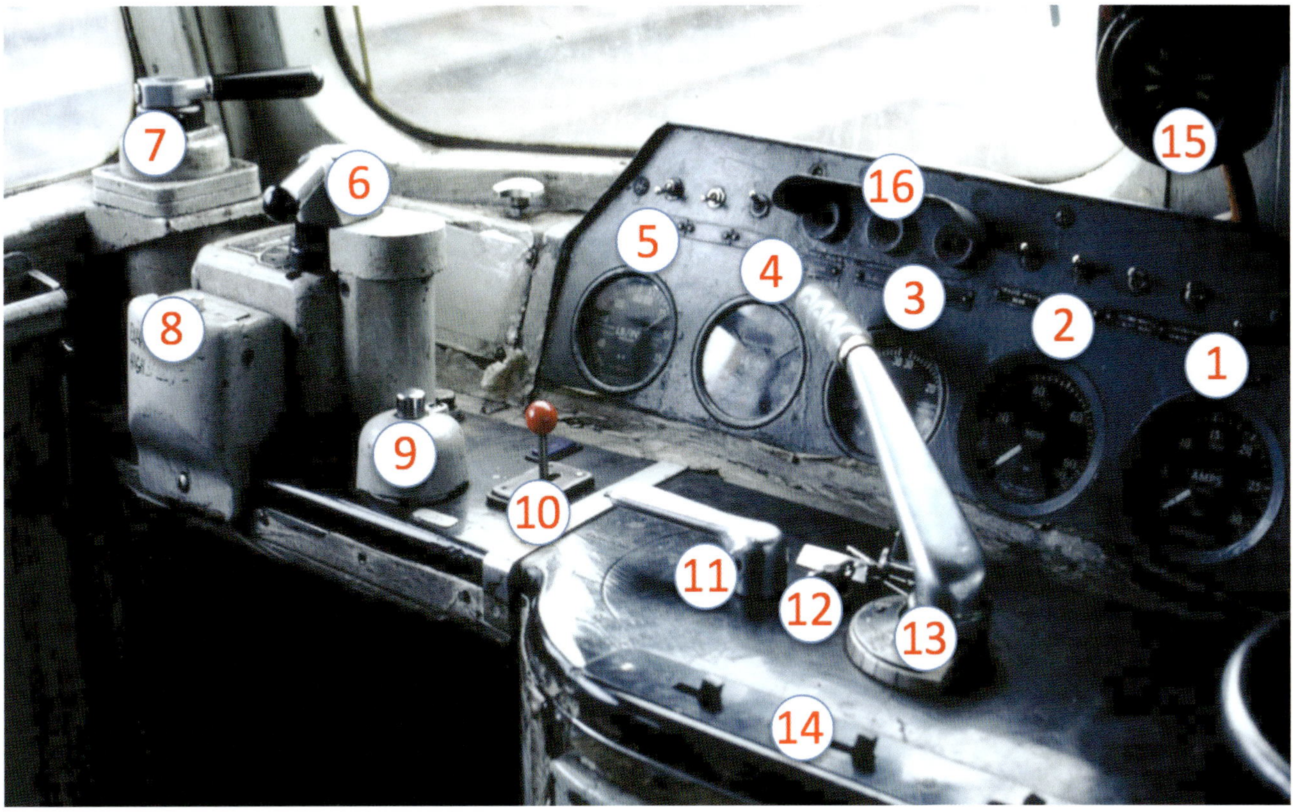

Above: Class 33/1 1550hp Type 3 'Crompton' Cab Layout:
1. Ammeter 2. Speedometer 3. Vacuum Gauge 4. Brake Cylinder Gauge 5. Main Reservoir / Brake Pipe Pressure Gauge 6. Driver's Brake Valve 7. Straight Air Brake 8. High Speed Vacuum Exhauster 9. AWS Reset 10. Two-Tone Horn 11. Master Switch 12. Master Key 13. Power Controller 14. Auto-Engine Start / Engine Stop Switches 15. AWS Warning Sunflower 16. Engine / Slip / Fault Lights (Red / Yellow / Blue).
Photo: The Author's Collection.

Below: An unidentified Class 33/0 1550hp 'Crompton' runs through platform 5 at Guildford with an empty stone train from Redhill to Woking Yard circa 1982.

Photo: Ken Oxlade - Julie Hogben Collection.

Passed Secondman Days - Woking MT

Woking Up Yard had its own PAD (Pre-Assembly Depot) where the lengths of track were made up in advance. Therefore, Woking MT depot had quite a number of turns which involved the renewal and replacement of permanent way. Stone trains, cable trough trains, long-welded rail trains, ballast and material trains with track-relayers, cranes, etc. and also spoil trains where the dirty ballast that had been taken away from the track bed was transported to various locations to be emptied.

The most local site was Farnham Tip which was situated behind the electric stabling depot just the other side of Farnham station - other locations were at Godstone and Woolston.

During the week, the jobs would normally be carried out following the last train service and would be completed before the first train service the following morning. However, a lot of work would be carried out at weekends where the lines in question would be under engineer's occupation and the crews relieved by conveying their relief to the site by taxi.

Our usual taxi driver was Gerry Ford and he knew the locations of the sites very well. Sometimes though, it would be necessary to clamber over fences and down embankments, walking along the cess or troughing to reach the locomotive which sometimes proved quite hazardous.

Invariably, you'd be stationary for long periods of time in the middle of nowhere so it was always a good idea to take with you a good supply of food and water for making a can of tea when necessary. All the locomotives had an electric cooker - situated in the engine room on a Crompton and electro-diesel and in the cab on a Brush type 4 locomotive.

Above: A Ballast cleaning machine. Cleaned ballast would be returned to the trackbed and the dirty ballast conveyed to open wagons on the adjoining line.

Below: Track Relayer with a new length of track.

Photos: Bob Hind Collection.

There were no such things as P.T.S. (Personal Track Safety Certificates), HVVs (High Visibility Vests), safety helmets, power lighting, steel-capped boots or leather gloves issued to staff. Lifting old 'panels' (60 foot lengths of 'bullhead' rail) with very old sleepers hanging down from the 'chairs' only held on by a couple of bolts secured into rotten timber whilst dropping ballast as the panel passed over the heads of track workers who were spreading out the old stone ready for the new 'panel' to be dropped into place, was extremely hazardous. Doubtless, this practice was against regulations but expediency was desired by all of the gang to enable an early finish.

The relaying gang for our area, (known as the Wokingham Gang), covered all routes south and west from Waterloo down to Havant via Guildford, Reading, Basingstoke and Alton lines were also covered.

The man in charge of 'our team' on site in those days was Stan Hoar a white haired gentleman who lived at Rowland's Castle. His subordinate, Mr Martin, usually wore an old railway issue gabardine mackintosh, his pate crowned with a battered brown trilby hat. Unlike the others, Mr Martin was issued a forward facing tilly-lamp instead of the usual 360-degree version supplied on site each night to the workforce. His lamp was better for examining the work done. (One individual was always detailed to prepare these tilly-lamps in advance; perhaps thirty or forty for each night's work.

Above: Renewing a bridge just outside Woking in the days before wearing HVVs (High Visibility Vests) became compulsory!

Below: An Alton to Waterloo train crosses from the Up Through to the Down Through because of weekend engineering works. The track having been slewed over to join up and alleviate the problems usually associated with single line working where points would have needed to be plugged and clipped.

Photos: Bob Hind Collection.

There would be perhaps five or six bogies of 'prefab', one track-relayer, mess vans, tool vans and depending on the job at hand, four or five stone hoppers. If the length of track to be relayed was very long then there would be more prefabs and a larger stone train would run separately with a further locomotive. But that was usually on 'weekend jobs.'

On arrival at its destination, Petersfield for example, the train would be shunted, the material with the stone hoppers and brake vans placed on the line to be relayed with one engine while the locomotive attached to the track-relayer would shunt to the other line before both sections ran to the site of work under engineer's occupation, one on the up road and one on the down road. (The engineers under the direction of Stan Hoar, would take charge of the section of line to be relayed, and the conductor rail current isolated under special arrangements).

When renewals were complete, the locomotive on the stone train portion, which hadn't turned a wheel all night, had to run the stone after the men had positioned themselves on each hopper to operate the control gear. If all went well, this manoeuvre could be completed in about 20 minutes. Very occasionally a problem might arise, for example: if the loco crew hauling the hopper stopped or slowed down below 2mph and the men on the control wheels couldn't shut the hopper doors, the stone would run out far too much in one spot and would have to be spread around by hand, much to the disgust of the 'gang.' On occasions the stone would pile up to such an extent that a hopper may even be derailed. Re-marshalling the train at the end of the night would take up to an hour or so before running back to Woking Yard; the locomotive/s being berthed on 'Hurdles Road' or if there wasn't enough room, left in the yard.

Above: Not the place to berth your locomotive!

Photo: Pete Beyer and Andy Gibb.

Below: A stone train laying ballast. The hopper doors were opened on the move and careful slow speed was of the essence otherwise it meant a lot of hard manual work.

Photo: Bob Hind Collection.

Above: Weekend engineering work in 1982 featuring Class 33/0 'Crompton' 33029. Notice the regulation HVVs (High Visibility Vests).

Photo: Ken Oxlade - Julie Hogben Collection.

Below: Class 73/1 electro-diesel 73134, Class 33/0 'Crompton' 33002 and Class 73/1 electro-diesel 73118 rest at Woking Hurdles Road Berthing Point on 23rd September 1978.

Photo: David Hird.

Above: JA Type electro-diesel E6001 approaches Guildford with an engineering train from Woking PAD (Pre-Assembly Depot) consisting of mess vans, track relayer, loaded bogies of prefab and ballast cleaner on 18th July 1970. The locomotive was one of six prototypes built at Eastleigh and was such a success, that a further forty-three were built (with slight modifications) and were classed JB type.
Later, the JA Type locomotives were all reclassified 73/0 and renumbered 73001 - 73006; the JB type reclassified 73/1 and renumbered 73101 - 73142 (except E6027 which had been withdrawn because of accident damage).

Above: North Box sidings are evident in the middle of the photograph and in the background, a new factory site is being constructed on what was part of Dennis Brothers Ltd factory, famous for its car, lorry and fire engine production.
Initial construction of Guildford University can also be seen on Stag Hill to the left of the photograph.

Photo: Gordon Edgar.

Above: A view from 'Twin Bridges' looking towards and across Woking Up Yard. The area was a Pre-Assembly Depot (PAD) for engineering trains; the crews' green-coloured mess coach is shown in the middle of the photograph.

Wooden and concrete sleepers wait to be unloaded and re-assembled for a job during the night or weekend. Note the lengths of track stacked in the background waiting to be dismantled.

Photo: Bob Hind Collection.

Passed Secondman Days - Woking MT

I was now passed for driving but but still had to learn the routes and although I knew most of them, I didn't sign up straight away. In the meantime, I would also be booked secondman duties.

Mick Sparrow and I were booked together one evening and Mick kindly offered to pick me from home in his car and give me a lift to work. We went 'pass' to Clapham Junction and were required to wait for a locomotive (type 3 Crompton) and take it light-engine to Eastleigh. Whilst we waited, we took refuge in Clapham 'C' signal box which stood on the end of the platform on the Kensington side of the station adjacent to the 'Kenny' sidings. Mick and I made a can of tea and we ate the sandwiches we'd brought with us. About 1am, the locomotive duly arrived and we set off to Eastleigh chatting about different things along the way as Mick and I had lots in common.

Above: Driver Mick Sparrow on JB Type 1600/600hp electro-diesel E6013 at Guildford Yard.

Photo: Alex McClymont.

As we approached Litchfield Tunnel, Mick said to me that he wasn't feeling well and felt quite sick; he then proceeded to hang his head out of the cab window. I said to him to be careful as there was a tunnel approaching and said that it would be better if he came over to the secondman's position to avoid possible injury. I took over the driving as we entered the tunnel and proceeded towards Popham tunnels just before Micheldever station. The next thing I saw was Mick standing up, his eyes were fluttering with his face looking contorted with his tongue protruding and suddenly he fell forward and slumped over the driver's desk. My mind was racing fast and I was thinking what to do next - should I get him into a recovery position on the floor? (Not an easy task as Mick was quite heavily built).

By this time we had entered the first tunnel and as there was a signal with a telephone at the other end of the second tunnel, I decided to stop there and get assistance.

By the time I had stopped, Mick had regained consciousness and I explained to him what I was going to do.

I stopped the locomotive next to the signal (WA315) and contacted the signalman telling him that I needed an ambulance and the best place for it to come to would be Micheldever station. The signalman agreed and I climbed back onto the locomotive and explained to Mick what was going to take place. Mick seemed to have recovered his composure by this point and I moved the locomotive into the platform and we waited for the ambulance.

Some thirty minutes must have passed and in the meantime Mick had rolled a cigarette and was smoking it.

The ambulance arrived so I said to Mick that I would meet the crew and direct them safely across the crossing to the down line.

I met the ambulance crew and explained what had happened and they climbed into the cab to assess Mick's sudden illness. One of the crew was taking Mick's pulse and the other was asking him questions when all of a sudden, Mick stood up with his fists clenched and his eyes went into a trance again just as they had before!

They were both giving each other puzzled looks and asked me if he was an epileptic? I explained that he couldn't be as we had strict medicals and this would have been picked up. I was quite worried at this point as I thought Mick was going to become violent and with that Mick suddenly came out of his trance-like state and was violently sick out of the cab window.

Mick also asked if he could visit the toilet and as luck would have it, there was a 'Gents' toilet on the up side platform. The ambulance crew escorted Mick to the toilet and I contacted the signalman again to report on progress. When Mick returned, it was decided that the ambulance would take him to Winchester Hospital for a further examination and that another driver would be required to take the light locomotive onwards to Eastleigh.

This was arranged and an Eastleigh driver was dispatched from Eastleigh in the cab of a freight train that was going to Basingstoke and duly dropped him off at Micheldever station. . When we arrived at Eastleigh, I was able to get a lift back to Woking with Driver Ray Beeson (at that time Woking men worked a night freight to Eastleigh and return).

When we got back to Woking, I found out that Mick had been released from Winchester Hospital and was returning by taxi. Gerry Ford (our regular taxi driver) had been given orders to collect Mick and bring him back to Woking.

I decided to wait for Mick to return and on seeing him, I was quite relieved to see that he looked much better. He then offered to give me a lift back home in his car and I must say that after the previous experience, I was reluctant to do so. However, I did accept the lift and reached home safely. What an eventful night!

Above: The down sidings at Micheldever, close to where I stopped to contact the signalman to call for an ambulance. The sidings were originally used to serve an underground fuel depot built prior to WW2, and at the time this photograph was taken in January 1971, were used as storage sidings. In this instance, 6TC 601 is seen in the company of 4SUB 4292, both withdrawn from service.

Photo: Gordon Edgar.

Below: Southern Electric 1925 built 4SUB 4338 stored at Micheldever in July 1963. The headcode indicated a special working code on the Central and Western sections, specifically empty trains on the latter.

Photo Mike Morant Collection.

Above: Platform 6 & 7 at Guildford viewing North - the platforms being either side of a single line which was locally known as 'Up the Gulley'.
The 6+8 Car Stop mark board served platform 5 as well as platform 6 & 7.

Photo: Alex McClymont.

One day I was working a 'juice' turn from Woking to Portsmouth Harbour and return to Waterloo; the train consisting of 2 x 4COR Portsmouth Express Stock. On my return trip from Portsmouth Harbour, I arrived at Guildford and stopped my train on the 8-car mark on number 6-7 platform 'Up the Gulley.' The starting signal was displaying a green aspect and when it was time to depart, I looked back for the guard's green flag to start my train.

On receiving the guard's signal to start, I released the brake and put the reverser key switch to 'For' and opened the controller. As I started away, I noticed the starting signal's green aspect extinguish (along with the starting signals on platform 5 and platform 8) and then all the signals show a red danger aspect. I made an emergency brake application immediately and my train came to a stand just in front of the starting signal. I then noticed the facing points in front of me (that were set for the Up Woking line) suddenly move over and set themselves for the Up Reading line. I then noticed a down train from Woking running into platform 4 and unbeknown to the driver, his train had run through a pair of trailing points that had originally been set correctly.

There was a phone situated in a cabinet below the starting signal so I contacted the signalman and reported what I'd just witnessed.

He sounded quite flustered and told me not to move my train until he gave permission. Some time went by before I was given permission to move my train and continue my journey to Waterloo. At the end of my shift, I had to make out a written report regarding the incident.

Apparently, it turned out that the signalman was trying to save time and had gone downstairs to the switch room to 'short circuit' a back-lock of some description. I count my lucky stars that I only had an 8-car train that day because if I'd been working a 12-car train, I would have already passed the starting signal (the 12-car mark being at the end of the platform) and the facing points would have opened several coaches back along my train. This would have caused a catastrophic derailment where part of my train would have traversed across the facing points and continue up the Reading line!

Above: 'Nelson' 4COR 3123 and 4BUF 3081 leaving Guildford on a Portsmouth to London Waterloo fast service with sister unit 4COR 3114 stabled in the up sidings on 18th July 1970. Photo: Gordon Edgar.

Below: Drewry 204hp diesel-shunter D2041 stands in the East-End mail dock at Woking station whilst the driver takes a meal break. A couple of mail bags are left strewn on the down local platform next to the loco, and a screw coupling is just waiting to trip someone over! The Drewry shunter was a regular locomotive utilised for attaching and detaching mail and parcel vans from trains from London for loading and unloading purposes. Photo: Bob Hind Collection.

Above: A Waterloo - Reading service leaves Waterloo headed by 4COR 3161 in October 1971. A 'Warship' Class locomotive is berthed in the sidings.

Below: 4SUB 4107 at Waterloo, circa 1971/72.

Photos: Stuart Ray.

Above: Driver's side view of an electro-diesel - this being a JB type (Class 73/1). If an 'EP' key was inserted and turned, the Master Switch could be opened. This would also unlock either of the power controllers.

Below: Positions of the Master Switch.

Photos: Courtesy of South West Trains.

Following my Type 3 1550hp diesel course, I was booked to attend an electro-diesel course at Waterloo South Side training school. Again, I was joined by Bill Tickner and another of my colleagues from Woking, Frank Saxby.

The course lasted three weeks and we had a variety of instructors teaching us. On our static sessions we visited Stewarts Lane depot and I can remember one of the instructors being George Bowman. Our training trips were conducted with a set of TC units from Clapham Yard to Weymouth and with various freight trains on the South Eastern Division from Tonbridge Yard to Hither Green via Hoo Junction.

We had a two-day exam with our examiner (Wally Ward), the first day based in the classroom with an assortment of fault and failure questions; one of the questions being 'Assisting a failed EMU train with a electro-diesel hauled vacuum-fitted van train'. Wally wanted to know what brake tests were required and the readings that one would expect to see on the gauges of the electro-diesel and also in the cab of the failed EMU after coupling procedures had taken place. Out of the twelve of the group present, three of the drivers failed the first part of the exam. The second part of the exam involved working a loose-coupled freight train with a fitted-head on diesel and electric conditions on the South Eastern Division and I'm not sure now which route we took. I was only in the driver's seat for about half-an-hour and when I stopped at a signal at a station, Wally said that I'd passed the course and I was to make my way home.

Low Level Connections:

1. Engine Speed Control
2. Main Reservoir Air
3. Automatic Brake
4. Vacuum Pipe
5. Electric Train Heat Supply Jumper & Receptacle
6. Diesel Control Jumper Receptacle
7. Buckeye Coupling

High Level Connections:

1. Automatic Brake & Main Reservoir Duplex Control
2. Multiple Unit Control Jumper
3. Multiple Unit Control Receptacle

Photo: George Woods.

Coupling two electro-diesel locomotives together in multiple was quite a difficult operation. The first thing was to ensure that the buffers were retracted on both locomotives and the buckeye couplings lifted to their raised position (with one jaw open). Note: It was always a good idea to couple one of the ends of the diesel control jumper (stored in the engine room) into one of the receptacles at this stage.

The locomotives would then be coupled together and a 'pull away test' carried out. After clambering into the little space provided, it would then be necessary to connect the other end of the diesel control jumper to the other loco's receptacle. If working a vacuum-fitted train, the vacuum pipes would also be connected. Finally, to complete the low level connections, the engine speed control pipes would be connected, not forgetting to open both nose end cocks.

The high level 27-way multiple unit control jumper would be now be connected and finally, the duplex main reservoir and brake pipe connection not forgetting to open both dual control isolating cocks.
Both the locomotives' engines could now be started by operating the Auto-Engine Start switch and once started, power could be applied to both locos by using the diesel controller. Once the electric controller was moved away from Lock Off to Off, both locomotives' shoes would lower onto the third rail and electrical power deployed on both locos by operating the electric controller.
A total of 3,200hp on electric conditions and 1200hp on diesel conditions.

Above: JA Type 1600/600hp electro-diesel E6006 approaches Raynes Park hauling an EMU on 25th July 1964. One of six prototype electro-diesels with slight differences to the JB type. These locomotives could pre-heat attached trains using electrical current generated whilst the diesel engine was running. The JB type could only pre-heat an attached train using current from the third rail supply.

Photo: George Woods.

Below: JB Type 1600/600hp electro-diesel E6041 runs into New Cross Gate Yard circa 1968.

Photo: Ken Oxlade - Julie Hogben Collection.

Passed Secondman Days - Woking MT

One of the night turns we had at Woking was to work a van train from Guildford to Willesden via Brentford and Acton Wells Junction and return to Woking with a similar train. Although I was already passed for driving, I was acting as secondman to Driver Gordon Ballard for the week and because the turn involved working most of the night, and also involved working overtime, it was a very good paying turn. On the Wednesday (3rd June 1970), we were returning with the train from Willesden and came to a halt at a red signal at Lyne Crossing (between Virginia Water and Chertsey). Wc stood at the signal for a few minutes and I then got down on the signalpost telephone to carry out Rule 55 (Detention of trains on running lines). The signalman informed me that there had been a collision at Chertsey involving the previous train that had been running in front of us and an empty passenger train that had been just leaving the down platform.

Above: Gordon Ballard on a JB type electro-diesel locomotive.

Photo: Alex McClymont.

Left: Chertsey level crossing and the aftermath of the collision with the breakdown crane in situ.

Below: Concertina effect of the wagons caused by the impact.

Photos: Pete Beyer & Andy Gibb.

It was not known how long that we would be delayed but some of the train involved in the collision had become derailed. I think that the collision had taken place at about 05.30 and our guard (John Beeson) volunteered to walk to Chertsey station and contacted our respective wives to inform them that we would be delayed (no mobile phones in those days).

After several hours, 'Control' decided that we would be relieved by another set of men and Gordon and I walked to Chertsey station, and whilst waiting for our relief to arrive, had breakfast in the café outside the station.

When I eventually got home and contacted my wife at work, she informed me that the message she'd received from John was "Mrs Burch? There's been an accident but Geoff's alright!"

That week turned out to be the best paying week I'd ever had during my railway career – total hours worked 100 hours + 12 and three-quarters of an hour mileage; a total of 112 and-three-quarters hours!

The accident turned out to be a freight train (hauled by an Class 74 electro-diesel failing to stop at the outer home signal at Chertsey and running into the rear of an EPB unit (that was just leaving for Weybridge that morning).

Luckily, there were no injuries but several wagons had become either buffer-locked or derailed. The locomotive hauling the freight train suffered little damage considering the impact.

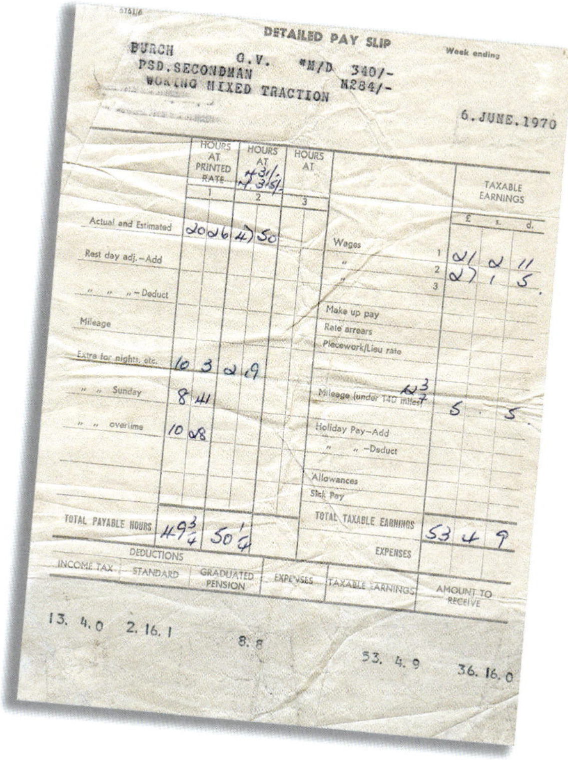
DETAILED PAY SLIP
BURCH G.V. *M/D 340/-
PSD.SECONDMAN M284/-
WORKING MIXED TRACTION
Week ending 6.JUNE.1970

	Hours at printed rate (1)	Hours at 43/- 47/3/8 (2)	Hours at (3)		Taxable earnings £ s. d.
Actual and Estimated	20 26	47 50		Wages 1	21 2 11
Rest day adj.–Add				" 2	27 1 5
" " "–Deduct				" 3	
Mileage				Make up pay	
				Rate arrears	
				Piecework/Lieu rate	
Extra for nights, etc.	10 3	2 9			
" " Sunday	8 41			Mileage (under 140 miles) 12¾	5 . 5
" " overtime	10 28			Holiday Pay–Add	
				" " –Deduct	
				Allowances	
				Sick Pay	
TOTAL PAYABLE HOURS	49¾	50¼		TOTAL TAXABLE EARNINGS	53 4 9
				EXPENSES	

Deductions: Income Tax	Standard	Graduated Pension	Expenses	Taxable Earnings	Amount to Receive
13. 4.0	2. 16. 1	8. 8		53. 4. 9	36. 16. 0

Above: The Author's payslip for the week following the incident.

Below: The Class 74 electro-diesel locomotive and train and EPB stock involved in the collision.

Photos: Pete Beyer & Andy Gibb.

Passed Secondman Days - Woking MT

On the 23rd March 1972, G Barnham (my secondman) and I booked on duty at 05.45 to take a Crompton locomotive light-engine to Stewarts Lane depot to take fuel and then work a van train from Clapham to Woking. After preparing the loco, we left Woking 'Hurdles Road' siding and with a clear route, proceeded through Woking station and onto the up through line towards West Byfleet.

With green signals all the way to Berrylands and approaching New Malden, I saw a carriage door open on the offside of a stationary train in the up local platform. I sounded the two-tone horn as a warning and noticed a figure climb down and crouch under the running board of the train. I applied the emergency brake but as we'd been travelling at around 60mph, we were unable to stop. Luckily, our locomotive missed the person by inches and came to a stand some 25 yards on the other side of the station.

I jumped down onto the track and walked back to the person (now standing in the track) whom I now recognised as being a large black lady. She was in a bit of a panic and was becoming hysterical not knowing what to do next and as she was standing in the four-foot next to a live rail and realising she was in immediate danger, I told her to stand still and stay exactly where she was. I approached her and held onto her arms to reassure her but she took no notice and then placed one of her feet onto the conductor rail. I immediately let go of her arms and as luck would have it, she didn't get electrocuted - this was probably because the weather conditions were dry and she was wearing rubber soled shoes. By this time, the driver of the train that she had alighted from had heard the commotion and although he'd received the Guard's signal to start, hadn't moved his train. The guard of the train had also appeared at the open carriage door and with our combined effort, (my secondman and I pushing and the guard and driver pulling), we collectively managed to get the lady back into the carriage.

Above: New Malden station and the exact place where the incident occurred.

Photo: Steve Poole.

Below: Letter from Area Depot Master Arthur Coe inviting my wife and I to attend a presentation and lunch at Waterloo with David Binnie the Southern Region General Manager.

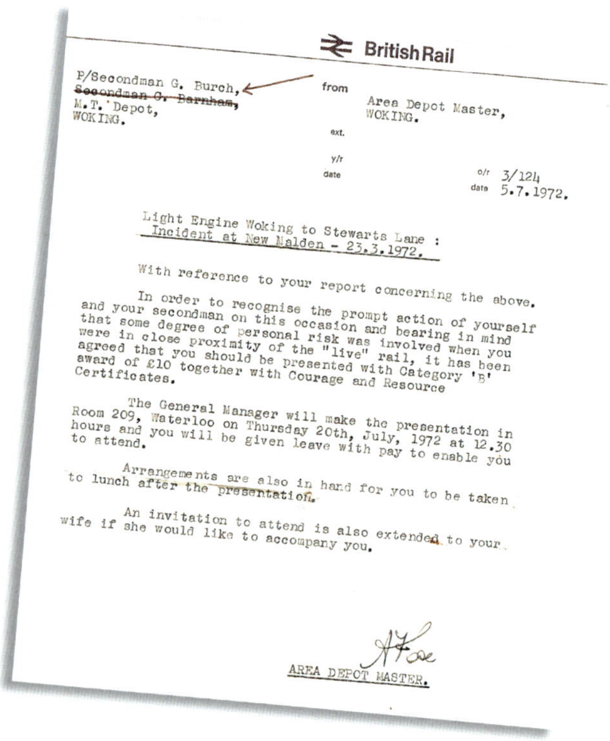

British Rail

P/Secondman G. Burch,
~~Secondman G. Barnham,~~
M.T. Depot,
WOKING.

from Area Depot Master,
WOKING.

ext.

y/r
date

o/r 3/124
date 5.7.1972.

Light Engine Woking to Stewarts Lane :
Incident at New Malden - 23.3.1972.

With reference to your report concerning the above.

In order to recognise the prompt action of yourself and your secondman on this occasion and bearing in mind that some degree of personal risk was involved when you were in close proximity of the "live" rail, it has been agreed that you should be presented with Category 'B' award of £10 together with Courage and Resource Certificates.

The General Manager will make the presentation in Room 209, Waterloo on Thursday 20th, July, 1972 at 12.30 hours and you will be given leave with pay to enable you to attend.

Arrangements are also in hand for you to be taken to lunch after the presentation.

An invitation to attend is also extended to your wife if she would like to accompany you.

A Coe

AREA DEPOT MASTER.

Above: Just in case you don't recognise me, I'm the one with the long hair and droopy moustache! Other's include from left to right: Mr Weedon, my secondman that day - G Barnham, my wife Pauline, Southern Region General Manager David Binnie, the guard on the passenger train and his wife and the driver of the passenger train and his wife.

Photo: The Author's Collection.

I later found out that the train (which consisted of two 4SUB units) had earlier worked down from Waterloo to Hampton Court and one of the coaches had been used to carry parcels and all of the doors on both sided of the carriage had been locked out of use. When the train had reached its destination at Hampton Court, the doors had been unlocked on the platform side of the train and the parcels had been unloaded but the doors on the 'left hand' side of the train hadn't been unlocked. The train then departed from Hampton Court and when it arrived at Surbiton, passengers were able to enter the carriage because Surbiton station has an island platform; the up local platform being on the 'off" side. When the train arrived at New Malden (with the platform on the left-hand side) the lady in question tried to open the carriage door and upon finding it locked, proceeded to exit the train from the door she got in – hence her position on the track in front of a locomotive bearing down on her at speed!

On returning to my depot, I submitted a written report of the incident and some weeks later, received a letter from my Depot Master saying that my wife and I were invited to attend a luncheon at Waterloo where I would receive a Courage & Resource certificate and an award of £10 from David Binnie (BR Southern Region General Manager).

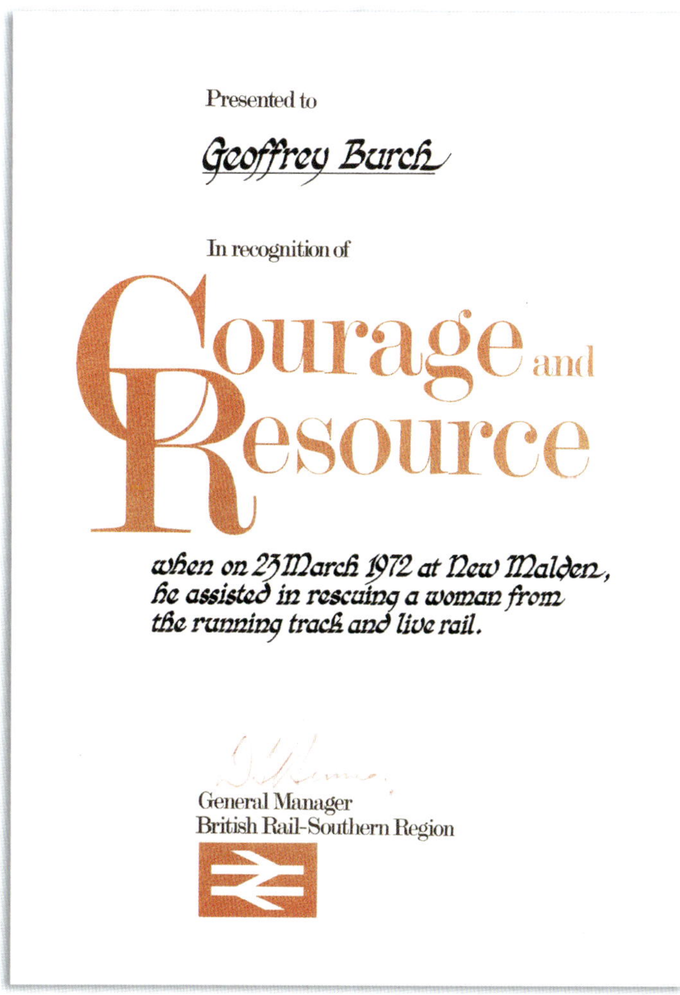

Presented to

Geoffrey Burch

In recognition of

Courage and Resource

when on 23 March 1972 at New Malden, he assisted in rescuing a woman from the running track and live rail.

General Manager
British Rail-Southern Region

Passed Secondman Days - Woking MT

Some of the drivers at Woking had previously learnt the Class 74 electro-diesels and I was quite often booked to ride secondman on this type of locomotive.

Two occasions come to mind; one turn where we had to take a locomotive from Guildford to Aldershot (light-loco) and work a freight back to Woking Yard.

We came out of Guildford Down Yard on diesel power and once over the third rail, the Driver shut the diesel down and continued on electric power. He swung the controller round fully and the locomotive took off like a rocket and as we climbed the bank round the curve towards Dennis's factory, the framing of the locomotive was swaying and banging from side to side as we continued our uphill climb towards Pinks Hill. I was astounded at the acceleration (as I think my driver was) and it wasn't long before we turned the top of the bank at a speed that was quite frightening. I hasten to add that the brakes on any light locomotive running light weren't at all good and luckily my driver started braking early enough at Wanborough for us to round the curve at Ash Junction at the correct speed.

The other occasion that I can remember quite clearly was working a boat train with Driver Bob Stuckey. Bob had transferred to Woking Mixed Traction from Chertsey where he had been a Motorman for quite a number of years. We worked the train both ways; first from Waterloo to Southampton Old Docks returning with another service to Waterloo.

Delivering 2,500hp on electric conditions, these journeys also attained high speed.

The Paxman engine of the Class 74s was marginally more powerful than the Class 73 English Electric engine but it was nowhere near as reliable. The Paxman engine was also extremely noisy and difficult to start on occasions. Until four additional 4REP units were built in 1973/74, class 74s had regular daytime passenger turns including the 15.30 Waterloo-Weymouth (as far as Bournemouth). Subsequently their only regular non-freight workings were on night mail and newspaper trains to and from Bournemouth, and the Weymouth boat trains.

Class 73 locomotives had a simpler electrical system arrangement for control of the dual power sources on the driver's desk; one for diesel and one for electric. The complex control system of Class 74 (with a single dual-purpose controller) was sometimes problematic and the class were dogged with electrical system failures.

Together, the three complaints of poor reliability, difficult engine starting and excessive noise made Class 74 locomotives unpopular with crew and fitters alike.

All of the locomotives had been withdrawn between June 1976 and December 1977 and were scrapped between 1977 and 1981.

Below: Class 74 electro-diesel 74004 stands at Woking with a down parcels working in the early hours of 3rd December 1977. The locomotive was withdrawn at the end of the year.

Photo: David Hayes.

Above: Class 74 electro-diesel 74007 passes through Farnborough on the up slow line just east of the station with a long van train on 4th January 1975.

Below: Class 74 electro-diesel 74003 passes Southampton's old terminus having been in the docks on the R.P.P.R. Class 74 Farewell Tour on 3rd December 1977.

Photos: David Hird.

Above: With the P&O Oriana in the background, a boat train heads out of Southampton Old Docks bound for Waterloo headed by Class 74 electro-diesel 74007 in May 1975.

Oriana held the Golden Cockerel trophy for the fastest ship in the P&O fleet until she retired in 1986, when it was handed over to the Canberra.

Photo: George Woods.

Above: A rather dilapidated 4BUF 'Nelson' 3077 at Ascot on 5th December 1970. The service would continue after the Guildford portion had attached to the rear of the train to form an 8-car stopping service to Waterloo.

Photo: Gordon Edgar.

Above: A view of the concourse at London Waterloo station in December 1973. The Christmas tree receives admiring glances from two ladies in head-scarves. In the background we see advertising for the Hastings & Thanet Building Society. They were merged with the Anglia in 1978, who in turn, were taken over by Nationwide in 1987.

Photo: Kevin Lane.

Above: Having been displaced from the 'Pompey' line services by 4CIG units, some 4COR units were cascaded onto suburban services. Blue-liveried 4COR Units 3149 and 3150, forming a Reading and Guildford service from London Waterloo via Ascot is seen at Clapham Junction on 22nd November 1970.

Photo & Caption: Gordon Edgar.

Below: 4VEP 7706 with the small yellow warning panel and the all-over blue livery as delivered, working a down stopping service near Hook on 2nd May 1970.

Photo: Gordon Edgar.

Above: 4COR 'Nelson' 3133 clatters into Camberley station on 22nd June 1971, working between Ascot and Guildford via Aldershot. Very much the last knockings for these pre-war units, the last running in 1972.

Photo & Caption: Alec Swain / Kevin Lane Collection.

Below: Frimley Junction Signal Box and its surrounds showing the line that went to Woking (via Sturt Lane Junction), the single line to Ash Vale and the line to Farnborough Main. Photo: Jack Hills / Steve West Collection.

Above: Ash Vale Junction Signal Box - the single line leading to Frimley Junction where it progressed as a double line to Ascot and eventually London Waterloo.

Below: Frimley Junction Signal Box - the wooden platform staging and post that was used to surrender the single line token is shown in the foreground.

Photo: Jack Hills / Steve West Collection.

Above: Mick Stokes of Farnham driving 2BIL 2147 cautiously approaches Frimley Junction Signal Box to collect the single line token from Signalman Jack Hills which will give him authority to pass over the single line section to Ash Vale.

Below: Block Regulation 5 is in place (signalman's green flag held steady - meaning section clear, junction blocked) as Mick Stokes collects the token. Always a difficult manoeuvre as the DSD had to be held down with the other hand with considerable pressure!

Photos: Jack Hills / Steve West Collection.

Although I had passed for driving on electric and Type 3 Crompton traction in 1969, by the end of October 1972, I realised that it would be a long time before I could get a driver's position at Woking MT. When the vacancy sheet came out the following month, I noticed that there were two vacancies for drivers' positions at Effingham Junction EMUT depot so I decided to apply for one of them.

Ray Bartlett was also in a similar position to myself and so he applied for the other. The vacancy list closed and Ray and I were both sent a letter to say that our applications were successful and we would be transferred to Effingham on 11th December 1972.

The depot worked on a two-shift system (early and late turn); the earliest turn signing on at 05.00 to work the first train from Effingham Junction to Waterloo via Epsom.

This wasn't a route that I was conversant with (as well as some of the other suburban routes) so I was booked 'route learning' for several weeks so that it would be possible for me to cover all turns at the depot.

The routes I had to learn were:

Guildford - Hampton Court Junction via Cobham
Surbiton - Hampton Court
Wimbledon - Chessington
Wimbledon - Effingham Junction via Epsom
Epsom - Holmwood via Dorking
Wimbledon - Shepperton
Waterloo - Waterloo via Hounslow
Waterloo - Waterloo via Kingston

The other drivers on my shift were quite a nice bunch and I got to know them better when I rode in their cabs whilst route learning.

Some of the men I worked with were: Len Rickard (nicknamed the 'Boy Scout' as he had a lot to do with the Scout movement), Peter Foster, George Baker, Ron Cooper, Sammy Rowe (whom I'd worked with at Guildford in my firing days), Alfie Hamblin, John Cane, Nelson Parsons, Jack Farrow, Terry Drudge, Ron Chaffey, Bob Black and Ray Bartlett. Most of the trains we worked were made of 4SUB or 2 x 4SUB stock whilst working on most of the suburban routes and EPB stock and occasionally VEP stock when working to Guildford via Cobham or Guildford via Woking. There was one turn though where we would work a 2 x 4COR stock to Holmwood and berth the train in the sidings for its return trip to Waterloo in the morning.

Driving from other than the leading cab was normal practice in those days and once an 8-car SUB had been prepared in the shed at Effingham, it would be set-back towards the stop block in the neck road with the shunter (John Cates) in the rear of the train. Once the front cab was clear of the ground signal, that was the position to stop your train.

I'd only been at Effingham Junction Depot a few months when ASLEF called a 'work-to-rule.' As the SUB stock didn't have a speedometer (or any safety related equipment besides a DSD) e.g. AWS / Vigilance Device, all of the trains in the depot were 'blacked' and didn't move out of the depot. This meant that we didn't do much work over the following two weeks and in the end, were ordered to stand spare at Waterloo.

I'm not sure whether it was the union or management that won the argument in the end but it wasn't long before we started driving the SUB units again.

My mode of transport at that time was a 750cc Norton Commando which I'd bought after returning from seeing the TT Races in the Isle of Man. I can honestly say that it didn't ever let me down and I was never late for work during my time at Effingham Junction.

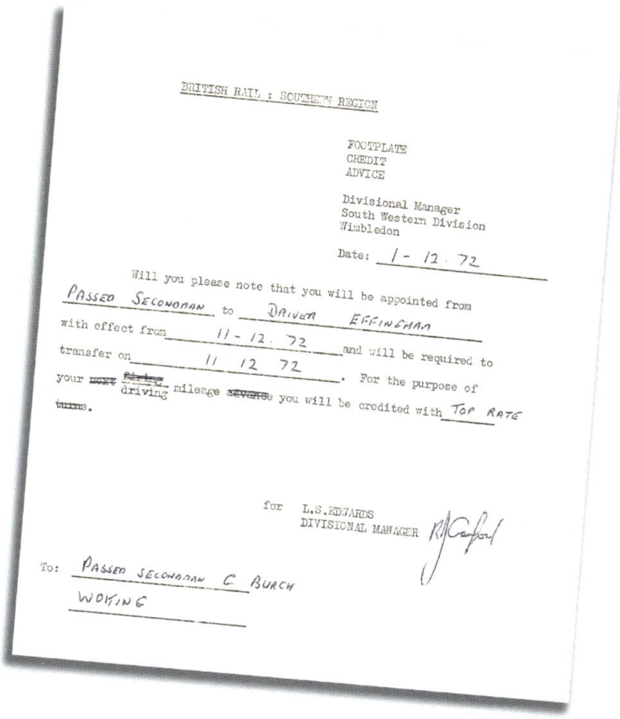

BRITISH RAIL : SOUTHERN REGION

FOOTPLATE
CREDIT
ADVICE

Divisional Manager
South Western Division
Wimbledon

Date: 1 - 12 . 72

Will you please note that you will be appointed from PASSED SECONDMAN to DRIVER EFFINGHAM with effect from 11 - 12 . 72 and will be required to transfer on 11 12 72. For the purpose of your ~~next~~ ~~firing~~ driving mileage ~~advance~~ you will be credited with TOP RATE ~~turns~~.

for L.S.EDWARDS
DIVISIONAL MANAGER [signature]

To: PASSED SECONDMAN C BURCH
WOKING

Left: Letter of confirmation regarding my appointment as Driver at Effingham Junction.

Below: The Author and 750cc Norton Commando.

Photo: Author's Collection.

Above: The driver of a Dorking - Waterloo service headed by 4SUB 4668 looks back for the guard's green flag at Clapham Junction.

Photo: Ken Oxlade - Julie Hogben Collection.

Below: Passengers scramble aboard a Hampton Court - Waterloo stopping service at Wimbledon headed by 2HAP 6072.

Photo: Ian Docwra.

Above: The train departure board at Waterloo station.
An ingenious device that was manually operated by inserting a series of hole-punched cards. Some of the destination names would occasionally get stuck and would need a gentle prod with a long wooden pole!

Photo: David Hird.

Below: Elaborate calligraphy and vinyl stickers!

Photo: Ian Docwra.

As well as the route knowledge, station stopping patterns had to be learnt thoroughly as well. Most of the trains that we worked at Effingham stopped at all stations but there were some exceptions, especially at weekends.

For instance, the first train up in the morning via Epsom stopped all stations to Waterloo and the stops were the same with the return trip. If you worked a train from Guildford via Cobham, the stopping pattern would be all stations to Wimbledon, and then fast to Waterloo.

However, on the 23rd February whilst working No. 133 duty which involved working a Guildford service via Weybridge, I completely forgot to call at Hersham. It wasn't until I was half way down the platform (with the controller still open) that I realised. It was far to late to try to stop so I continued to Walton station. On stopping, a rather irate lady in the front carriage jumped out waving her brolly and said that she wanted to get out at Hersham. I apologised profusely and seeing a train approaching on the up local line, directed her to catch the train back to Hersham.

I was fully expecting a letter demanding an explanation but luckily, the incident wasn't reported.

Driving Days - Effingham Junction

The one good thing about driving SUBs or BILs or Portsmouth Main Line stock was that you were guaranteed not to fall asleep whilst driving! The seating arrangement wasn't at all comfortable (except on the 4COR stock) and the deadman was such a pressure to hold down, it was more comfortable to stand up. Heating arrangements weren't too clever either with draughts coming into the cab from poorly fitting doors and windows. I personally loved using the Westinghouse brake (good job really as it was the only brake available on 2BIL, 4SUB or 4COR stock). I hated the clicking noise whilst operating the EP brake's magnet valves and when driving EP stock I would use the Westinghouse brake instead.

Using the Westinghouse brake on the 1963 VEP stock (termed AUTO Brake) was quite an easy operation and with the flick of a switch, the 3-position brake valve could be transformed immediately but with 1957 EPB stock you'd have to trip the mcb (miniature circuit breaker) or on 1951 stock remove the EP fuse. However, the Westinghouse brake could still be applied on EPB stock by moving the 5 position brake handle smartly round to position 3 (Lap) and using the service application position and back to position 1 to release the brake. This took a lot of practice and was also a rule book requirement at certain points of one's journey e.g. carrying out running brake tests.

You must test that the automatic brake is working properly:
• at the first opportunity after starting the journey, and
• again in good time before approaching:
(a) the first stopping place
(b) a crossing place where the train has to stop
(c) a steep falling gradient
(d) a terminus or dead-end platform line

When a running brake test is made in any of these circumstances, you must check that deceleration is taking place.

4.5.2 Running brake test during, and in, snow conditions
4.5.2.1 When:
• snow is falling, or
• fallen snow is being disturbed by the passage of trains,
you must make sure:
A full service brake application is made every three to five minutes
The speed of the train is reduced by at least 10 m.p.h.

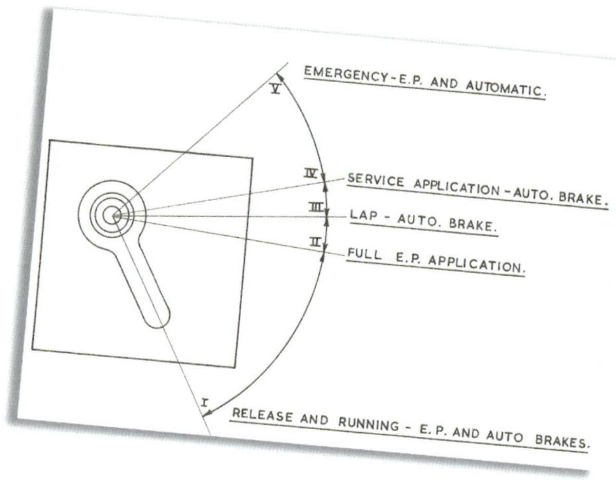

Above: 5 Position Brake drawing on 1951 & 1957 stock.

Below: Litter strewn tracks between Waterloo's platforms 2 and 3.
Another trip to Chessington - train ready to start - green signal with indication ML (Main Local line).

Photo: The Author's Collection.

Above: An assortment of EMU stock in Wimbledon Maintenance Depot, Durnsford Road. Following the early morning 'rush hour', most ECS (empty coaching stock) ran from Waterloo to Wimbledon Park via East Putney.

Photo: Ian Docwra.

Below: A Waterloo W (Windsor side) - Waterloo M (Main side) via Kingston (Round the World) stopping service headed by 4SUB 4653 runs into Twickenham.

Photo: Stuart Ray.

Driving Days - Effingham Junction

One of the late turns at Effingham entailed finishing the shift by working the last train from Waterloo to Effingham Junction via Epsom. After leaving Epsom, I came to a stand at an intermediate signal between Epsom and Ashtead.

After a few minutes, I secured my train and got down on the track and attempted to phone the signalman by using the signal-post telephone provided. When I opened the telephone cabinet, I found that the phone had been left off the hook and the line was dead. I walked back to see my guard and asked him to walk back to the signal-post telephone on the up side and try to contact Epsom signal box. Some time went by and eventually the guard returned with a message from the signalman that as he couldn't raise the signalman at Ashtead either; to pass the signal at danger and proceed towards Ashtead and stop prior to reaching the crossing gates. With the guard in the cab, I proceeded with caution and stopped just short of the gates and the guard jumped down and climbed the steps to the signal box. All of sudden there was a commotion in the signal box – the signalman being suddenly raised from his slumber and not knowing which way to turn! All of this was in clear view of my cab and to passengers in the first carriage of my train – goodness knows what they must have thought!

When the crossing gates were eventually opened, I was able to continue into the station and let the passengers disembark.

Once I reached Effingham Junction shed, I then had to make out a written report of the incident.

I learnt later that the signalman in question had a part-time job as a coach driver and was so tired, he'd lie down on the couch between trains and go to sleep.

The previous train to mine had also been stopped at the intermediate signal and the driver (annoyed that he'd had to get down to use the phone to raise the signalman), had deliberately left the phone off the hook so that it would keep ringing in the signalbox. The signalman had then taken his phone off the hook to stop the ringing noise, which subsequently rendered it useless.

There were other instances of the signalman's tiredness (on the first train service up in the morning I'd had to use the signal-post telephone to wake him on several occasions) and following an enquiry, he was relieved of his signalman's duties and removed from the box.

Above: Ashtead signal box in 1974.

Photo: John Scrace.

Below: A superb painting (oils on board) of a Victoria to Portsmouth express (via Dorking) formed of 6PAN 3022 as it rushes through Ashtead in Surrey in the summer of 1959. This painting features in the book 'Emotions of Railway Art', published by the Guild of Railway Artists.

Artist: Ian Docwra.

For some unknown reason, the stopping services from Waterloo M (Waterloo Main side) – Waterloo W (Windsor side) via Kingston and vice-versa nicknamed 'Round the World' and the Waterloo W (Windsor side) – Waterloo W (Windsor side) via Brentford nicknamed 'Round the Loop' had anomalies in their stopping pattern.

In one direction you would stop at Queens Road (Battersea) and Wandsworth Town on the down journey and stop there on the up journey. On reaching Clapham with a 'Round the Loop' (via Brentford), I'd always run the front of my cab past the 4car/8car stop mark so that I wouldn't have to explain to anyone when questioned "does this train stop at Barnes Bridge?" the answer being "yes it does, but on the way back!"

As mentioned in my 'Secondman Days' chapter, route indicators on SUB stock were made out of metal stencils and these would be inserted into a metal frame and clipped into place on the front of the headcode panel. Once you'd reached your destination, the frame would be removed and if the platform wasn't on the driver' side, the non-driver's side window could be opened (this was hinged and held secure by two butterfly nuts) and the frame retrieved through the window.

The headcodes for the suburban routes were as follows:

01	ECS Clapham yard
03	ECS to Wimbledon Park
16	Waterloo M - Effingham Jn via Epsom & return
17	Waterloo M - Dorking & return
18	Waterloo M - Chessington & return
21	Waterloo M - Waterloo W via Kingston
24	Waterloo M - Shepperton & return
28	Waterloo W - Guildford via Ascot & return
30	Waterloo M - Hampton Court & return
32	Waterloo W - Waterloo M via Kingston
36	Waterloo W - Reading & return
42	Waterloo M - Guildford via Cobham & return
73	Waterloo M - Portsmouth & Southsea & return
87	Waterloo W - Waterloo W via Hounslow
89	Waterloo W - Waterloo W via Brentford

***Left:** Queens Road Battersea (the station name was later changed to Queenstown Road on 12th May 1980).*

***Photo:** David Hird.*

***Below:** A Shepperton service consisting of 4SUB 4639 disgorges its passengers at Sunbury on a cold winter's morning in 1979. The British Cardboard factory can be seen in the background.*

***Photo:** Stuart Ray.*

Above: 4SUB 4630 runs into Clapham Junction with a Waterloo - Shepperton service. Clapham Junction A signalbox which spanned the Windsor-side lines can be seen in the background.

Below: Travelling in the opposite direction with 4SUB 4651, the driver of a Hampton Court - Waterloo service ponders on whether other passengers will dash up the steps from the subway to board his train as this was normally the case.

Photos: David Hayes.

Above: Epsom Signalbox on a cold winter's day.

Photo: Ian Docwra.

Below: This set of ECS (Empty Coaching Stock) with 4EPB 5123 is ready to depart from Waterloo for Wimbledon Park Depot. The route was normally via Clapham Junction and East Putney.

Photo: David Hayes.

Above: 4EPB Unit No. 5105 heads a Guildford - Waterloo via Cobham stopping service from the down bay (No. 1 platform). The Down Yard is still kept busy with a variety of goods traffic including wagons of scrap metal shown on the left of the photograph.

Below: Judging by the open guard's compartment door and carriage windows it looks like a really hot summer day as 4EPB 5116 + 4VEP passes Woking signal No. WV56 working a semi-fast Portsmouth - Waterloo service. Even the driver has his sleeves rolled up!

Photos: Michael Thorne.

Above: 4SUB 4632 working a Waterloo W - Waterloo W stopping service (via Richmond) heads towards Chiswick station having just left Kew Bridge station and passed under the Richmond - Kensington line.

Below: Working in the opposite direction (Waterloo W - Waterloo W) 4SUB 4633 has just left Brentford station heading for Syon Lane.

Both of these services were an Effingham driver's 'bread and butter' and the routes were nicknamed 'Round the Loop'.

Photos: Michael Thorne.

Above: A beautiful spring morning and the driver is about to make another perfect stop at the 8-car mark at Teddington using the Westinghouse brake. The 8-car train is headed by 4SUB 4660. This unit was one of the few that had roller blinds fitted as route indicators.

The headcode 24 denotes that it is a Shepperton service and will call at Fulwell, Hampton, Kempton Park (on race days), Sunbury, Upper Halliford and Shepperton.

Photo: Stuart Ray.

Above Top: Waterloo Up Main Local Home Signal (WB2) displaying a green aspect and theatre box indication to enter platform 5 circa 1973.
Above: Waterloo Up Main Slow Home Signal (W2) displaying a yellow aspect with theatre box indication to enter platform 3 circa 2009.

In the photograph at the top, note the home signal's green aspect. All home signals on the approach to a 'dead-end' terminus are now restricted to a one yellow caution aspect. This change became necessary after the Moorgate disaster on 28th February 1975 when a London Underground tube train failed to stop at the terminus and forty-three people, including the driver, lost their lives.
Photos: Author's Collection.

Driving Days - Effingham Junction

When I applied for a driver's vacancy at Effingham, I'd also elected to return to Woking Mixed Traction Depot as my first preference when a vacancy arose. On 21st December 1973, I received a letter to say that my transfer was going to take place on 7th January 1974.

I'd had a really good time being a driver at Effingham but now it was time to move on. My last turn of duty at Effingham was on Friday 4th January 1974 working a late turn; 144 duty signing on at 16.28.

On Monday 7th January, I returned to Effingham Junction mess room for the last time as a driver, said goodbye to the resident cabin cat and transferred my locker contents back to Woking.

Right: A Waterloo - Guildford service approaches 'Yorkies' Bridge headed by 2EPB 5773.

Photo: Gordon Edgar.

Below: Effingham Shed in later days; the 4SUBs having been replaced by Class 455 units.

Photo: Steve West Collection.

On my second day back at Woking I was booked route refresher (signals) signing on at 10.00 and travelled in the cab with Driver Ray Reed. I was also booked signals the rest of the week but on the Thursday, ASLEF had called for strike action so I didn't go into work and helped my brother instead.

I still had to refresh my memory on a lot of routes and was booked signals to Portsmouth the following week but that was interrupted by another day's strike action on the Tuesday. However, on the Thursday, I did go to Portsmouth Harbour with my old regular driver in the steam days, Stan Harms. It was nice to be back with Stan again; putting the world to rights and it felt quite strange being in the cab with someone else as it had been a lonely existence being in a cab of EMU at Effingham for the past year.

The next three weeks I was again booked signals; going to Alton and Eastleigh and also back over routes I'd not been over for a long time. Guildford to Waterloo via Aldershot and Ascot and from Ascot to Reading and because I was now back at a mixed traction depot, I had to refresh my memory of routes over non-electrified lines such as Guildford - Redhill - Three Bridges -Tonbridge and also Guildford to Reading and Basingstoke to Salisbury.

As I'd only been away from diesel traction for a year, it wasn't deemed necessary for me to have a refresher course on 'Cromptons' or Class 73s so it wasn't long before I was working the various turns worked by this form of traction. I'd already had a REP and 350hp shunter course before my transfer to Effingham so that wasn't necessary either.

Above: Driver Ray Reed in his Acting Train Crew Supervisor role at Woking MT.

Photo: Alex McClymont.

Below: The signal gantry at Redhill - London end. A place where I'd worked trains on many occasions during my time at Guildford Loco and Woking MT Depot.

Photo: Gordon Edgar.

Driving Days - Woking MT

I had also sold my Norton Commando; this was bought by Ian Newall (who was the son of Jim Newall, a fellow driver at Guildford). I'd borrowed a few bikes from friends for rides out occasionally - Brian Davis's Kawasaki 500cc Triple and Bill Scott's Honda 500cc Four but thought that the time had eventually come for me to settle down to four-wheeled transport. In December 1974, I thought that the only way I would convince myself was to apply for my driving test and I had a bit of a shock when a letter came back saying that the test was five days later!

I contacted BSM driving school and they fixed me up with four 'crash course' lessons and I passed first time. I'm sure though that my years of motorcycling experience helped tremendously. My first car was a mini and it felt quite strange driving with passengers and having conversations. Quite alien to what I'd been used to on the bikes! It wasn't long though before I decided to buy my first 'sports car'. This was a Teal Blue MGB GT and was a wonderful car to drive.

George Langhorn, a friend of mine that worked at Maranello Concessionaires at the time, gave it a re-spray in the 'oven' there and it looked fantastic. This was to be my mode of transport for the next few years.

Above: Brian Davis's Kawasaki 500cc Triple. Being a two-stroke with triple cylinders, this bike had phenomenal acceleration. Unfortunately, the handling wasn't as good and the model had a nickname of 'widow maker'.

Right: Bill Scott's Honda 500cc Four. A superb bike to ride.

Below: The Author's MGB GT.

Photos: The Author's Collection.

Above: De-icing Unit 012 at Fratton in October 1972. Originally this was a 4SUB 4340 and was converted in 1959.

Photo: Gordon Edgar.

Below: 4VEP 7708 leaves Woking on the Down Local line towards 'Twin Bridges'. These were to be my 'bread & butter 'units, working most passenger services for the next 20 years.

Photo: Bob Hind Collection.

Driving Days - Woking MT

Above: Class 33/0 'Crompton' at North Camp Oil Sidings.

Below: Shunter Horace Bishop removes the tail lamp on the tanks at North Camp Sidings.

Photos: Steve West Collection.

Apart from the stone trains and engineer's trains that were regular turns at the depot, there were also a number of freight turns.

At North Camp, there was a small oil terminal and the train would arrive at Guildford from Ripple Lane. We would then work the train (usually with a Class 73/1 electro-diesel over to North Camp.

There was always considerable excitement displayed by the Guildford Yard shunters with a lot of shouting "the tanks are coming - the tanks are coming" as if everything else became unimportant!

As the load was quite heavy, considerable amps would be drawn whilst climbing the bank towards Pinks Hill and care would need to be exercised under electric conditions especially where there were gaps in the conductor rail. At that time, North Camp had a level crossing with barriers and there would be considerable delay to traffic when propelling the tanks back over the crossing towards the stop blocks.

Unfortunately, one of our drivers was propelling the tanks back a little bit faster than he should have been and one of the wagons (fully laden with fuel) went over the buffer stops and punctured one of the depot's main fuel tanks! The Fire Brigade were called and emergency procedures were immediately put in place; cordoning off the area and even evicting residents from some nearby homes.

Luckily, the fuel tank that was ruptured wasn't holding high-octane fuel.

Another one of our regular freight turns was from Aldershot to Norwood Yard via Redhill - this being an evening turn returning in the early hours of the morning. I already knew the route to Redhill but had to learn the route from Redhill to Norwood Yard and also Selhurst depot just in case we needed to change locomotives or replenish the fuel tanks.

The Class 33 'Crompton' hauled train was normally loose-coupled with a fitted-head of vacuum-fitted wagons to give a good brake force which was necessary when working over the Surrey Hills to and from Redhill. The turn was originally double-manned and one New Year's Eve I can remember my driver and I both taking some whisky with us and seeing in the New Year on the way over to Norwood Yard!

Above: The Top Deck part of Woking Mess Room and it looks like there's a PN break in progress. From left to right - Woking Drivers: Lew Wooldridge, George Lynam, John Burr and Bernie Knibbs.

Below: Driver Bill Brain exhales cigarette smoke from one of his 'roll-ups' as he exchanges banter with fellow Woking Driver Brian Pickett in the driver's mess room. The room's resident teapot can be seen on the table in the foreground.

The door led out to a room containing the notice cases and to the washroom and toilets.

This was to be my place of work for the next thirteen years.

Photo: The Author's Collection.

Above: Farnham starting signal and Farnham Signal Box in the distance. Always an awkward place to perform shunting. An engineer's trolley is in the up siding.

Below: Farnham outer home signal and to the left of the photograph, the carriage sheds. Unofficial lifts to the station would be conducted from this foot crossing and if you needed to be picked up, a waving of a rolled up newspaper to attract the attention of the driver of an up train from Alton would most certainly be a necessity!

Photos: Steve West.

Above: The Driver of Class 33/0 33004 conducts a shunt movement from Farnham Tip. This was just one of many places where 'dirty ballast' (spoil that had been cleaned from the track bed by a ballast cleaner) was deposited.

Class 33/0 33020 returns from Farnham Tip with a string of empty wagons to Farnham Up Yard under the supervision of Steve West.

Photos: Steve West.

Driving Days - Woking MT

Above: With an autumnal mist in the air, Class 73/1 No. 73111 stands at Waterloo with the 22.52 service to Southampton on 14th October 1977.

Below: An autumn evening at Eastleigh catches Class 33/1 No. 33113 absorbing the sun at the rear end of a 4TC unit heading for Waterloo on 16th October 1977.

Photos & Captions: David Hayes.

Above: An empty low-flat train passes through a snow covered Sheer Heath on its way back from Redhill to Woking Yard.

Photo: The Author's Collection.

Below: An empty stone train hauled by Class 33/0 33029 emerges from St Catherine's Tunnel outside Guildford on its way to Woking Yard.
St Catherine's Chantry Chapel is perched on the sandstone outcrop through which the 'Crompton' has just emerged; this was built in the 14th century.

Photo & Caption: Gordon Edgar.

Above: Blue blue and grey slam door stock abound in this scene at Waterloo. 4 BR-designed 2EPBs leave on a 'Round the World' Waterloo W - Waterloo M working via Richmond and Kingston, while a 4CIG brings up the rear of an arriving train (probably from Reading).

On the far left, a Class 33 locomotive lurks in the long-removed yard which became the Eurostar terminal, while a Class 73 locomotive stands in No. 2 dock between platforms 11 and 12.

Photo: Ian Docwra.

Driving Days - Woking MT

Apart from the usual freight we'd work from Woking Yard to Aldershot and Farnham, one of the regular turns that ran two or three times a week was to Aldershot Government Sidings. The sidings were situated on the up line between Aldershot and Aldershot North Junction and were operated by a ground frame. The train was marshalled at Aldershot and the Aldershot shunters (Frank King, Bill Padgett or Danny Curley) would accompany you to the sidings and operate the ground frame once your train had passed over the points. The train was then propelled back into the siding, with the shunter closing the ground frame points to allow normal traffic to pass.

In the steam days, Aldershot Government Sidings was very busy, with a train visiting the area every day. One of the sidings went down adjacent to the Basingstoke Canal (where coke would be placed for a huge boiler); another to the bakery, where you would deliver wagons of flour, and finally the field stores which were situated across the other side of a main road that lead to Aldershot Cambridge Military Hospital.

Before any movement was made across the road to the field stores, the shunter(s) would have to stop the traffic by displaying red flags.

The field stores area was quite large and had platforms with covered canopies. In the Great War, horses and troops were loaded into trains and departed from here to the front.

On one occasion, whilst at the field stores sidings, my secondman Nigel Cummins and I noticed an old leather medicine ball laying near the track in the sidings. One of the seams was split but thinking that it would be an invaluable aid for keeping us mixed traction men fit when standing spare in the mess room, we decided to take it back to Woking. Nigel and I had quite a bit of fun with it on the train when travelling passenger back to Woking and it stayed in the driver's mess room for some considerable time before ending its days on a skip.

Above Top: Aldershot Government Sidings call plunger.

Photo: Courtesy of Great Central Railwayana Ltd.

Above: A medicine ball similar to the one the Author brought back from Aldershot Government Sidings.

Below: Aldershot Signalbox's illuminated track diagram showing Aldershot Government Sidings.

Photo: David Ingham.

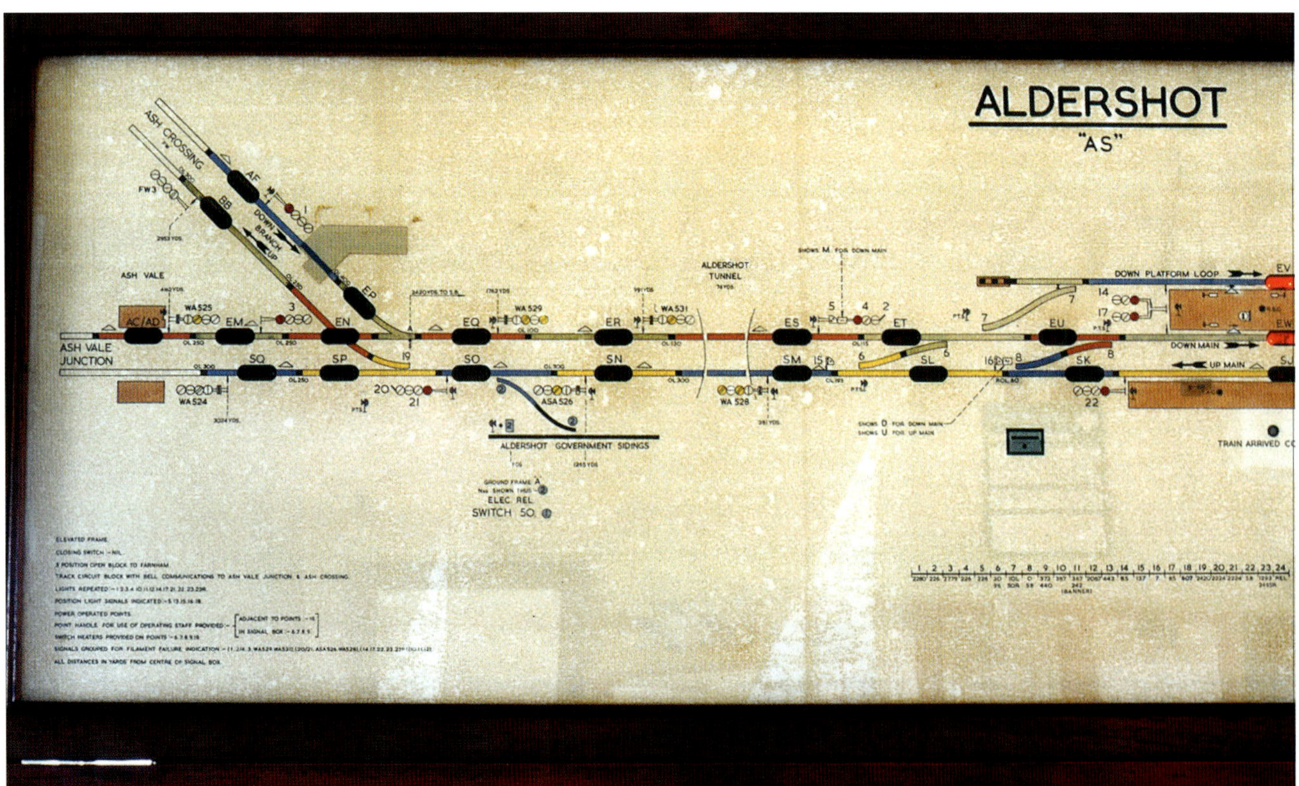

Between 1975 and 1985, the M25 Motorway was under construction and one of the many obstacles in its path was the railway line that ran between Chertsey and Virginia Water.

In order to allow a suspension bridge to be built that would carry the line over the roadway, the railway track was diverted away and then back to join up again with its original connection. A curvature of the track was made that went to the right for 200-300 yards and then curved back to the left and joined again with the original line. Because the roadway was going to take two to three years to complete, the alterations and the curvature demanded a 20mph speed restriction be imposed; later termed as a Temporary Speed Restriction.

Although drivers were warned about the speed restriction alterations in the Periodical Operating Notice (PON) and the Weekly Operating Notice (WON), it wasn't deemed necessary to mark the area with Temporary Speed Restriction boards.

One of the early turns that had been introduced at Woking at the time was a staff train that ran from Basingstoke to Staines and return. It left Basingstoke at around 04.30 and a Woking driver would relieve the previous crew at around 05.00 and complete the turn.

It was the first time that I'd been rostered the turn and having relieved the Basingstoke driver, I set off from Woking. The EMU that I was driving was of the 2HAP variety and as the guard's van was at the London end of the train, the guard rode in the cab with me for company. After we left Chertsey, my guard asked me if I'd like some coffee and proceeded to get a flask out of his bag. I had turned the cab light on so he could see what he was doing and after he'd poured out the coffee, I said to him that I was going to extinguish the cab light as I needed to look out for the deviation and speed restriction. As I turned out the light, the train lurched to the right and then after a couple of seconds lurched to the left; the guard's flask and cups of coffee taking on a mind of their own spilled everywhere and smashed the vacuum flask in the process! Luckily the 2-car train stayed on the rails which was quite surprising as we must have been travelling in excess of 40mph.

Several other incidents occurred at the deviation following my misdemeanour and because of this, a permanent AWS warning magnet and warning board were placed at each end of the deviation.

Above; Lyne Suspension Bridge over the M25 at Chertsey.

Photo: Stacey Harris.

Below: 2HAP 6096 calls at Byfleet & New Haw station making its return journey from Staines to Woking. The M25 overbridge can be seen in the background.

Photo: Ian Docwra.

Above: Two 4REP Units in the middle sidings at Bournemouth. 3004 and 3009. Headcode 91 would denote this was a fast service stopping at Southampton & Waterloo only. Headcode 92 denoted that this was a semi-fast service.
Unit 3004 would move into the up platform and stop on the 12-car mark and the driver would place his master switch to OFF and remove his EP key (to isolate the train heat supply).
The rear portion of the train (which had worked up from Weymouth (Push/Pull with a Class 33/2 - TC leading) would then attach to the rear of the REP Unit. Once coupled (and 33/2 locomotive uncoupled at the rear), the shunter would then give an indication to the driver of the REP unit that it was safe to open the master switch (for train heating to re-commence). A brake continuity test would be made.

Photo: Ian Docwra.

Imagine it – the start of a beautiful spring day and you're working! This was the case on Tuesday 25th May 1976 when Les Mills and I were booked together on a Bournemouth turn. In fact, Les was booked with me for most of the week. Les was then a 'passed man' and also knew the electric traction that we were working on this day.

After reaching Bournemouth, we decided we should take it in turns to have a couple of hours off during the week and on our way back to Waterloo, I got off at Woking and went home early. Les continued with the train to Waterloo and prepared himself for the final trip from Waterloo to Woking. The train worked was the 17.14 semi-fast passenger service from Waterloo comprised of three 4VEP units. Unfortunately, when Les reached the other side of New Malden, he experienced an uncontrolled brake application with loss of power, main-reservoir air and line-volts indication. After coming to a halt, Les examined the train and realised that two collector shoes on the middle unit were missing and that there was damage to an air reservoir tank below the motor coach. The conductor rail had also been displaced. Les started remedying the problem to the best of his ability by firstly obtaining a traction current isolation, tying up the loose ends of the power cables and closing off the main-reservoir angle cocks on either side of the burst to stop the air leak. In the meantime, considerable delay to trains that were behind him occurred. After phoning the signalman to have the current restored, Les was able to drive the train to Surbiton, de-train passengers and run ECS to Woking to get the train out of service.

When Les eventually got home, he rang me to say what had happened and I commended him for doing a good job in getting the train out of service. The following day, after listening to Les's story of events again, I decided to write out a report to say what had happened and thought that might be the end of it.

A few days later, a traction inspector came to see me and asked me to give him a further account of what happened. Well, as you can imagine, that's quite a difficult task to perform when you weren't at the scene! He asked some very pertinent questions such as "which telephone did you use to contact the signalman when I reached Surbiton? Was it on the up side platform or the down side?" I should have realised then that he knew damned well that I wasn't anywhere near Surbiton at the time but I still continued with 'Les's story of events' and afterwards, signed his written report.

Another month went by before Les and I learnt that there was going to be a Head Office inquiry into the incident because there had been cases of passengers jumping down from trains, walking all over the tracks and climbing over neighbouring garden fences and even a case where the traction current was still live!

I mentioned to Les that if we have to go to an inquiry at Wimbledon, we would both be interviewed separately and the truth would come out that I wasn't there and we decided we'd just as well come clean and say that you were on your own at the time of the incident. I went to see our Depot Master and admitted to him that I wasn't present but he said that we'd still have to attend the inquiry.

On the day of the inquiry, we both travelled up to Head Office at Worple Road, Wimbledon and the first persons that were called into the inquiry were members of the CM&EE department. They immediately admitted responsibility as upon inspection, it was found that the shoe-beam holding the collector shoe that had caused the incident had not been set correctly which resulted in the shoe running up the side of the conductor rail (instead of on top of it). This is what displaced the conductor rail for several hundred yards. The inquiry was immediately concluded and Les and I didn't have to be interviewed.

However, on 18th June, I was issued with a Form No 1 charge sheet containing the following charges:

On the 25th May 1976:

1. Failing to work the 17.14 Waterloo to Woking passenger service in accordance with my rostered duty (No. 817).

2. Allowing Relief Driver Mills of Woking to work this train without authority.

3. Making a false statement to the Inspector

Both Les and I had to go to Wimbledon Head Office at Worple Road again for a disciplinary hearing and we were interviewed by Bill Neal, the Chief Motive Power Inspector. The whole thing was rather unfortunate because had we kept quiet, we would have received a commendation for getting the train out of service in good time. Instead, the actual phrase he used was "You both want your arses kicked!" On 7th July, I received a Form No 2 saying that as punishment, I would be suspended from duty for one day with loss of pay. Les was more fortunate and received a written caution.

We were the most talked-about couple at the depot for weeks!

Below: 4REP 3005 and associated 4TC unit powers through Basingstoke with a Waterloo - Bournemouth service on 25th August 1981.

The high powered (3,200 hp)EMU tractor units were classified 4REP (Restaurant Electro-Pneumatic brake).
Initially, eleven 4REP units were built to propel the TC units to Bournemouth and haul them back to Waterloo. Four more units followed.
The 4REPs were, as a result, the most powerful third rail type EMUs in the world, with a total of 3,200 hp (2,400 kW) available, in order to be able to provide the traction for up to eight trailer cars – just 100 horsepower (75 kW) less than the famous 'Deltic' Class 55 diesel locomotives.
Each REP unit had eight traction motors, and because of this, to avoid an overload, a REP could only work with another powered EMU or electro-diesel locomotive if sufficient traction motors in the overall formation were first isolated. Each power bogie had a shoe beam with two pick-up shoes since there were two power circuits.

Photo: Stuart Ray.

Above: After detaching from the 4REP Tractor Unit at Bournemouth, the 4TC portion of the train from Waterloo thunders away towards Weymouth headed by Class 33/1 No. 33111 on 25th August 1981.

Photo: Stuart Ray.

On Monday 16th January 1978, I was booked to attend South-Side Training School Waterloo for a Class 47 'Brush Type 4' diesel-electric course. This was of five days duration (classroom and static) with a couple of practical handling days during the week. This was termed a 'conversion course' as all attendees had already passed an examination on a diesel course of some description. The exam was held the following Monday (23rd January) when I had to make my way to Southampton to meet the examining instructor (Cyril Sweet) who had taken charge of the train at Poole earlier that morning. I took charge of the train from Southampton to Basingstoke which only necessitated stopping the train at Winchester and Basingstoke which was farcical when I think about it now.

I then got out of the driver's seat and another driver took the train to Reading. We then went down to Reading Depot and were asked a few questions about the locomotive and were then sent home.

A couple of weeks of other mixed traction turns went by before I was booked on my first 'Brush' turn (28th January) and this was a ballast turn (Spl. 107) signing on at 00.18 with secondman Dave Morgan. We were also booked the turn the rest of the week - rest day off on the Saturday.

I loved working on the Brush Type 4 locomotives; they were extremely powerful but did have certain drawbacks. There was a bulkhead behind the driver's seat, which made it difficult to drive in the opposite direction as you had to lean out of the cab window so far. Another draw-back was that they had a very restricted clearance when walking through the engine room. In fact, I'd always change-ends via the ground rather than walk through. The locomotive's engine room was also a very oily place and we were even issued a long dark blue cotton coat as protection. Finally, the cabs were quite draughty and you'd notice masking tape would be stuck around the gaps to try to seal the draughts!

Above: Waiting for the road at Reading Spur with Class 47 No. 47415 and a Cross-Country service.

Photo: Nick Waite.

Below: A cold winter's day as the Author passes Shalford Meadows with Class 47 'Brush' Type 4 diesel-electric No. 47626 'ATLAS' hauling a Leeds - Portsmouth Harbour service.

Photo: Pat Kinsella.

Driving Days - Woking MT

However, the driving controls were great and with a very good forward vision through the front windows. They weren't 'dual control' though so it was difficult to perform shunting manoeuvres without a secondman present. Some of the locomotives even had a 'slow-speed' control switch in the cab which was quite handy if you were laying stone with a ballast train and wanted to keep to an even speed between 1 -3 mph.

There were other creature comforts too such as a urinal in the engine room! Just goes to show how the male species dominated the footplate scene in those days. However, one day whilst using the urinal to relieve myself, I didn't notice that the drain pipe had a fracture in it and I consequently ended up with a wet trouser leg!

In my mind, the best jobs at Woking with this locomotive were the cross-country turns from Reading to Portsmouth Harbour and vice-versa.

Sign on at Woking and go pass to Guildford. Relieve and work the Manchester/Liverpool train to Reading.

Relieve and work the Liverpool/Manchester train from Reading to Portsmouth Harbour stopping at Guildford, Havant, Portsmouth & Southsea High Level and Portsmouth Harbour. You were then booked your break in which time the locomotive was shunt-released and placed onto the other end of the train, You'd then relieve the driver and work the train back to Reading stopping at Portsmouth and Southsea High Level, Havant, Guildford and getting relief at Reading. You nearly always had a good run (both ways) so maximum speed over the route was often attained.

Above: My brother David stands next to Class 47 'Brush' Type 4 No. 47592 'County of Avon' at Portsmouth Harbour upon my arrival from Reading with a cross-country service.

My nephew Jonathan visits the cab of a Class 47 at Guildford before I depart for Reading with a cross-country service.

Photos: The Author's Collection.

Above: The driver looks back for the guard's 'right away' before leaving Guildford with the 08.05 Portsmouth Harbour to Manchester cross-country service headed by Class 47 'Brush' Type 4 No. 47107.

Below: Class 47 'Brush' Type 4 No. 47322 heads away from Guildford towards Pinks Hill bank with the 08.05 Portsmouth Harbour to Manchester service after carefully negotiating the up main to up Reading crossover's 20mph speed restriction on 14th June 1983.

Photos: Gordon Edgar.

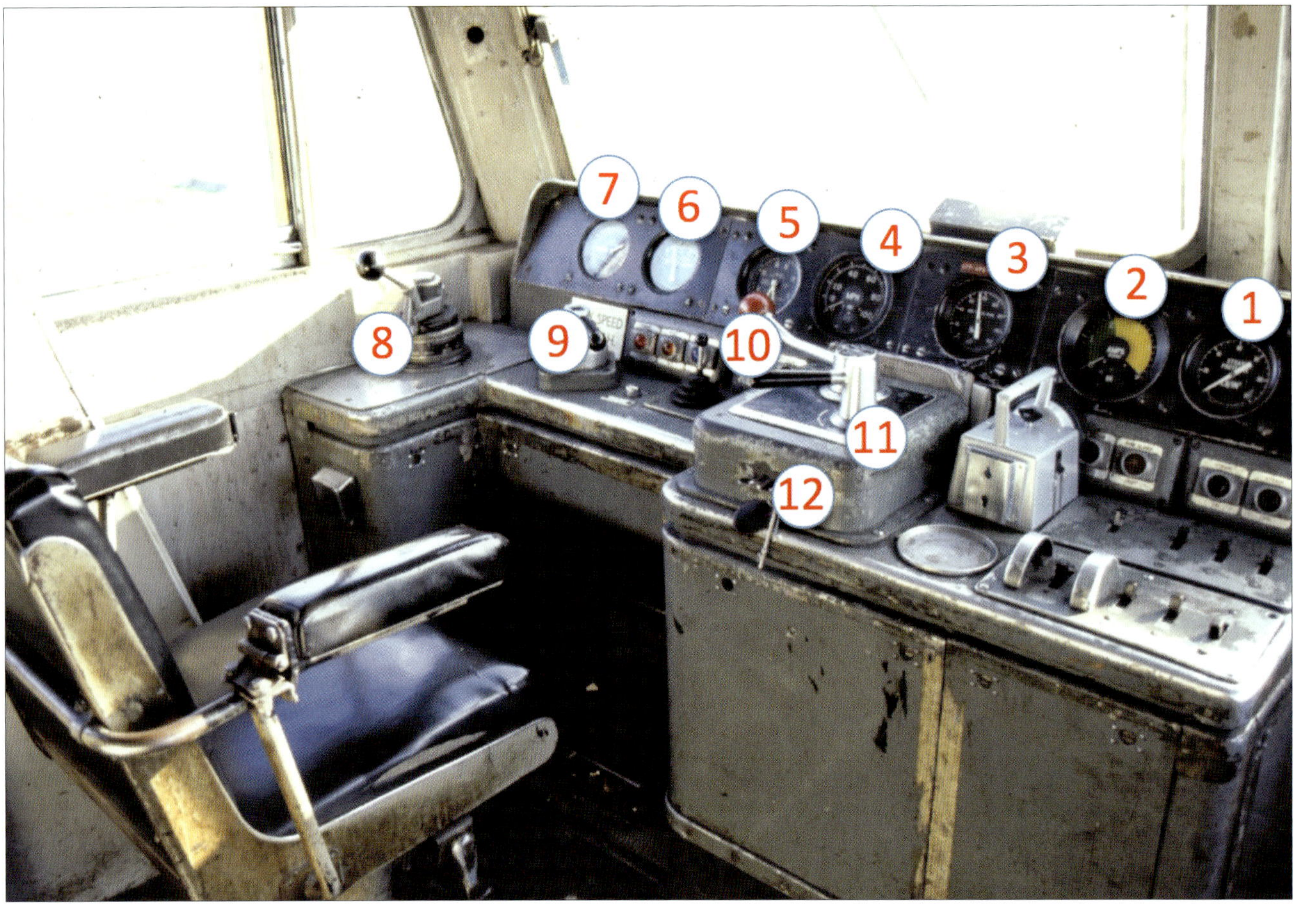

Above: Driving Cab of a Class 47 'Brush' Type 4 locomotive. Evidence of peeled masking tape can be seen around the joints in the Driver's desk.
Legend: 1. Steam Heating Pressure 2. Amps 3. Brake Pipe Pressure 4. Speedometer 5. Vacuum Brake 6. Brake Cylinder Pressure 7. Main Reservoir Air Pressure 8. Main Brake Valve (Air or Vacuum) 9. Straight Air Brake (Locomotive only) 10. Power Controller 11. Master Switch 12. Master Key.

Below: The evening sunlight glints on the Master Switch as the Author waits for the road at Worting Junction whilst working an empty stone train to Salisbury.

Photos: The Author's Collection.

Above: The Author aboard Class 47 'Brush' Type 4 No. 47020 at Woking Up Yard after returning from Salisbury with a stone train.

Below: At maximum speed with a Class 47 'Brush' Type 4 locomotive.

Photos: The Author's Collection.

Class 47 'Brush' Type 4 diesel-electric No. 47483 emerges from St Catherine's tunnel, Guildford with a cross-country service from Liverpool to Portsmouth Harbour circa 1985.

Photo: The Author's Collection.

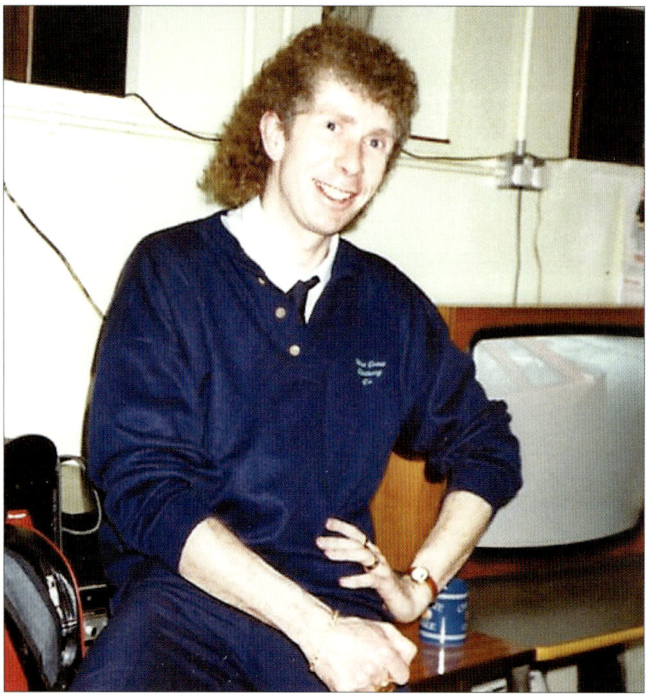

Some of my work colleagues at Woking Depot.

Opposite page clockwise from top left: Doug Dunstall, George Michie, Lew Wooldridge, Alex 'Mac' McClymont, Tony Channon and Martin Peakall.

Photos: Steve West & Alex McClymont Collection.

Above from top to bottom: Les Mills 02.00 cover (this sofa was a comfort to anyone on the cover duties), Charlie Holter and Jim Soal and finally, Eric Clarke (on his last day at work before retirement).

Photos: Steve West & Alex McClymont and the Author's Collection.

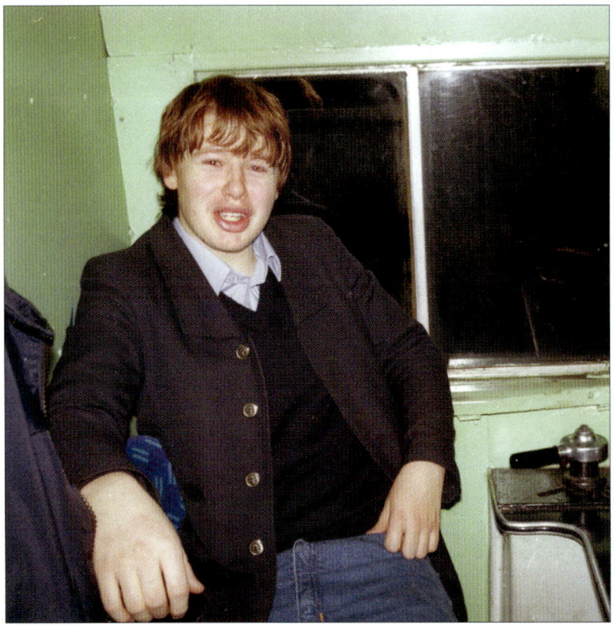

Some more of my Woking associates.

Above from top left corner: Dave Champion, Pat Kinsella, Charlie Hampshire and Mick Sparrow and finally in his Acting Train Crew Supervisor role, Ian Coles.

Ian was a real entrepreneur as regards 'bargain' merchandise that he'd acquired at various sales. So long as you bought a dozen items at a time, Ian was the man to do business with!

Photos: Alex McClymont Collection.

Above: Les Mills at his 'leaving do' at Woking Railway club surrounded by his workmates.
From left to right: Graham Redrup, Alex 'Mac' McClymont, Les Hayden, Les Mills, Ray Bartlett, Doug Dunstall and Brian Cobbett.

Below: A retirement party at Woking Railway club with the Woking contingent whom most of which I worked with whilst there.
Back Row: Fred Garnham, Alex 'Mac' McClymont, Mick Lockyer, John Berriman, Ray Bartlett, Jim Lester, Ron Baird, Chris Berriman, Alan Ackehurst, Barry Foster, Dave Hewson, Mark Taylor, Frank Saxby, Bill Flahive, Terry Butwell, Ian Verrinder, Alan Johns, Sue Kinching, Bernie Knibbs, Len Boxall, Alan Hughes, Steve West, Lew Wooldridge, Colin Watkins, Alan Nichols and Derek Gane.
Front row seated: Dave Jackson, Dave Newberry, George Michie, Pat Kinsella, Terry Aylesbury and Bill Tickner.

Photos: The Author's Collection.

Above: Class 33/2 'Slim Jim' Crompton with a possible van train to Clapham waits for the road in Woking Down Yard long siding. Only twelve of these locomotives were built in this form for the narrow tunnels on the Tonbridge - Hastings line.

Below: Class 33/0 33028 hauls a string of hyfits and opens of various designs from Woking Yard bound for Eastleigh Yard on 17th June 1978.

Photos: Michael Thorne.

Above: A Basingstoke - Waterloo semi-fast service headed by 4VEP 7832 kicks up the snow as it approaches Woking on 31st December 1981.

Below: Replacing the scheduled Class 50, this Waterloo - Exeter service is in the more reliable hands of a Class 33/0 Crompton as it leaves Woking on 31st December 1981.

Photos: Michael Thorne.

Driving Days - Woking MT

I can remember a couple of incidents involving platelayers that were working on the line between Winchester and Eastleigh.

The first was when I noticed a gang of workers some way ahead of me so I sounded the two-tone horn as a warning of my approach. The workers moved to a place of safety but as I watched them from my cab as I approached, I noticed that they were all picking up pieces of ballast and frantically throwing them at an object that was propped against the running rail. As I got nearer, I could see what they were aiming at – a fishplate! Too late to stop, I bore down onto the offending fishplate and as I went by, the guard iron on the front of my train hit the fishplate which rebounded under the first coach of my train making several 'metal against metal' noises. Luckily, my train didn't suffer any effects and I continued on my way.
The platelayers had obviously completely removed the fishplate for its annual inspection and left it propped against the running rail. History doesn't relate to whether it was damaged beyond replacement after my train had hit it!

The other occasion of platelayers working alongside the line was again when working a passenger service to Bournemouth. This time, the men were cutting down some small trees alongside the line. As I approached, a tree that they were cutting fell straight across the four-foot in front of my train. There was nothing I could do but wait for the inevitable crunching sound of branches being chopped to pieces by the front of my train as I hit it at speed. Luckily, I was driving the train from the TC unit and not from the REP unit as I'm certain we would have sustained damage to the shoegear. When I ran into Bournemouth station, the shunter came up to me and asked me where I'd collected all of the camouflage.The front of my train still had branches and foliage wrapped around it!

Sometimes it was necessary to conduct drivers of Plassermatic on-track tamping machines (mostly working at night) as they didn't know a particular route they were working over. Some had an open-fronted cab so it was imperative to wear warm clothing especially in the winter months.

There was a also a track recording machine made by 'Matisa' and got the nickname 'Neptune' because of the trident logo carried on the back of the cabs.

There principal purpose was to record track defects and they sprayed out red or yellow coloured paint to mark the track at sites requiring attention. They assessed gauge, line levels and cross levels that could then be matched up to previous records to identify areas of deterioration.

Above: Fishplate joining two rails.

Photo: The Author's Collection.

Below: Plassermatic and Matisa Machines berthed in Hurdles Road siding circa 1967.

Photo: Bob Hind Collection.

Above: With the BAT (British American Tobacco) building dominating Woking's skyline, Class 47 No. 47118 gets the road on the down fast with a Ripple Lane - Micheldever Elf Oil Terminal train on 30th December 1981.

Photo: Michael Thorne.

Above: A Class 33/0 locomotive heads a long Reading - Redhill parcels train - probably returning empties - east of Ash on Saturday 6th January 1979.

Below: 4VEP 7800 is seen between Ash and Wanborough on a Waterloo - Ascot - Guildford service. 4CIGs were the usual stock on these workings. The site of Ash Junction signal box can be seen on the left of the photograph; the original line to Farnham junction via Ash Green and Tongham was removed in the early 1960s.

Photos: Tony Watson.

Above: Approaching Woking, Class 33/0 No. 33019 heads a fuel tank train on 29th May 1979. A lengthy string of mostly 36 ton tanks in the twilight of their operating years. This train is 6V95 14.47 ex Fawley Refinery. The headcode DF denotes cross London freight via Clapham Junction and Kensington Olympia to the LMR but the end destination was actually on the Western Region. It was a dual destination working being Monday and Thursdays only to Acton Yard and Tuesday to Friday only to Old Oak Common Sidings.

Below: Class 73/1 No. 73135 hauls the cement empties from Northam Yard to Northfleet Cement Works on 20th July 1979. Woking drivers were rostered a return working of this train and with each wagon being 102 tons loaded, you had to very careful driving under electric conditions with traction motors pulling high amps. A good knowledge of where the conductor rail gaps were situated was also necessary! Photos: Michael Thorne - Train information: thanks to Adrian Nicholls.

Train services to London were seriously disrupted on Friday 23rd February 1979 when the 13.13 Hampton Court to Waterloo eight-car electric multiple-unit passenger train, after making its scheduled stop at Thames Ditton, was driven past the branch exit signal at danger onto the up slow line on which the 12.20 from Alton coupled with the 12.28 from Basingstoke to Waterloo eight-car electric multiple-unit passenger train was passing at speed. An extract from the Department of Transport report on the incident is below:

The Hampton Court train struck the rear three cars of the Alton train and the leading car of the Hampton Court train was diverted down a steep embankment with its trailing end, to which the second car remained attached, some twelve feet above the ground. The rear six cars of the train remained on the branch line.

The Alton train came to a stand with the seventh car derailed and the trailing bogie of the rear car detached. The rear two cars struck and demolished the brick parapet of Angel Road under-bridge which crashed onto the road below. Luckily nobody was passing at the time, but the roofs of several houses adjacent to the line were damaged by flying debris.

The emergency services were quickly called by a householder beside the line and thirty ambulances were soon on the scene, but only one passenger and the crew of the Hampton Court train and four passengers of the Alton train were taken to hospital suffering minor injuries. All were discharged after treatment. The guard of the Alton train was also slightly injured. A fifth person travelling on the Alton train suffered injuries which he did not report until the next day.

All the main lines, as well as the Hampton Court and Cobham lines, were blocked following the collision but normal services were resumed at 12.20 on 24th February and the Hampton Court line was restored by 04.00 on 26th February.

The report concluded that the driver failed to look at signal WA75 and assumed that it was displaying a green aspect as it most often did when he drove on the branch line. Having made that assumption, it was natural for him to assume that signal S39 was displaying a proceed aspect so he allowed his attention to be distracted by the thrust boring going on beside the railway when he should have been looking at the signal above it. He alone was entirely responsible for the accident.

Below and the following page show the aftermath of the incident where the Hampton Court - Waterloo stopping service failed to stop at the signal protecting the junction and collided with the Alton - Waterloo service which was passing at considerable speed.
Although the signal was fitted with AWS equipment, the 8-car train consisting of 2x4SUB units 4662 (leading) and 4628 was not. This type of stock was due for withdrawal when the Class 508 was introduced later that year. Had AWS been fitted on this train, it probably would have prevented the accident.

Photos: Pete Beyer & Andy Gibb Collection.

Above: With shunter 'Ginger' Patterson hanging on the handrail, the driver of Class 73/0 No. 73005 shunts the Goods Yard at Guildford circa 1980. This scene wasn't to last much longer before the whole of this area became a vast car park.

Photo: Kevin Lane.

Above Right: Class 73/1 No. 73116 rushes through Worplesdon station with a special charter on 25th February 1979.

Photo: David Hird.

Right: 4CIG 7425 passes through North Sheen with a Waterloo - Reading fast service. As a keen horticulturist, I always admired the fine crops that were grown on the allotments that ran parallel with the railway line. However, one does wonder whether the brake dust from the trains improved the flavour!

Photo: Kevin Lane.

99

7425
7425
36
TICKET
OFFICE

Driving Days - Woking MT

In October 1980, I was booked to attend Waterloo South Side Training School for a Class 508 Course and our instructor was Ken Norris. I enjoyed working on the stock as it didn't require a signal from the Guard (by green flag or green light at night) but by buzzer instead. This didn't however exempt you from looking back to make sure your train was still in order.

The units were based at Strawberry Hill depot, and soon became unpopular due to wheel slip/slide problems. This was eventually overcome by fitting a wheel slip/slide override button. Later, once a new build of Class 455 EMUs were complete, the 508s were slowly sent back to their originally intended home on the Merseyrail network.

I also quite liked the rheostatic (dynamic) braking that was available on the motor coaches; normal disc braking switching in when the train speed dropped below 18mph.

Above Top: The old and the new - Class 508 508 018 alongside a 4SUB at Clapham Junction. Note the passengers standing in the guard's van, common in the days of this stock when trains were packed in the peak periods.

Above: Class 508 508 004 runs into Clapham Junction with a Waterloo - Chessington service circa 1980.

Photos: Ian Docwra.

There was one incident on 21st April 1982 where the brakes didn't operate as the driver might have expected. The night previous to the incident, brake testing trials were being carried out on the Shepperton line. To simulate slip/slide conditions, a solution had been applied to the rails to simulate leaf-fall conditions. Following the trials, the solution should have been removed but allegedly, the solution was still on the rails when the first train in the morning worked down to Shepperton. Unfortunately, the driver was completely unaware of the state of the railhead and the train overshot the buffers at Shepperton and ended up with the front coach overhanging the wall bordering the high street.

***Above:** Class 508 508 031 at the end of the line at Chessington North Station. Trains had a 25 minute wait here before returning to Waterloo.*
Note the distinctive art deco canopies that were standard along this line.

***Photo:** Michael Thorne.*

***Below:** Class 508 508 031 overran the buffer stops at Shepperton station because of a rail adhesion problem on 21st April 1982.*

***Photo:** Pete Beyer & Andy Gibb Collection.*

Driving Days - Woking MT

On 29th July 1981, Lady Diana Spencer and Charles Prince of Wales were married and the first part of their honeymoon was to be spent at Broadlands near Romsey in Hampshire which was the former home of Lord Mountbatten. Hundreds of people turned out to see the Royal Train and my wife Pauline and I and our neighbours Liz & Colin Stovold, their children and some of their friends went to Brookwood station to see it go by. The train was hauled by Class 73/1 electro-diesel 73142 aptly named 'Broadlands' with the headcode 'CD' signifying the initials of Charles and Diana.

***Below:** With hundreds of well-wishers looking on, the Royal Train hauled by Class 73/1 electro-diesel No. 73142 'Broadlands' rushes through Brookwood station on 29th July 1981.*

***Photo:** The Author's Collection.*

***Bottom:** The Royal train passes through Worting Junction on its way to Romsey as more well-wishers look on.*

***Photo:** Adrian Pink.*

In July 1982, ASLEF called a strike for two weeks (a conflict with management regarding the introduction of flexible rostering). One of the weeks I should have been on the 'Big-Bomo' turn for two of the days so not only did I lose two week's pay but also two day's mileage.

However, I had a lot of work to do at home so this turned out to be a blessing in disguise. I also did a decorating job at my neighbour's house which also helped pay the bills.

I'm not sure now who won the argument but I do know that we started Flexible Rostering on Monday 4th September 1982. This meant that on an early turn you could start work any time between the hours of 00.01 and 12.00 and for a late turn, any time between 12.01 and 23.59. My signing on times for early turn were as follows:

Monday 4th September	00.24
Tuesday 5th September	03.27
Wednesday 6th September	06.45
Thursday 7th September	05.17
Friday 8th September	RD
(Rest Day Off)	
Saturday 10th September	05.29
Sunday 11th September	04.00

Above: An assortment of the Author's ASLE&F Badges from left to right: 30 years, Branch Centenary and 20 years.

Photo: The Author's Collection.

Below: A photo of the Author taken by his secondman whilst we were on a night ballast.

Photo: Doug Dunstall.

Sometimes, when working on ballast trains on nights or weekends you might not move your train for hours and sitting in one position would become quite uncomfortable. To alleviate this, you'd either stretch your legs out onto the desk or lay on the floor to try to get some shuteye. However, stretching out whilst remaining seated did pinch a nerve and make your legs go numb!

We had one single manned turn where we would work stone train empties from Woking Down Yard to Salisbury East Yard with a 1550hp 'Crompton'. After coupling up to your return loaded stone train in the Up Yard, you'd have several hours wait before working the train back to Woking. To make things more comfortable, I'd slide out the bottom parts of a seat from the back cab and place them together on the floor with the other two in the front cab to form a comfortable bed. In the winter, the engine ticking over would not only provide heating but would also rock you off to sleep! The early turn Salisbury guard would then wake you up to give you the load sheet after he had looked round the train.

Driving Days - Woking MT

On Saturday 28th August 1982, my secondman Nick Waite and I were booked to work a football special from Woking to Fratton (where Portsmouth City football club were playing a home game against Sheffield United at Fratton Park).

The train with the 'away' supporters had come from the Midlands and when it arrived at Woking, was hauled by a Class 45 'Peak' locomotive. The driver didn't know the route from Woking to Fratton and although the Rules said he should have driven the traction (with me conducting him) he let me do the driving. The controls were fairly straightforward - the controller being the same type as a Class 33 1550hp Crompton and the brake handle being the same type found on a Type 4 Brush-Sulzer locomotive.

We had a good run down and when we reached Fratton, once the football supporters had disembarked, we placed the empty coaching stock in the sidings at Fratton ready for the return journey. I was booked to conduct the train back to Woking so as we had several hours to wait and it was a nice day, Nick and I caught a train to Portsmouth Harbour.

When we got there we ate our sandwiches and had a cup of tea and then decided to take a trip on a local boat round Portsmouth docks. Several other people took advantage of the nice weather and joined us and when the skipper of the boat noticed we were railway staff, kindly waived our fee.

We chugged around the various ships that were moored up - with the skipper giving us a running commentary when required. A lot of the ships in the docks had just returned from the Falklands conflict – one in particular being *HMS Glamorgan,* a County Class Destroyer that had been hit by an Exocet missile with a loss of fourteen lives. The skipper pointed out the position of where the missile had struck and the temporary repair that had been made to the hull.

When we returned to Fratton, we found that there wasn't a driver for the train as the previous driver had gone home. Luckily, a driver from Eastleigh was available (he had transferred from a depot that knew the traction) and we departed right-time. However, he too didn't know the route from Fratton to Woking which again gave me the opportunity to drive the train from Fratton back to Woking where the Eastleigh driver took over.

For those of you that are dying to know the score - Pompey beat Sheffield United 4-1.

Below: Class 45 No. 45119 leaves Sheffield Midland on 2nd September 1982.

Photo: Kevin Cooke.

One of the worst jobs (mixed traction wise) was to take a 350hp shunting diesel anywhere other than within the confines of a shunting yard. However, they occasionally needed servicing and the nearest depot was Stewarts Lane. The trip was normally completed at night so as to keep disturbance to other traffic at a minimum.

Les Mills and I were booked 20.00 cover and were given the task of taking a 350hp shunter up to Stewarts Lane Depot for fuel and once this was completed, bring the loco back light to Woking Yard.

Off we went – a laborious task as the speed of the loco was restricted to 20mph. When we reached the depot and the fuelling point, there wasn't a fitter to be seen so Les and I decided to take fuel ourselves. Les connected the fuel line to the loco's fuel pipe and turned the motor on. As the main tank was filling, I mentioned to Les that once the outside fuel tank was completely full, the fuel would also automatically start to fill the header tank (which would save us using the hand pump). As the gauge on the main tank headed toward the full position, I watched the header tank gauge for movement and as soon as I saw the fuel gauge move up to the 'red-line' position, I'd shout down to Les to turn off the pump's motor. That was the plan anyway.

From then on, everything happened so quickly. As soon as the main tank became full, the header tank fuel indication needle shot round to the 'full' position and diesel oil cascaded out of the breather pipe on the top of the tank and ran down the sides of the loco's framing! Les quickly shut off the supply but there was diesel oil everywhere. After disconnecting the supply pipe, Les and I thought it would be a good idea to use the 2-inch hose pipe to wash the loco down and try to get rid of some of the diesel oil that seemed to be everywhere. The 2-inch hose was an extremely powerful piece of kit and as we were directing the jet of water at the diesel engine's framing (and everywhere else) the depot fitter suddenly appeared! He wasn't too happy with us at all and I thought that we'd be reported but luckily, nothing else was said.

Above: Timothy Saunders on 350hp shunter 15228 circa 1968 when he was a young secondman. The fuel gauge also indicates the loco is low on fuel!

Below: Stewarts Lane Depot - the fuelling point was situated in the shed on the right of the photograph.

Photos: Timothy Saunders.

Above: Battersea Power Station provides a striking backdrop to this photograph of Class 33/0 33004 as it awaits entry into Stewarts Lane Depot circa 1989.

Below: A line up of diesel-electric locomotives at Stewarts Lane Depot on 1st December 1993. From left to right: 47631, 37235, 37009 and 47517. Class 33s 33020, 33040 and 33113 are withdrawn, awaiting disposal.

Photos: Timothy Saunders.

One of our better paying turns at Woking was a turn nicknamed 'The Big Bomo'. The turn would only be rostered three days in one week and the other two days in another week. Drivers were being paid mileage then and this was our biggest weekday mileage turn totalling 264 miles.

Signing on at 11.16 you would relieve and work the 11.31 semi-fast Bournemouth service from Woking to Waterloo. This would then make the 12.30 fast service to Bournemouth calling at Southampton and Bournemouth only (this was the old Bournemouth Belle timing). You were then booked a meal-break and afterwards, you would relieve and work another fast service to Waterloo calling at Southampton and Waterloo only. The duty finished by working a semi-fast service back to Woking and then get relief.

12.30 Waterloo - Bournemouth - Incident 1.

My first instance of a problem on this turn was when I was waiting to leave Waterloo with the 12.30 Bournemouth service on Friday 12th November. After performing the necessary brake tests, an American gentleman knocked on the non-driver's side cab window (we were standing on platform 13) and when I slid the window open, he asked me where the 'engine' was? I explained to him that the train was made of two 4-car TC (trailer–coaches) and a 4REP 3,200hp Tractor Unit (situated at the rear of the 12-car train).

He seemed quite happy with my explanation and disappeared from my view. As soon as the time reached 12.29, my starting signal cleared displaying a green aspect with the MT indication (Main Through). At 12.30, I received the starting bells from the guard and I released the brake and opened the power controller to 'series' and back to the 'shunt' position. After the train started to move, I then hand-notched the power and we moved out towards Westminster Bridge at 20mph. As I passed the next signal, the driver of an incoming service was gesticulating with one hand as he passed by, I thought to myself, did I forget to change the red blinds for the usual 91 Bournemouth headcode? I leaned across and opened the headcode box door and looked inside. No, the 91 headcode was set so I closed the door and concentrated on my progress out of Waterloo and the signals ahead of me towards Vauxhall. The driver of the next incoming service on the Up Main Through line did the same thing as the first driver and my first thought went back to the American that had asked me the question about where the 'engine' was. I then had this awful vision in my head – when he disappeared from my view at Waterloo station – had he gone round to the front of my train and was sitting on one of the buffers?!!

Below: 4REP 3011 leads the 09.32 Weymouth to Waterloo service past Worting Junction on 24th May 1986.
These units were the 'top of the range' of SR EMUs, complete with a full buffet car (the third vehicle). They were also easily the most powerful, being equipped with eight traction motors giving a total of 3200hp. This high power output was needed when they were required to haul or propel TC units.
The electrical equipment from the REPs was obviously built to last, as all the traction motors were salvaged from the units to build the much more modern looking Class 442s in the 1980s.

Photo & Caption: Martin Loader.

Driving Days - Woking MT

By this time, we had gone through Vauxhall and were on the right-hand curve when the next driver of an incoming service pointed at my train as he went by and the next thing I knew was that the emergency brake was being applied from somewhere other than in my cab, so my train came to an abrupt stand. I contacted the guard on the loudaphone to find out if he'd applied the brake. He said that he hadn't and would investigate to see if a communication cord had been pulled. Sure enough, a passenger in the second coach back from my cab had pulled the communication cord and when I went back along the inside of the train I could see why. One of the offside passenger doors was missing completely! It had been left open when we left Waterloo and hadn't been spotted by the platform staff. As we left Waterloo, it had been hanging in the breeze and the first two trains that had passed us had narrowly missed hitting it. As we rounded the curve after Vauxhall the angle of degrees was more pronounced and the third train had hit it and ripped it off its hinges. The door was laying in the 'four foot' between the two tracks. The Guard then had to ask the passengers to move to another coach further down the train and after locking the doors and resetting the communication cord, we continued to Clapham Junction where the train was taken out of service.

12.30 Waterloo - Bournemouth - Incident 2.

The second time that I had an incident with this train was again after leaving Waterloo with the 12.30 Bournemouth service. As I was approaching Clapham Junction (roughly where the carriage washing machine is situated) a van train hauled by a Class 33 Crompton had just left Clapham Yard and a door on one of the vans was swinging open. It missed the two 4TC units of my train but again, I noticed an uncontrolled reduction of brake pipe pressure on my brake gauge and the brakes going on in an emergency. We came to a stand and the guard contacted me on the loudaphone to say that the door had smashed into the side of the buffet car window (on the 4REP unit) and the impact had caused a metal catch of the one of the windows to fly across and smash the glass mirror in the buffet car and a couple of spirit optics in the process! There was also considerable damage to the window but luckily no one was injured. After the communication cord had been reset, I continued into Clapham Junction station and again the train was taken out of service.

Below: A passenger chats to the driver of a Weymouth - Waterloo fast service at Southampton. The train is headed by 4REP 3001 which would have taken over at Bournemouth once the rear portion from Weymouth had been attached.

Photo: Ian Docwra.

12.30 Waterloo - Bournemouth - Incident 3.

My third incident regarding this train but at least this time, I did get beyond Clapham Junction!

As I was hurtling down towards Winchester, at 90mph, a van train approached on the up line with a door wide open on the off side! I thought to myself 'not again' and waited for the inevitable to happen. As the van train went by me, I looked at the Line Indicator which would give me an indication whether or not the collector shoes of the REP unit might get damaged should the door get knocked off. Sure enough, the Line Indicator went from ON to OFF so I instantly initialised a brake application so that I could at least stop my train in the confines of Winchester station. After I came to a stand, I observed that the Line Indicator was still OFF so I contacted the guard and after securing my train, started to walk back looking for damage. Some of the shoes on the REP unit on the off side were still intact but two were missing and bits of debris were still wrapped round what was the remainder of the shoe gear. It was obvious that the train wasn't able to continue so after obtaining a current isolation and detraining the passengers, I set about the task of isolating the rest of the shoes from the conductor rail. Assistance was also obtained and a Class 33 locomotive came light from Eastleigh depot (travelling wrong-road) and after coupling up, hauled my train back to Eastleigh where it was taken out of service.

Now you might think that I was a bit of a 'Jonah' whilst working this train but must emphasise, these incidents happened over a three to four year period - other trips were pretty straightforward with nothing untoward happening, thank goodness!

The other mileage turn was known as the 'Little Bomo' and again was shared on the roster - three days one week and two days another. This was also an early turn, booking on at 05.55 - (635 duty) work a stopping service to Bournemouth and then get relief. After your PN break, you would then walk to the middle siding, bring the train out into the platform and after the Weymouth portion had coupled, work a semi-fast service back to Woking and get relief - a distance of 216 miles.

Above: Class 430 4REP Detail.

Below: 4REP 3004 waits to leave Bournemouth with a fast service to Waterloo.

Photos: Ian Docwra.

Driving Days - Woking MT

On the 31st March 1983, I was again booked to attend the Operations Training Centre at South Side Waterloo for a Class 455 Course.

Having already learnt Class 508s, this was classed as a conversion course lasting two days as the 3-step braking system was very similar. Originally, there was only one type of 455 but more joined the fleet in later years. They all had the same driving controls but with subtle differences in the layout of the equipment and isolating cock positioning under the coaches. Some of the units also had a different power control system thyristor control instead of a camshaft governed by a CLR (Current Limit Relay). One of the types (57XX series) was also easily recognisable as having a flat-roofed coach that was originally fitted to a Class 508.

However, there were drawbacks to the braking system employed (as with the Class 508).

Older style EMUs had a braking system where the brake blocks would press against the wheels whereas Class 508 and 455 units had brake discs and pads. During adverse weather conditions e.g. leaf-fall, the older style of brake system would burn a certain amount of residue from the wheels with the friction involved. This of course didn't occur with the brake disc and pad system and it was a common occurrence for the wheels to 'pick up' and slide.

To combat this, a blow-down system would detect that the wheels were about to pick-up and would release the brakes accordingly. It was important though to let the apparatus (called the logic box) do its work and not to 'fan the brake' (repeatedly putting the brake on and releasing it). If the wheels started sliding, you were instructed to place the brake controller to step 3 and leave it there.

Another important factor was the weight of the train (especially on a commuter run where more passengers were boarding as the journey progressed towards Waterloo). As the loading increased, suspension and braking pressures were also increased but a certain amount of care still had to be undertaken when braking.

The units proved very reliable and are still in service today.

Above: Class 455 5853 causes a few sparks as the train heads away from Woking with a Guildford - Waterloo stopping service.

Photo: The Author's Collection.

One of the regular mixed-traction turns at the depot was 808 duty which usually involved working a freight from Woking Yard to Eastleigh Yard and then either working an engineer's train back or a long-welded rail train from Redbridge Yard to Woking Yard.

On this particular day, my secondman Ian Verrinder and I booked on at 14.42 and worked the train to Eastleigh as planned but were instructed to take the locomotive to Eastleigh diesel depot and pick up a fresh locomotive. This was also a Class 73 and had just come out of the shops. Looking resplendent with gleaming paintwork, the locomotive looked in fine fettle.

We ran light to Eastleigh Down Yard and picked up our fully-fitted train and after we were given the load by the guard (who rode in the back cab) and had the signal to go, proceeded out onto the up line towards Shawford.

Ian was doing the driving and as soon as we were over the conductor rail, he eased the diesel controller back to 'Off', pressed the shoe-down button and placed the diesel controller to 'Lock-Off' and opened the electric controller to a 'Run-Up' position and at the same time stopped the diesel engine by using the 'Engine Stop' switch. As soon as the locomotive took electric power, the Line Indicator went from ON to OFF. Ian waited a few seconds for the Line Indicator to return to ON (which meant that power to the conductor rail was restored) and again opened the electric controller. Exactly the same thing happened so I said to Ian, "restart the diesel engine and we will continue on diesel power." Ian complied with my request and as we had quite a heavy load, continued through Shawford and Winchester at a fairly slow pace. On the approach to Weston, we were put away in the long relief siding, coming to a stand at the signal at Wallers Ash. I decided to let the guard know that we had a problem and as I walked back through the diesel engine compartment (we were driving from No. 1 end of the locomotive - diesel engine end) as I opened the communicating fire-door to the electric compartment, I noticed a strange burning smell but I put this down to new paint.

I mentioned to the guard what had happened and he decided to have a look round the train and straightaway noticed a chain hanging down from one of the wagons. As there wasn't a conductor rail on this side, he managed to safely secure the chain and realised that this was the cause of the sub-station circuit breaker blowing and losing the current supply. I phoned the Signalman to tell him know what we'd found and that it was now OK for us to continue.

The signalman gave us the road and we then continued out onto the main line towards Micheldever on electric power. As we continued towards Basingstoke, the smell I'd experienced became more noticeable so we stopped at the first available signal to request permission to go into Basingstoke Yard via the Winkleberry sidings entrance. As soon as we arrived there I decided that it was probably best not to continue and that the locomotive receive a fitter's attention. I duly made an entry in the log book to report what we had experienced.

The following day, I was contacted by the head of the CM&EE department at Eastleigh for a more detailed report and after an examination back at Eastleigh it had been discovered that the Traction Motor Blower upon installation had been wired up incorrectly - hence the burning smell of the traction motors overheating!

Class 33/0 33020 trundles into Tonbridge West Yard from Redhill with a long welded rail train. This type of train was restricted to a 25mph speed for obvious reasons!

Photo: Timothy Saunders.

Driving Days - Woking MT

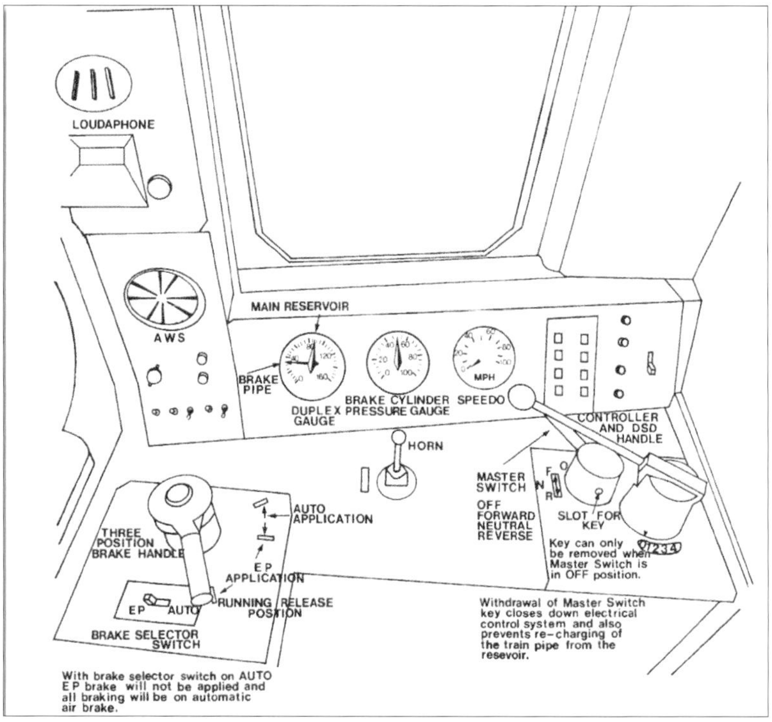

There were three other incidents that I recall whilst being at Woking MT. The first involving a runaway train consisting of 2 x 4VEP units from Woking towards West Byfleet on 30th March 1978.

The driver of the ECS that had worked the train into Woking didn't apply the automatic brake correctly when leaving his cab and thinking that the relieving Driver that was going to take the train into East End sidings, was already in the cab at the other end, didn't think any more about it when he heard the brakes release as he stepped out of the cab onto the platform.

Because of the falling gradient, the train started to move and instead of going into East End sidings, proceeded to run away 'wrong line' back towards West Byfleet on the Down Fast line. This was noticed immediately by the signalman on his panel and he stopped the next train on the Down Fast line at West Byfleet station. A shunter who had also noticed the runaway tried to run after the train but unfortunately, tripped and fell.

Quick action was taken at West Byfleet to get all but four of the passengers out of the train before the inevitable collision, the train colliding with the other at an estimated speed of 15 - 20mph. These four passengers including the driver suffered slight injuries.

This incident was to come in handy at the Training School at Waterloo later on as a 'real life experience' when teaching drivers the correct way to leave a 1963 type EMU cab being:

1. Apply the EP Brake by placing the 3-Position Brake handle to the Full Service position
2. Place EP / AUTO Brake Selector Switch to the AUTO position
3. Observe the Auto Brake applies on the Brake Cylinder Pressure gauge to 50psi and brake pipe needle on Duplex gauge drops below 50psi
4. Place Master Switch to OFF and remove EP Key
5. Return Drivers Brake handle to the Running Release position
6. Observe that Brake Cylinder Pressure is holding at 50psi.

A previous incident involved another 'runaway' of sorts in July 1975. It involved 4CIG 7346 that was in the depot at Durnsford Road, Wimbledon Park alledgedly being worked on by a fitter. I'm not sure what the fitter was doing but it suddenly took power and moved out of the shed of its own accord. Once out of the shed and onto the third rail (pulling the shed socket cable out of its housing in the process) it continued under power up towards another 4CIG 7378 that was standing foul. The offending unit side-swiped the other, ending up against the parapet of the up local flyover.

Above: Drawing of a 1963 4-VEP driving cab showing the controls especially the Brake Selector Switch.

Graphic: MOT Document.

Right: The coming together of two 4CIG Units at Wimbledon Park Depot, July 1975.

Photo: Pete Beyer and Andy Gibb Collection.

The third incident in November 1970, involved a loaded stone train consisting of 10 Whale hoppers hauled by a 'Crompton' 1550hp diesel electric locomotive travelling from Woking Yard to Redhill.

On the descent from Dorking Town to Deepdene, a number of Whale hoppers became derailed, emptying their contents onto the busy A24 road below.

Above and Below: *The aftermath showing the derailed Whale hoppers and the ballast deposited in the dual carriageway of the main road below, blocking the traffic.*

Photos: Pete Beyer and Andy Gibb Collection.

Driving Days - Woking MT

I once worked an Officer's Special from Aldershot to Waterloo (via Guildford and Cobham) with a Class 73/1 electro-diesel locomotive. The GM Saloon coach had its own driving cab (similar to a 1963 Unit) and I drove the unit from this cab from Aldershot to Guildford. Fred Smith was the Inspector with me and it felt quite strange to 'listen in' to the conversation of the 'top brass' that were assembled round the meeting table. As we approached Guildford, Fred (whispering in my ear) asked me if it was possible for the train to go up to Waterloo via Cobham from any of the platforms that we could have entered. I informed him that it wasn't possible as we could only enter platforms 5, 6&7 and platform 8 and we would be required to shunt into the tunnel and proceed back up platform 3 (the Up Cobham).

One day, Les Mills and I were booked to take two Class 33 Crompton locomotives in multiple, light to Eastleigh Depot.

It was a warm day so I said to Les, that I would shut the diesel engine down on the leading loco and to stop the pump-set from running, I turned the Engine Control switch to the 'Off' position. This then enabled me to propel the leading locomotive with the trailing locomotive doing all the work. We were in the No. 1 end of the loco and I'd noticed that Les had also got his feet on the DSD treadle on his side. As we entered Popham Tunnels at Micheldever and went into darkness, I quietly got up, opened the engine room door and stepped into the engine room closing the door behind me. As we came out of the tunnel and into the light, I could see Les sitting in the secondman's position gazing ahead through his front window. After a few seconds, Les looked around to where I'd been sitting and suddenly did a 'double-take' when he realised I wasn't in the cab! I couldn't control my laughter for very long and opened the engine room door and stepped out into the cab. I couldn't have played this trick if the diesel engine had of been running as Les would have heard the engine noise get louder as I opened the engine room door.

Above: The General Manager's saloon at Alton.

Photo: David Timothy Collection.

Below: Class 33/0s 33048 and 33052 coupled in multiple at Tonbridge Yard.
Between locos: Coupling, main reservoir and & brake pipes, 27-way diesel jumper, engine speed control pipes.

Photo: Timothy Saunders.

I was booked 15.00 cover one day and the Acting Running Foreman came into the mess room and asked me to take a Class 47 locomotive light to Waterloo as one of the locomotives that was to work an Exeter service had broken down.

My secondman and I walked across to Hurdles Road siding where the locomotive was berthed and after a quick preparation made our way behind the ground signal in the Up Yard. I decided to let my secondman do the driving as he was already passed for driving on Class 33 traction and once the ground signal cleared, we made our way towards the London end of Woking station on the Up Local line.

At the same time, an ECS train had come out of the East End sidings and had started away from the Down Through platform towards London. We both had green signals ahead and it wasn't long before we were moving at the same speed as we headed towards West Byfleet. We both continued at the same pace until we reached Hersham where the signals become repeating signals (because of their distance apart). At Esher, our signal became 2 yellows and repeated two yellows whereas, the ECS train had green aspects. Unfortunately, although my secondman had started braking, it wasn't sufficient and we hadn't reduced the speed of our locomotive enough before the next signal (which was at caution). The ECS train was now disappearing fast and it wasn't realised until too late that we weren't going to stop before reaching the next signal which was at danger. We ran past the red signal a couple of locomotive lengths, stopping before the track-circuit which was situated in front of the next set of facing points.

I said to my secondman "go back to the signal telephone and tell the signalman that we've slipped by the signal." As he was doing so, I noticed the facing points in front move across to allow us to go from the Up Local to the Up Through line. My secondman came running back and said that the signal showed one yellow with diversion lights and after he climbed aboard, we continued on our way to Waterloo.

I think that my secondman learnt a valuable lesson that day regarding the poor braking qualities of locomotives running light (especially Class 47s).

Below: Class 47 No. 47716 heads away from Woking with an Exeter service on 6th September 1991.

Photo: Stuart Ray.

Driving Days - Woking MT

On Sunday 24th March 1985, my secondman (Nick Waite) and I were booked on at 09.03 to work a special ballast train from Woking Yard to Guildford. We then proceeded into the site of work accompanied by a PICOP (Person in Charge of Possession) and were then under his orders to move the train when required. As they were working within St Catherine's Tunnel, we didn't have to move the train very often which gave Nick the opportunity to take a couple of photographs of the site of work.

Above: PICOP Armlet.

Photo: Network Rail.

Right: Class 33/0 33062 outside St Catherine's Tunnel, Guildford.

Photo: Nick Waite.

Above: Under the orders of the PICOP, the engineering train headed by Class 33/0 33062 outside St Catherine's Tunnel, between Guildford and Shalford Junction. There are two tunnels - St Catherine's, bored through layers of sandstone and the other bored through layers of chalk.

Photo: Nick Waite.

One of the most embarrassing moments of my life occurred one day when I was rostered to relieve a driver on a ballast train at Basingstoke in the early hours of the morning.

I was booked to sign on the previous evening and catch the last train to Basingstoke and relieve the ballast train at 05.30 in the morning.

Well, as readers might already know, Basingstoke station isn't the nicest of places to spend the night – being the same height as St Paul's Cathedral, it's a cold windy place to be at any time.

I had a plan and signed on duty at Woking but instead of catching the last train to Basingstoke, nipped off home to spend a few hours in bed, returning to Woking to catch the paper train to Basingstoke which left at around 04.30 – plenty of time to get there and relieve the Driver at 05.30. All went according to plan and I returned to Woking and jumped on the paper train.

Busying myself reading a newspaper, I was horrified to find that the train had been diverted and we were just passing 'Moons' timber yard (just outside Guildford)! I hurried to find the guard on the train but by this time we were entering the chalk tunnel and heading towards Farncombe. I explained to the guard what had happened and he applied the emergency brake just before we entered the station at Farncombe. I jumped out onto the platform and after the train had left, walked up to the signal box and asked the signalman if I could use his phone to contact the Running Foreman at Woking. Here's the embarrassing part – Peter Bunce was the Acting Running Foreman and when he answered the phone I explained what had happened and when I said that I was at Farncombe signalbox and not at Basingstoke he wasn't at all pleased with me! Luckily, the ballast train was ready to leave earlier than expected and the Driver worked the train back to Woking. I had to walk back to Guildford from Farncombe catching a train from there to Woking!

Below: Class 73/1 electro-diesel No. 73134 waits on the down local platform at Woking before leaving with the 22.52 Waterloo - Southampton on 4th November 1977. Primarily a parcels working it also carried coaching stock for the few travellers who wanted the ride. I'd quite often let passengers ride in the cab of the early morning paper train to Aldershot or Farnborough.

Photo: David Hayes.

Driving Days - Woking MT

Above: Class 73/1 electro-diesel No. 73102 (formerly E6008) pauses at the semaphore starter signal at Salisbury on 6th March 1985.

Photo: David Mant.

Below: 'Warship' Class No. 812 'Royal Naval Reserve 1859 - 1959' at Waterloo in October 1971.

Photo: Stuart Ray.

One turn we had at Woking was to work a passenger train to Basingstoke and then PC (prepare circuits) a Type 3 1550hp Crompton that was left in the down bay with a 4TC unit and work a passenger service to Salisbury.

This particular day, my secondman and I climbed into the cab of the Crompton only to find that the locomotive had developed a bad water leak coming from a ruptured water pipe in the engine room. The only locomotive that they had 'spare' at Basingstoke was a Class 73/1 electro-diesel so after detaching the Crompton and placing it in the yard utilising the Class 73/1 locomotive, we went back on the train. After isolating the collector shoes, I worked the train using auxiliary diesel power; the 600hp engine coping admirably and managing to time the train. We then worked the train back from the cab of the TC stock (Push-Pull) with the same locomotive on the rear of the train.

The only time that I ever worked on a 'Warship' class locomotive was when I had to conduct a Basingstoke driver from Woking to Merstham (near Redhill) with a loaded stone train. The M25 was being built at the time and a rail-head had been put in place at Merstham to allow trains to deliver road stone 'on site'. Not long after that Basingstoke men didn't need the services of a conductor as they had signed for the route.

Sometime in the autumn of 1984 whilst working a Waterloo - Reading passenger service, I was cautioned by the signalman to search the line between Wokingham and Winnersh. A passenger on a previous train had reported seeing a fox with what was thought to have been a child's arm in its mouth running along the railway line.

The police officer that accompanied me in the cab said they were especially interested as a seven-year-old boy called Mark Tildesley had gone missing after visiting a fun-fair at Wokingham some months before. His parents had searched for him but only found his bicycle chained to a fence and despite a national publicity campaign, his body has never been found.

On a lighter note, I again was cautioned to search the line, this time by the signalman at Aldershot as there was a report of persons on the track walking through Aldershot tunnel.

There was a 'home' match being played at Aldershot Football Stadium (which adjoins the line towards the tunnel) and it was thought that supporters were trying to gain access to the stadium via the railway line. It was absolutely chucking it down with rain as I left the station and as I approached the tunnel, I noticed a police officer standing near the portal. Unfortunately, as I came to a stop just prior to where he was standing, rain water that had gathered on the roof of the train suddenly rushed forward along the gutter on the roof of the carriage and cascaded over the police officer scoring a direct hit! Luckily, he was wearing a helmet and trench coat which stopped him from getting a soaking!

Above: Class 73/1 electro-diesel No. 73112 emerges from the Guildford Chalk Tunnel with a permanent way train for Three Bridges on Saturday 11th February 1978.

Photo: Gordon Edgar.

Above: Regular turns at Woking MT were to work stone trains from Woking Down Yard to either Tonbridge Yard, Three Bridges Yard or New Cross Gate Yard. You would then return with the empty hoppers / wagons to Woking Yard for their onward journey to the stone quarries in the West of England. Here we see Class 33/1 No. 33113 leaving Woking Down Yard with a mixed train of loaded Whale hoppers and Grampus wagons.

Photo: Michael Thorne.

Below: A variety of wagons bask in the sun at Tonbridge West Yard on 2nd March 1985.

Photo: Timothy Saunders.

Above: Resplendent in Trainload Freight Construction markings, Class 33/0 No. 33033 stands at South Godstone CCE Tip located in the old brick pits beside the Redhill to Tonbridge line. The locomotive is waiting to depart with the 14.20 to Tonbridge West Yard formed of empty Grampus wagons which would have arrived loaded from Redhill with ballast spoil. The waste stone was unloaded and cleaned at this location before being sold on as sub-base and road stone.

Below: Class 33/2 No. 33208 waits at the exit signal from Redhill Down Tonbridge Branch Sidings. The train is the 07.40 Redhill Yard to Godstone Tip and is made up of Grampus wagons loaded with ballast spoil for dumping in the former brickworks clay pit.

Photos & Captions: Adrian Nicholls.

Driving Days - Woking MT

Thankfully, I've never had to experience anyone jumping in front of my train intentionally but two instances of near misses spring to mind.

The first was when I was working an ECS train (consisting of 2 x 4SUB units) from Waterloo to Kingston (via Norbiton) and as I was passing through Norbiton station, I noticed a platelayer standing in the four-foot on the bridge at the other side of the station. I sounded the two-tone horn as a warning but instead of moving to the adjacent line, he didn't move out of the way. He assumed (wrongfully) that I was going to stop in the platform.

By this time, I was almost through the platform and then to his horror and realising the danger he was in, he flattened himself against the bridge parapet. I'd let go of the deadman by this time and luckily, my train missed him by inches.

The second incident was when I was working a Guildford - Waterloo (via Ascot) service. It was quite a foggy morning and as I was passing through North Sheen, I saw a woman in the four-foot on the down line walking towards Mortlake station. I sounded the two-tone horn as a warning but she continued walking so I applied the emergency brake and came to a stand some 400 yards past her. I looked back down the off-side of my train but she was nowhere to be seen but through the mist I could see a train leaving Mortlake station coming towards us. I quickly opened the emergency cabinet that contains red flags and detonators and started waving a red flag at the approaching train from the cab window. Luckily, the driver saw me in time and brought his train to a stand adjacent to my cab and I explained the situation to him. As far as I'm aware, the lady must have returned to the platform at North Sheen station.

Above Top: Norbiton Station looking towards Kingston.

Photo: Martin Addison - Wikipedia.

Above: The bridge where the incident occurred.

Photo: Damon Hart-Davis - Wikipedia.

Right: North Sheen station looking towards Mortlake.

Photo: Hassocks 5489 - Wikipedia.

Above: Woking crew Dick Bullen and Doug Dunstall head off to Salisbury with Class 33/0 No. 33025 'Sultan' on 4th October 1986 hauling a Woking Homes Special Charter.

Photo: The Author's Collection.

Class 33/1 No. 33106 races past Newton Tony (between Salisbury and Andover) with the 09.29 Salisbury to Waterloo service on 19th April 1986, comprising 4TC trailer set 423.

At this time the Salisbury trains were working in push pull mode using Class 33/1s, while the Exeter trains were principally in the hands of Class 50s.

Photo and Caption: Martin Loader.

Driving Days - Woking MT

Above: 4VEP 3159 works away from Woking with a stopping service to Alton. An unidentified Class 33 locomotive and Class 73/1 locomotive are berthed on Hurdles Road siding.

Below: An 8-car Alton service headed by 4VEP 3487 waits in platform 3 at Woking while 4CIG 1821 waits in platform 4 with a stopping service for Portsmouth and Southsea.

Photos: Matthew Taylor.

One of our regular routes at the depot was to Alton. It was whilst working one of these turns (from Alton to Waterloo) that proved to be a turning point in my railway career.

As mentioned in an earlier chapter, I didn't like using the EP (electro-pneumatic) brake and always used the Westinghouse brake. I found it a challenge and would always use it whether the train consisted of 4, 8 or 12 cars.

One of the instructors at South Side Training School (Phil Eke) would quite often catch this service and would ride in the cab with me to Waterloo. Phil had previously been a driver at Farnham and we got on very well. I think Phil was quite impressed with my driving and stopping skills using the Westinghouse brake and when we reached our destination asked me if I'd be interested in becoming an instructor myself and up until this point, I hadn't given it a thought. I said to Phil that I would indeed welcome the opportunity and Phil said that he would make inquiries.

A couple of days later he contacted me and said that I should write a letter to my Depot Master to apply for a position at South Side and this I duly did.

On the 6th February 1987, I received an acknowledgment from Roy Vigars (who was the Acting Depot Master at the time) to say that he had forwarded it to the Training School along with a recommendation.

Several months went by and on Friday 8th August whilst standing spare, Bill White (who was then Chief Traction Inspector) came into the room and said that he needed me to work a passenger service to Alton and back and that he was going to ride with me.

When the next service for Alton ran into Woking, I did the necessary splitting procedure (the Waterloo Basingstoke / Alton services split at Woking in those days) and after uncoupling the train and the front part had left) I got ready to work the rear part to Alton.

Once our signal had cleared and after receiving the Guard's signal to depart, we left Woking - next stop Brookwood. Whilst we were travelling along, Bill chatted away about the Training School and the possibility of me joining as an 'Acting Instructor' with the emphasise on the word 'If' e.g. "if you come to the Training School, etc." As per usual, I flicked the EP/AUTO brake switch to the AUTO position and after shutting off power and coasting towards Brookwood station, proceeded to brake the train to stop on the 4-Car mark on the down platform. As mentioned, I'd been using the AUTO brake on VEP stock for several years and came to a perfect stop releasing the brake at the last moment to avoid a jolt. Bill must have been impressed because when we chatted about the Training School from then on, the emphasise was on the word 'When' e.g. "when you come to the Training School!"

Above: Driver's eye view of Woking from the cab of 4VEP 7759 with the home signal displaying one yellow with a diversion to the Up Fast line. Notice Auto braking has been used.

Below: Acknowledgement letter from Roy Vigars - Acting Train Crew Manager.

Photo: The Author's Collection.

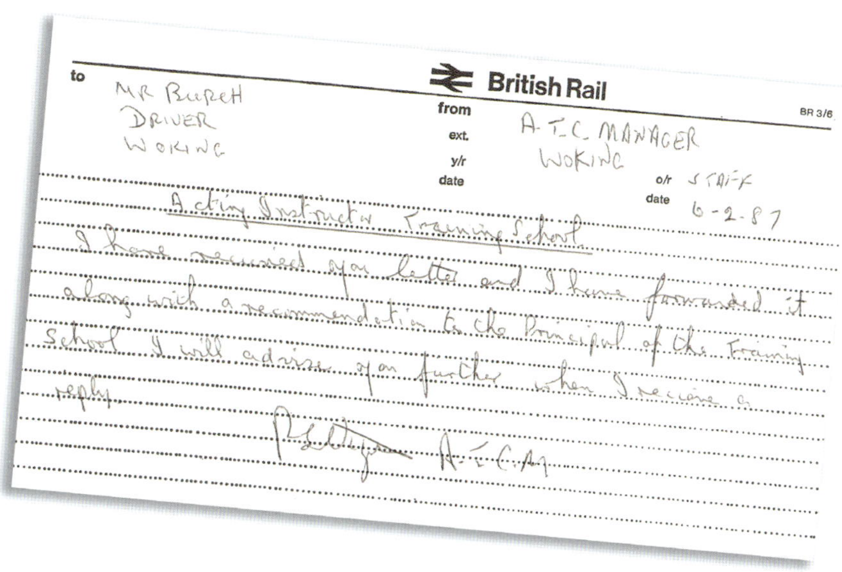

British Rail

BR 3/6

to MR BURCH
DRIVER
WOKING

from A.T.C. MANAGER
WOKING

o/r STAFF
date 6-2-87

Acting Instructor Training School

I have received your letter and I have forwarded it along with a recommendation to the Principal of the Training School. I will advise you further when I receive a reply.

A.T.C.M.

The rest of the trip also went according to plan and Bill and I mostly chatted about fishing (as I knew that he was a keen fisherman). Things started to happen very fast from then on as the following Monday (10th August) I was booked to attend Waterloo South Side Training School for an interview with the Principal, Tony Skilton.

My interview with Tony Skilton and Cyril Sweet went very well and afterwards I was told that the job was mine.

The rest of the week I was booked late turns / nights and on Thursday 20th August I went late-night shopping to Marks and Spencers for some new clothes for my new job as an Acting Instructor starting on Monday 24th August 1987.

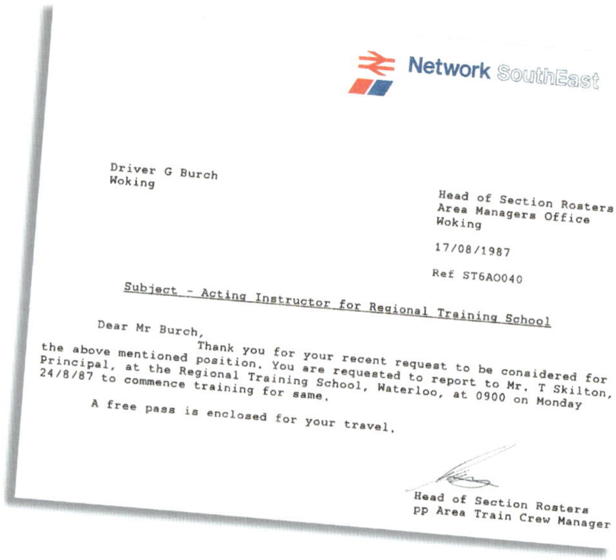

Network SouthEast

Driver G Burch
Woking

Head of Section Rosters
Area Managers Office
Woking

17/08/1987

Ref ST6A0040

Subject - Acting Instructor for Regional Training School

Dear Mr Burch,

Thank you for your recent request to be considered for the above mentioned position. You are requested to report to Mr. T Skilton, Principal, at the Regional Training School, Waterloo, at 0900 on Monday 24/8/87 to commence training for same.

A free pass is enclosed for your travel.

Head of Section Rosters
pp Area Train Crew Manager

Above: The Author's first day at the Training School.

Left: Appointment Letter from South Side Training School Waterloo.

Below: Alton - Waterloo service with 4VEP 3467.

Photo: Matt Taylor.

My first week at the Operational Training Centre (OTC) Side Side was spent meeting everyone (some forty-five full-time and acting instructors) and getting to know what was to be expected of me. Cyril Sweet (who was the senior instructor) said that I would first sit-in on a five-week Rules course but as I was still an acting instructor, this meant that I was still available to work Saturdays and Sundays as a driver back at my depot at Woking. Each Saturday was classed as a 'Rest Day' so the rate of pay would be at time-and-a-half and Sunday rate was time-and-three-quarters but I did have some weekends off.

Above: Hurricane damage at Five Oak Green, between Tonbridge and Paddock Wood.

Photo: Timothy Saunders.

Following the Rules course, I then had to sit-in on a six-week Traction Trainee course with Brian Hobby. This was quite interesting as there were quite a number of 'out days' covering various subjects such as signal box and depot visits to practise coupling / uncoupling of locomotives and train protection rules e.g. placing detonators. I was also allowed to do some of the instructing myself and I'm pleased to say that all nine trainees passed their course exam.

It was during this time (the night of 15th October 1987 and the following morning) that a hurricane struck the south of Britain and caused absolute turmoil to the transport system. Trees were blown down and were blocking railway lines and even the road to the station was blocked in several places so it took me all morning to get to work. The course had to be abandoned for the day as the trainees had also found it difficult to get to the training school.

In the meantime, another acting instructor had arrived at the OTC South Side, Dave Webb who lived at Dover.

Dave and I hit it off straight away; he was of similar seniority as myself and had been a fireman at Nottingham so we had a lot in common.

On 30th November, I was booked to instruct on my first Traction Trainee course with six trainees; five from Hither Green and one from Bournemouth.

On 12th December, Pauline and I attended my first 'office party' which was held at the BR Staff Association Club at Waterloo which was quite a social event and where we met some of the other instructor's wives and girlfriends.

On 22nd December, I had to sit my own Rules Exam with George Taylor, one of the Chief Traction Inspectors which I thankfully passed and this took a weight off of my shoulders before the Christmas period.

My course continued on 4th January 1988 but I did work some of the days preceding this back at Woking where I was booked route refreshers most of the week. All six students on my first Traction Trainee course were passed out by David Timothy with flying colours!

Above: Chief Traction Inspector George Taylor at Waterloo before heading towards Portsmouth Harbour with a Royal Train.

Photo: The Author's Collection.

UTILISATION

INSPECTORS	MON. 18/3	TUES. 19/3	WED. 20/3	THURS. 21/3	FRI. 22/3	MON. 25/3	TUES. 26/3	WED. 27/3
STEWARTS LANE								
W. WARD, Insp. I/C	DEMU	2ND WK	RD	A	→	DEMU	A	3RD WK
J. BARRETT	2750	→			→	BECK		ST III
D. INGRAM	L/B	MEETING KATE RM 350	→	→	EMV 2WK	ASST T.T (3)	L.B	ASST EMU
SOUTH SIDE, WATERLOO								
R. MILLS, Insp. I/C								
R. DRAPPER	204	S.GREEN R DYKES →		A		E.L	3 WK	→
G. BOWMAN	RD	ASST ED	LIT	→	FOSTER ROWE	1550 SCHEMATIC	LIT	ASST 1550
B. BYRNE	E.L.	→	2ND WK	→	E.L.	ED	2 WK	→
D. GANE	EMV	→	2 WK	→	RD	1550 DRS	1 WK	▲ →
D. TAIT	1550	SCHEMATICS		-(ROWE)		RD	1550	SCHEMAT
W. WARD	T.T (5)					T (5)		2 WK
SOUTHAMPTON								
C. SWEET Insp. I/C	EXAM 2750	MEETING KATE RM 350	A			EXAM 2750	A	RD WK 3
E. LENCH	T.T. (4)	→	WK 2		→	T.T. (4)		
F. JOHNSON	1550 DRS DT	DT	5 WK DT	DT	→ DT	1550 DRS	6 WK	→
ACTING INSPECTORS								
D. OTTIGNON	TT WK 7 (3)	VEP	DEMU	→	T.T WK (3)	TT (3) ▲		8 WK
W. WHITE	1550 S/M	→	3 WK		→	1550 S/M		4 WK
A. GREAVES-HURD	1550 S/M		6 WK		→	1550 S/M	7 WK	→
E. PEAKE	E.D	▲	1 WK		→	ED	2 WK	→
E. CHRISTIAN	EMU	→	2 WK		→	EMU	3 WK	▲
DRIVERS D. JUDGES	LEARN DEMU	→			→	LEARN DEMU		
A. ROWE	LEARN 1550	SCHEMATICS		→		LEARN 1550		SCHEMAT
C. MARSHALL	LEARN 1550	→	3 WK		→	LEARN 1550		1 WK
P. BASSETT	LEARN 1550	→			→	LEARN 1550		1 WK

SCHOOL COLOURS: STEWARTS LANE

1974 instructor's roster for the South Side Training School and its satellite training venues - Stewarts Lane and Southampton. There were twenty two names on the list - some of which were still at OTC South Side when I joined. Namely: Cyril Sweet, Bernie Byrne, Derek Gane, Fred Johnson, Don Ottignon, Ted Greaves-Hurd, Alan Rowe and Eric Christian. All others had either retired (or in one case passed away) and Bill White had become Chief Traction Inspector on the South-Western Division.

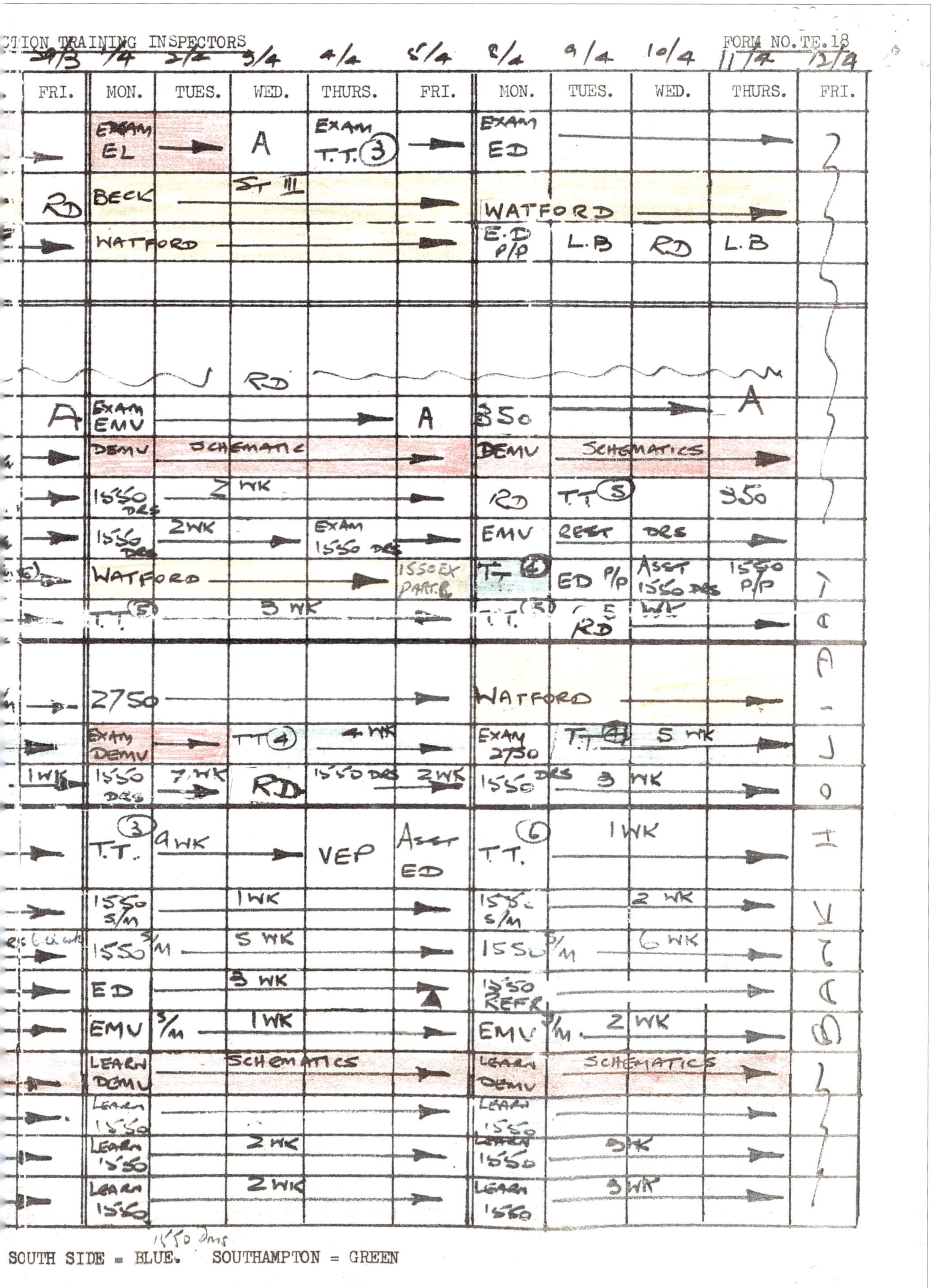

When I joined the Training School in 1987 as an acting instructor, there were fifty instructors at OTC South Side and six instructors at Basingstoke.

Graphic courtesy of Fred Johnson.

Instructing Days - OTC South Side

The training programme for train drivers at the time was called MP12 and trainees had to undergo the courses below:

- 5 weeks' training on rules
- 3 weeks' on the principles of route learning
- 9 weeks' traction training,(practical)
- 7 weeks' revision

The training programme then changed:

As a pre-condition, prospective Drivers must already have completed 90 turns as a trainman, i.e. as a Guard, Secondman or Driver's Assistant. At least forty of these turns must have been spent in the driving cab, this would permit some preliminary understanding of the driver's responsibilities, signals, routes etc;

- 4 weeks training on Rules
- 4 weeks traction training
- 2 weeks driving with instructor
- 8 weeks driving with a qualified 'minder driver'
- 2 weeks with the instructor

All training and progress was recorded by the trainee in a log book which was monitored and signed daily by the trainer.

At the end of each stage marked in the programme, the trainee took an examination to ensure full understanding and that they had reached the standard required. If unsuccessful, the trainee was allowed one further attempt; if they failed a second time they would be withdrawn from the training programme. The newly qualified driver then went to their own depot to learn the routes they were not familiar with. Their performance thereafter as a driver was monitored initially by the Training Centre but principally by the local Traction Inspectorate.

The names of the many colleagues that I worked with at the OTC South Side during the period I was there that aren't shown in the following photographs are listed below:

Tim Morgan
Brian Cook
Don Ottignon
Trevor Sprague
Phil Eke
Dave Webb
John Rutter
Len Price
Martyn Bowman
Peter Wensley
David Owen
Mick Oakley
Graham Allen
Roger Luckins
Dave Roussett
Paul Inge
Grant Gillingham
Paul Lemon
Tony Saunders
Neil Hickman
Derek Drage
Derek Gane
Ken Norris
Richard Pike
Alan Barnes
Ted Wickham
Fred Johnson
Peter Tyler
Ted Greaves-Hurd
Eric Christian
Peter Johns
Nigel Lacey
Mark Croucher
John Linge
John Saville
Brian Hobby
Colin Wood
Dave Tomlyn
Nigel Buck
Nigel Turner
Eric Harris
John Chambers
Mick Bassett
John Brookshaw
Eric Harris
Alan Cook
Peter Johns

Above: Some of the Instructors at OTC South Side - from left to right: Cyril Sweet, Chris Exley, Ian Verrinder, Mike Geall, Chris Foot, John Hartford, Tim Reynolds, Martin Squibb and Alan Brindley.

Photo: David Timothy.

Above: Some of the Instructors at OTC South Side - from left to right: Peter Delacey, Jim Samuel, Mark Medley, The Author, Dave Brown, Ralph Sullivan, Graham 'Inky' Penn, Gerry Waite and Alan Rowe.

Photo: David Timothy.

Above: Some of the Instructors at OTC South Side - from left to right: Peter Roberts, Ian Glover, Trevor 'Chopper' Harris, Ian Simmonds, Bernie Byrne, David Timothy, Tony Harper and Chris Haynes.

Photo: David Timothy.

Instructing Days - OTC South Side

For the rest of January, I was booked to cover a variety of days of a Rules course whilst one of my colleagues was on leave and on 12th February, I had to take my course notes, etc., to Basingstoke Training School as I was going to run another Traction Trainee course there starting on 15th February.

Basingstoke Training School was a satellite of the main one at OTC South Side and was situated on the up side of the station and Don Ottignon was the senior instructor in charge.

Don made me very welcome; I'd fired to Don when he'd been a driver at Guildford in the steam days and we got on very well.

There were ten trainees on my course this time - four of them (Neil Butcher, Mike Trodd, Stewart Barker and John Harrison) being from my home depot at Woking.

As each lesson progressed, I became more confident in my teaching methods and the 'sitting in' sessions on other courses and listening to other instructors had helped a great deal. There were quite a number of 'out days' and I was joined by fellow instructor Peter Roberts to assist me at Stewarts Lane for the coupling / uncoupling procedures and for the other depot visits.

Unfortunately, on the third week, I lost one of my trainees as he'd had an accident whilst riding his motorcycle suffering a broken collarbone.

On 24th March, the group were split into two groups for their exam (taken by Ken Norris and Don Ottignon) and eight out of the nine trainees passed, one failing on placing track circuit clips incorrectly.

On 28th March, I returned to the OTC South Side and was booked to sit in on another course, this time an MP12 EMU Traction course for Driver Assistants run by Martyn Bowman. Peter Johns (another acting instructor) was also going to sit in on the course. This course was of five week's duration (ten days longer than I received when I had my EMU course in 1969) but this did also cover the Class 455 element.

Above: Trainees on my first Traction Trainee course, this being held at Basingstoke.

Below: MP12 EMU course for drivers with Martyn Bowman in the foreground.

Photos: The Author's Collection.

The course structure started with the theory of Basic Electricity and how the current reached the unit via the third rail, then moving on to the 1951 EPB (Electro-Pneumatic Brake) type of unit. After teaching the theory part, the following day would be spent as a 'static' day at a depot (such as Victoria) teaching the practical part (cab and equipment layout / paddling up procedures, etc). Here again the group was split up: Martyn running one group and Derek Gane running the other.

Over the next two weeks, there were two more static days, the first being spent at Grove Park, this time covering main reservoir air bursts and the second day covering brake pipe bursts. All the procedures would be listed in the Faults & Failures books that were issued to each driver during the course. The other event covered on this day were coupling / uncoupling procedures and bearing in mind this was probably the first time that any of the trainees had actually moved a train, it sometimes proved a bit tense (for the trainee and instructor alike)!

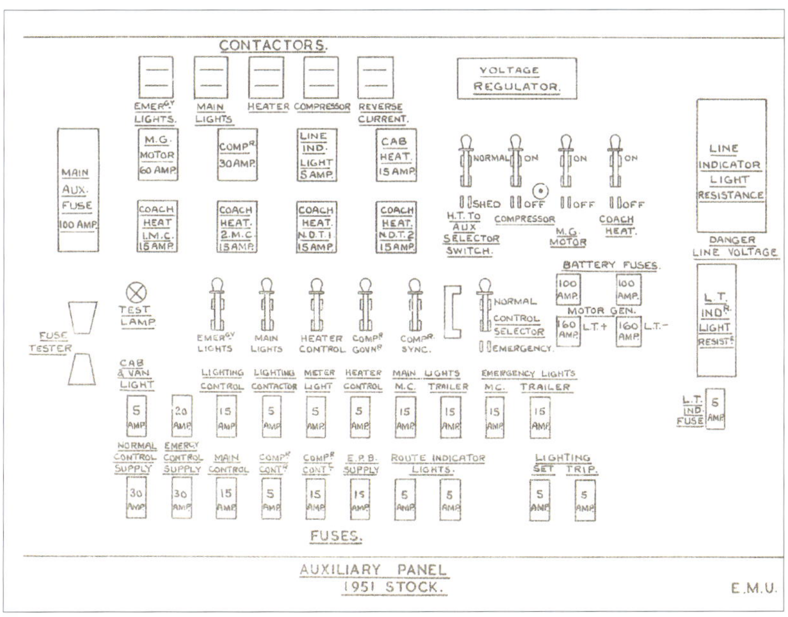

Following the 1951 EPB part of the course, the units built in 1957 were covered. Although similar in style and build, fuse cupboard layout and fuse changing procedures were totally different; the 1957 unit having MCBs (miniature circuit breakers) within the LT (low-tension) part of the fuse cupboard instead of cartridge fuses.

The following day was spent at a depot and we were joined by Mick Oakley. I had known Mick for a number of years before I joined the Training School as he'd been a driver at Guildford and I took a keen interest in his style of teaching.

Above: Instructor David Timothy with 4EPB 5437 at London Bridge.

Photo: David Timothy Collection.

Left: Auxiliary Panel of a 1951 EPB Unit.

Below: Generator End of Auxiliary Panel 1957 Unit.

The third static day was then followed by four days practical handling and as the South Western Division didn't operate any 1951 EPB stock, these days were spent over routes I'd never been over before - London Bridge to Redhill (via East Croydon) and from Victoria to Orpington and return. However, this was good for me as I needed to learn these routes before taking a group of students on my own.

All practical handling was completed by using service trains and in most cases, the driver would gladly let you take over and although they were supposed to stay with the train, quite often they disappeared to the mess room or had an 'early day.'

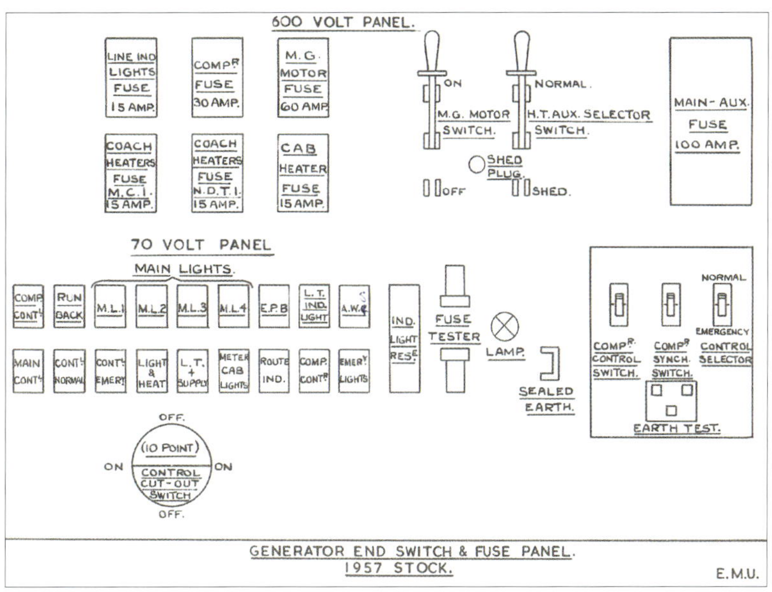

Above Top: Network SouthEast Operations Training Centre Sign.

Photo: Brian Cook.

Above: An abundance of SWT rolling stock outside of what was the OTC South Side, Waterloo. The huts were built on what was the Necropolis station that served Brookwood Cemetery with funeral trains. A further simulator block and further training rooms (D Block) were built to accommodate the Class 465 training programme for the South Eastern Division before the railway industry privatised in 1994.

Photo: Timothy Saunders.

The next part of the course was of the 1963 stock variety - 4VEP, 4BIG and 4CIG.

I'd been driving this type of stock since passing as a driver myself so I was completely familiar with the cab and equipment layout. The only stock that I didn't normally see were the 4CIG type with the electric parking brake so the day's static took place at Streatham Hill Depot.

The 1963 stock practical handling days were completed over familiar territory: Waterloo - Portsmouth Harbour, Woking - Alton, Woking - Basingstoke and Waterloo - Reading via Ascot. We did though have a change one day and worked from Victoria to Dover.

De-Icer Units were also covered and on another static day we went to Victoria to look at MLVs (Motor Luggage Vans).

On the final days of the course, the trainees were introduced to Class 455 units and on the 26th May, I was booked annual leave for two weeks but was told beforehand that Peter Johns and I would be commencing an EMU Schematic Course on 13th June.

Above: De-Icer Unit 005 makes its way through Wimbledon on its way to Guildford via Cobham.

Photo: Mike Morant Collection.

Below: A Network SouthEast livery sandwich at Sevington on 2nd June 1989. 'Jaffa Cake' liveried Class 4CEP 1548 heads the 12.30 Charing Cross to Dover Priory Network SouthEast service past the Channel Tunnel construction site, with a NSE unit and another 'Jaffa Cake' 4CEP bringing up the rear. The colour schemes pictured here are all now part of history, as are the 4CEP units.
Even the location has changed out of all recognition, with the high speed channel tunnel line running parallel on the right, making life in the small cottage even noisier!

Photo & Caption: Martin Loader.

Two admirers watch as Driver Barry Foster departs with a shuttle service from Woking Down Bay to Guildford with preserved 2BIL 2090 during the Woking 150 celebrations in May 1988.

Photo: Ian Docwra.

Instructing Days - OTC South Side

I returned from holiday in Thassos quite refreshed to learn that all of the trainees on the MP12 course that I'd been with had passed their traction exam, which was good news.

Peter Johns and myself were now going to learn EMU Schematics; passing the exam at the end being a necessary requirement for an instructor teaching any of the traction courses at OTC South Side. Apart from having to have an in-depth knowledge of the electrical equipment appertaining to the traction side of things, having an in-depth knowledge of how the various forms of braking systems operate was also a requirement.

The instruction was going to take several weeks to complete and when the instructor thought that we were ready, we would sit an exam with a member of the CM&EE department.

Unfortunately, the period of time given was interrupted by having to run different weeks of another Traction Trainee course at Basingstoke and Peter and I had one instructor that really wasn't interested in teaching us as he had his mind on another project - two Class 465 Simulators which were being built at OTC South Side for the training of South Eastern Division Drivers.

Another problem that interrupted our training was that a group of us (Dave Webb, John Brookshaw, Peter Johns and myself) were booked to attend a two-week residential 'Core Trainer Skills' Course at Watford commencing 25th July. This was Pauline's 40th birthday so I can't say that I was keen on being away from home but off I went to join the others

Above: Pauline's 40th birthday and the red roses!

Photo: The Author's Collection.

at the Management Training Centre at The Grove, Watford. I did however manage to get a bunch of red roses to Pauline via my nephew!

The first week, we were given various projects and had to choose subjects to talk about. My first subject was how to load a film into a 35mm camera and my second was how to operate a slide projector carousel. We had to demonstrate how it was done and then ask someone else to perform the task.

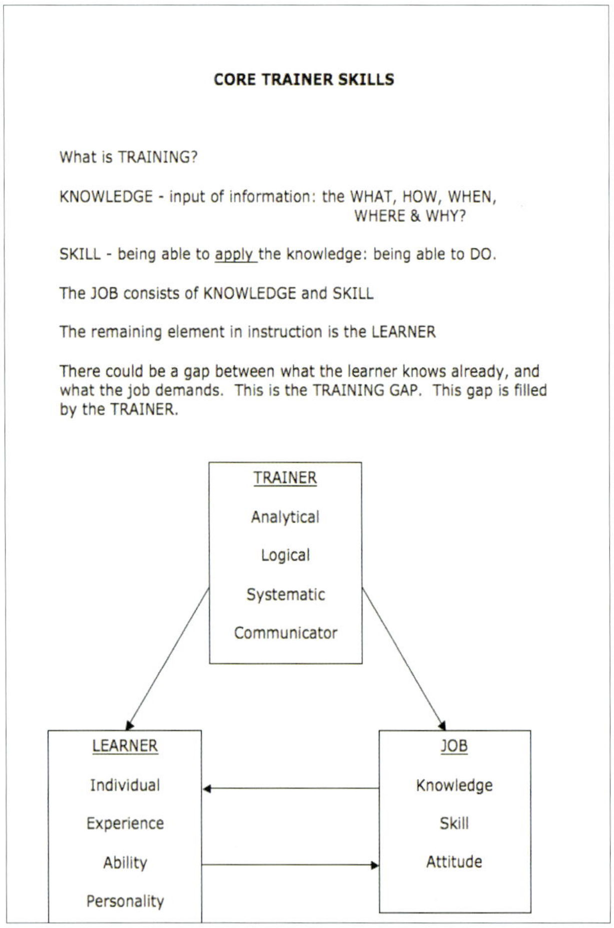

CORE TRAINER SKILLS

What is TRAINING?

KNOWLEDGE - input of information: the WHAT, HOW, WHEN, WHERE & WHY?

SKILL - being able to apply the knowledge: being able to DO.

The JOB consists of KNOWLEDGE and SKILL

The remaining element in instruction is the LEARNER

There could be a gap between what the learner knows already, and what the job demands. This is the TRAINING GAP. This gap is filled by the TRAINER.

TRAINER: Analytical, Logical, Systematic, Communicator

LEARNER: Individual, Experience, Ability, Personality

JOB: Knowledge, Skill, Attitude

Above: Core Training Skills Course literature.

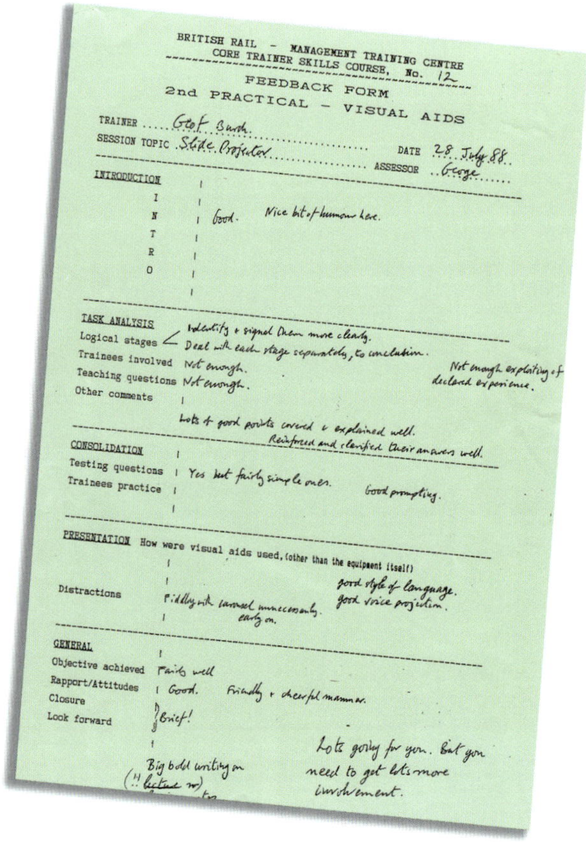

BRITISH RAIL - MANAGEMENT TRAINING CENTRE
CORE TRAINER SKILLS COURSE, No. 12
FEEDBACK FORM
2nd PRACTICAL - VISUAL AIDS

TRAINER Geof Burch
SESSION TOPIC Slide Projector DATE 28 July 88
ASSESSOR George

INTRODUCTION
INTRO | Good. Nice bit of humour here.

TASK ANALYSIS
Logical stages < Identify & signal them more clearly. Deal with each stage separately, to conclusion.
Trainees involved Not enough.
Teaching questions Not enough. Not enough exploiting of declared experience.
Other comments | Lots of good points covered & explained well. Reinforced and clarified their answers well.

CONSOLIDATION
Testing questions | Yes but fairly simple ones.
Trainees practice | Good prompting.

PRESENTATION How were visual aids used, (other than the equipment itself)
Distractions Fiddling with carousel unnecessarily early on. Good style of language. Good voice projection.

GENERAL
Objective achieved Fairly well
Rapport/Attitudes | Good. Friendly & cheerful manner.
Closure
Look forward } Brief!

Big bold writing on (!! lecture no)

Lots going for you. But you need to get lots more involvement.

Right: Feedback from Steve - one of the other attendees on the course.

It then went on to delivering a lesson plan that was work orientated and I chose a further two subjects - one on how electricity was transferred to the third rail from the National Grid and the second was how electricity was collected from the conductor rail and transferred to other equipment on the train.

Both of these presentations were captured on video and after seeing the first one, I certainly learnt by my mistakes!

I was really determined to do a good job on the second week and burnt the midnight oil to get it just right. On the final day, the second presentation went extremely well (apart from a motor mower cutting the grass outside) and I felt far more at ease with the audience. Upon interview with the Course Tutor, George Kershaw, I was very pleased to hear that I'd passed the course with no need for further assessment.

Above: The British Rail Management Training Centre, Watford.

Photo: The Author's Collection.

Below: Power Train Line of a Class 455 unit showing the flow of electrical current from the conductor rail to the PJB (Power Junction Boxes) via the pickup shoes and shoe fuses. Current would then be fed to the traction motors. If all conditions were met, the driver would open the power handle, the line switches would close and 750v would then flow to the traction motors.

Graphic: David Timothy.

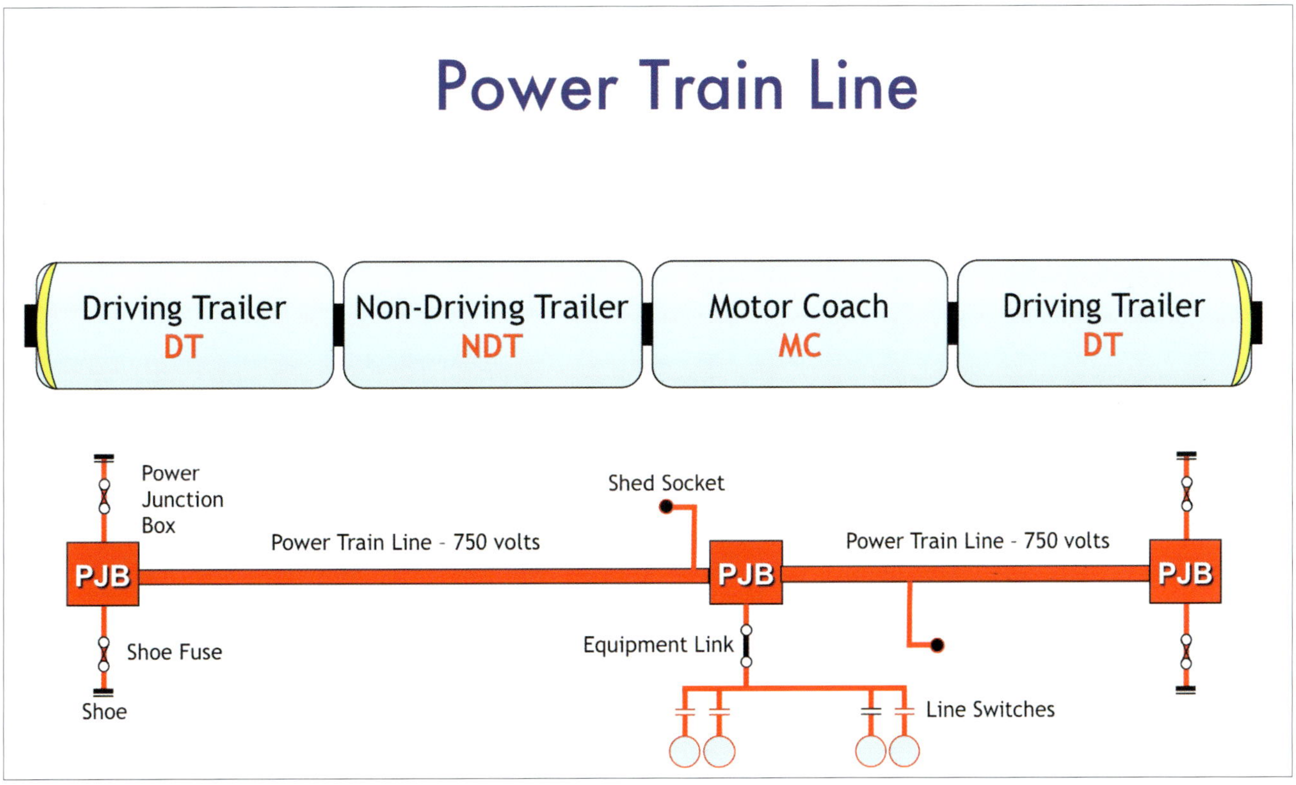

Instructing Days - OTC South Side

BRITISH RAILWAYS BOARD
TRAINING CERTIFICATE

This Certificate
records that
Geof Burch
has attended the
CORE TRAINING SKILLS COURSE
at BR Management Training Centre,
The Grove, Watford.

and has demonstrated a satisfactory standard
of training performance during assessment

For B.R. Management Training Centre

For British Railways Board

28th Nov 88.
Date

BR 9211/13

Above: The Author and Dave Webb after hearing that we'd passed the course!

Right: Core Training Certificate issued after the course.

Below: The course students flanked by Course Tutors George Kershaw and Ian Foot.

Photos: The Author's Collection.

Back at the OTC South Side on 8th August and it was decided Bernie Byrne and Mick Oakley were going to take over our EMU Schematic Instruction and for the next five weeks Peter Johns and I knuckled down to learn as much as we could.

Apart from working out the sequence of how everything worked on the schematic, we would go to various depots and examine everything in detail to get a good understanding of what the equipment looked like and its position on the train.

On the 14th September, I sat my exam - electric schematics in the morning and brake schematics in the afternoon and thankfully, both Peter and I passed. I remember it being one of the hardest exams I had ever sat and ending up having a splitting headache!

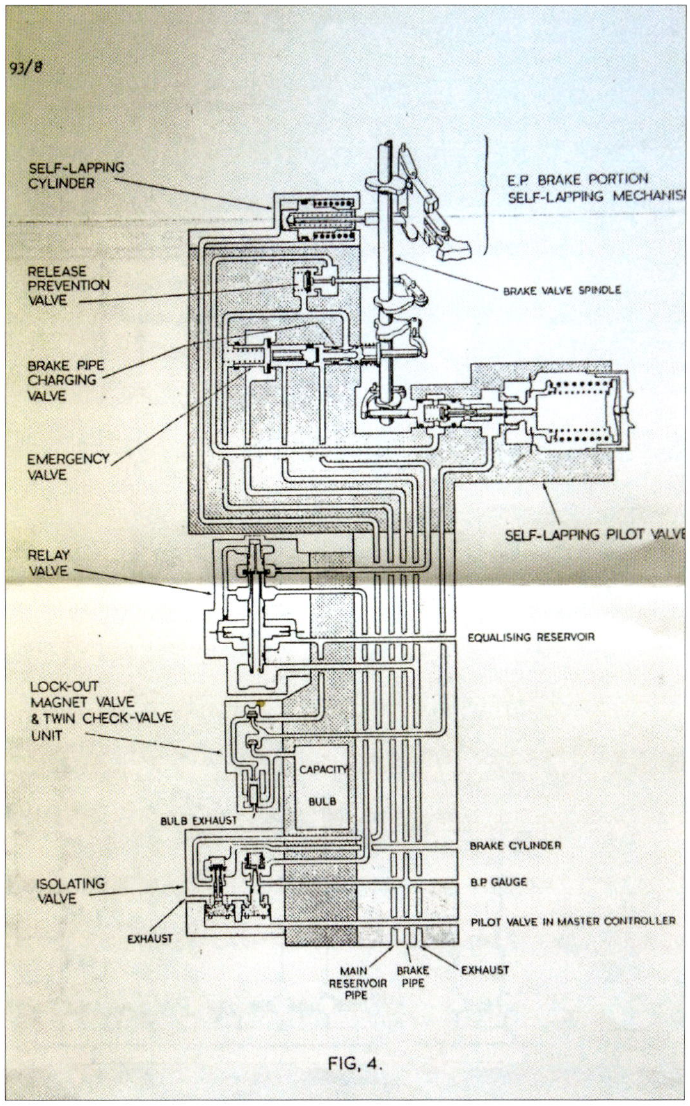

Right: Brake schematic - 1963 type stock.

Below: Power & Control schematic - 1957 stock.

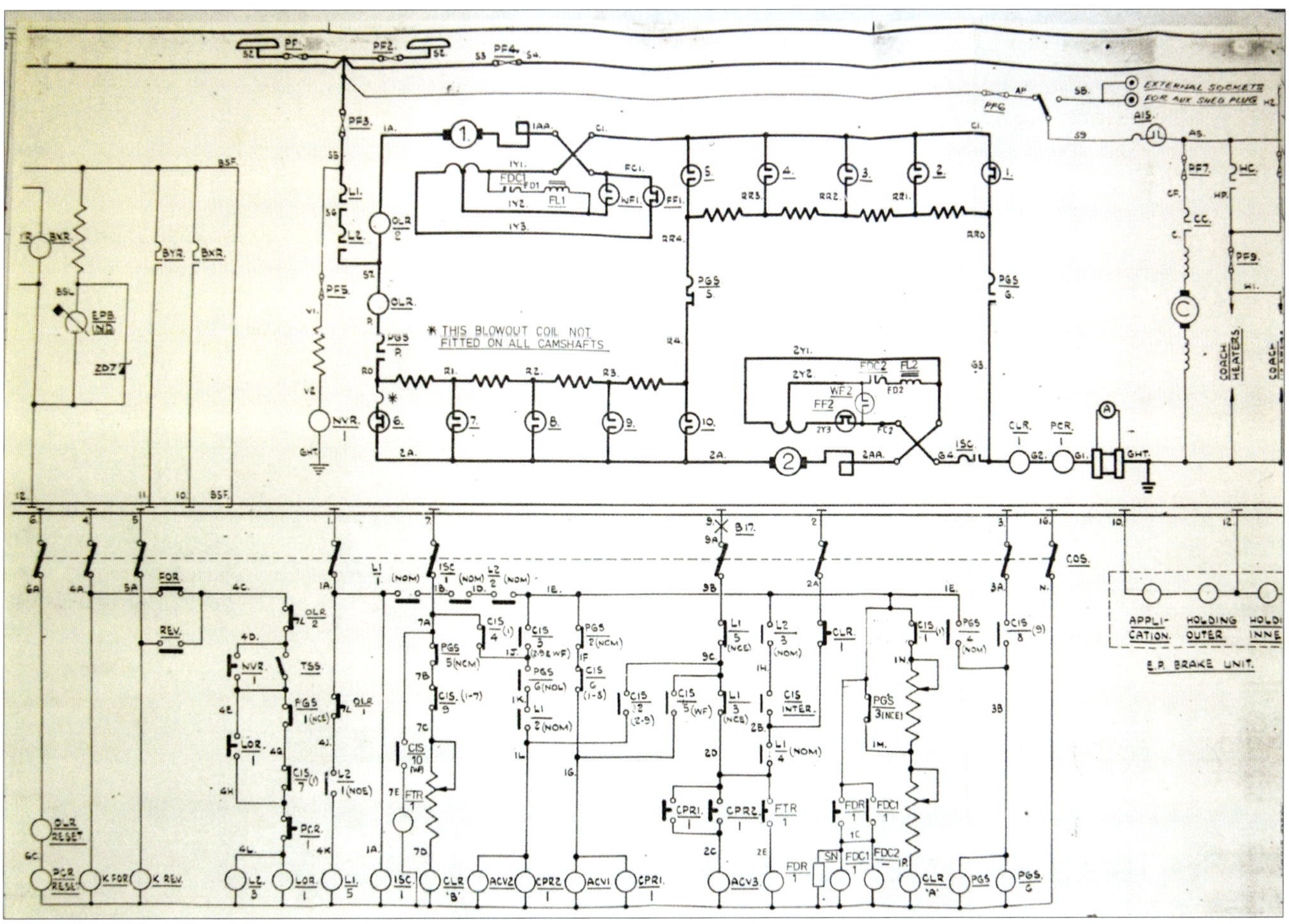

Instructing Days - OTC South Side

Afterwards, I had a further week annual leave and following this, I was booked along with Bernie Byrne learning the route from Charing Cross to Hayes and also on other routes on the South Eastern Division that I wasn't familiar with.

Because I'd missed the Class 455 part of the MP12 course I'd sat-in on earlier in the year, it was decided that I should sit-in on a further Class 455 course with Ken Norris.

By this time there was another MP12 EMU course running and for the next month I was booked to assist on static and driving instruction days before starting my first EMU course on 7th November. This was also going to be held at Basingstoke, so again, I had to move all of my course notes, etc.

There were eleven students on the course; namely:

P Birkett - Charing Cross
R Jones - Charing Cross
M Richardson - Strawberry Hill
R Oatway - Waterloo
G White - Eastleigh
A Watson - Eastleigh
B Richardson - Faversham
G Dodds - Gillingham
D Champion - Woking
G Fletcher - Slade Green
S Simmons - Brighton

As you could imagine, getting to Basingstoke was quite a trek for the South Eastern trainees.

I started the course off but missed the second week because of annual leave picked up the course again on the 28th November with a third 1951 static day at Victoria (assisted by two other instructors) and the rest of the week 1951 stock driving instruction with four students working trips from Victoria - Orpington and return or from Wimbledon - West Croydon (nicknamed the Spratt and Winkle line).

Above: The Author studying hard at OTC South Side.

Photo: The Author's Collection.

Right: 2EPB 6264 approaches Waddon Marsh on the Wimbledon - West Croydon branch. I used this route specifically for training the Westinghouse brake.
The power station in the background used to have a large coal traffic flow, but is now reduced to the chimneys marking the location of IKEA.

Photo: Ian Docwra.

On Monday 12th December 1988, whilst I was travelling from Woking to Waterloo on my way to the Training School, the train came to a stand between Weybridge and Walton. We stood at the signal for ages so I decided to make my way to the front of the train to see the driver and learnt that a disaster had occurred. A train that was travelling in front of us had run into the back of another at Clapham Junction and via the phone communication with the signalman, news filtered back that a Woking driver and colleague of mine (Alex McClymont) had been killed along with many other passengers.

I managed to reach the Training School some hours later by travelling from Wimbledon to Waterloo via Victoria and found that all training had been cancelled for the day.

Eventually, I made my way back to Woking station and had the shock of my life to see Alex walking along the platform towards me. He looked awful. It transpired that he had been the driver of the train that had stopped at the signal outside Clapham Junction to phone the signalman to inform him of a signal irregularity. As he was talking to the signalman on the signal post telephone, another train (driven by a Bournemouth driver) had run into the back of his train.

Alex had just been debriefed when I met him at Woking and I gave him a lift to Guildford to pick up his car that he'd left there that morning. I offered to drive him to his home in Liphook where he lived, but he declined the offer and said he wanted to be on his own for a while.

Up until this day, that tragedy has scarred his life and the horrors that he witnessed must have affected him deeply.

This accident had been until then, the worst railway disaster in recent years - thirty-five people lost their lives including the Bournemouth driver and another driver who was in the cab with him.

Above Top: Aftermath of the fatal collision.

Above: The view shows all four ex-LSWR tracks of the main Waterloo - Wimbledon - Woking and the West line blocked by the breakdown-train men at work more than 24 hours afterwards. The numerous casualties had been brought up the embankment on the right to Spencer Park Road.

Photo: Ben Brooksbank.

Left: The memorial at the site of the crash.

Photo: Edgepedia - Wikipedia.

Instructing Days - OTC South Side

Above: Class 455 5856 stands on platform 4 at Guildford on 16th June 1989. Unusual to see that one DT (driving trailer) of the unit is still painted in a different livery.

Photo: Timothy Saunders.

Below: Up Main Fast Home Signal at Waterloo.

Photo: The Author's Collection.

For the rest of the month the course continued but we were now a day behind and everything needed to be re-scheduled. We continued with a 1963 stock static on the Tuesday and De-Icer static on the Thursday and the driving instruction took place over the Woking - Alton route and also from Waterloo - Reading via Ascot.

The Training School closed on the 23rd December for the Christmas recess and I returned to Woking as a driver ("back to depot") as Cyril Sweet would say in his Welsh accent!

I worked on the Saturday (15.00 A/O) and again on the bank holiday Tuesday and the rest of the week working a Guildford duty signing on at 15.45.

The start of the new year saw me working an early turn (something I hadn't done for a while), 06.30 on the Tuesday and was booked route refresher the rest of the week before taking the reigns again with EMU Course 15 at Basingstoke.

The first day was Class 455 (in the classroom) and second day Class 455 static which we performed at Strawberry Hill accompanied by two other instructors. There had to be three instructors present due to an incident some months previously when a trainee moved the unit as an instructor was in-between an EPB and a Class 455 unit demonstrating emergency coupling procedures.

. The next two days were Class 455 Driving Instruction from Waterloo - Guildford and then finally, back to Basingstoke for revision of all subjects.

For the next four months I was booked a variety of work assisting different courses with Mick Oakley on statics and driving instruction from Victoria - Orpington for the EPB work and Waterloo - Portsmouth and Waterloo - Reading for the 1963 work.

It was on a return trip from Portsmouth - Waterloo when I had to take control of the train outside of Waterloo station. As we approached Waterloo home signal which was displaying a red aspect, the trainee made no attempt to stop so I had to jump across the cab and apply the emergency brake myself with the train just about coming to a stand underneath the signal! I asked the trainee what he was thinking of and he said that his mind was miles away. It was the only time that I'd had to take a person off a course but I think I made the right decision.

Two special ASLE&F branch meetings were called in March and April at Guildford and a ban on rest days and overtime was called for beginning on Monday 8th May. This would affect my weekend working as a driver at Woking at weekends.

Following a heatwave in the third week of May, I experienced a thunderstorm with such ferocity that I've never seen before or since. Because the car park on the down side of Woking station is completely covered in tarmac, the heavy downpour had nowhere else to go but into the station's entrance hall, through the ticket barrier and onto the platform! It was an incredible sight with passengers wading through the water trying to reach their destination.

Clockwise from top: The buffet girls enjoy a paddle!

The platform Inspector has the right footwear!

Woking Secondman Chris Berriman and Driver Jeff Tucker decide to wait a while.....

It says 'Luxury Land Cruises' on the poster but it's not what these passengers expected ....

Photos: The Author's Collection.

***Above:** Passengers wait on the stairs for the floods to abate as Farnham Guard David Brown looks on.*

***Below:** The sudden downpour doesn't hinder the 12.30 Waterloo - Bournemouth passenger service as it speeds through Woking with torrential rain bouncing off its roof.*

***Photos:** The Author's Collection.*

It had now come to the point where I had to make a decision regarding my future career. An instructor's vacancy had arisen at the Training School - some of my fellow 'acting men' had been there for longer than me but I was advised to apply. It was a big decision to make and meant that if I was appointed, I couldn't go back driving trains at weekends. However, I was loving the job so I applied. On the 18th July 1989, I received a letter saying that my application had been successful and my transfer was arranged for the 7th August.

The heatwave continued through the first part of June and I was booked to start a rules course on Monday 19th. The NUR (National Union of Railwaymen) had a strike day planned for the following three Wednesdays so that put the course a couple of days behind.

At the beginning of August, I had to sit-in on a rules examination with Phil Eke as it would now be necessary for me to conduct both rules and traction examinations for traction trainees and drivers.

On Saturday 5th August, I was booked to move the contents of my locker from Woking to the OTC South Side where I would take up residence as an 'E' Grade Traction instructor.

My last day driving at Woking was on Sunday 6th August 1989 where I was booked 06.00 A/O.

Network SouthEast

To: Mr G Burch
Driver
Woking

From: Area Manager
WOKING

Ext: 080 2217

O/R: WG/S/BU/G/10
Date: 18 July 1989

VACANCY S 980 LIST 18 INSTRUCTOR (TRACTION) 'E' WATERLOO

I am pleased to advise you that you have been appointed to the above position.

Your seniority step in Grade E will be from 14 June 1989, and your revised rate of pay £10,787 + £946 London Allowance will be from Monday 7 August 1989 when arrangements have been made for your transfer.

Congratulations.

M. Hibberd

M Hibberd
for Area Manager

Above: Appointment to Instructor at the OTC South Side, Waterloo.

Below: Class 455 5857 throws out a spark as it approaches Windsor and Eton Riverside station with the 09.20 Network SouthEast service from Waterloo on 10th December 1989. A typically dull autumnal day, but at least the view here is reasonably open, which is not what it is like now. The tree growth has been astonishing here, and in summer it resembles a green tunnel!

Photo: Martin Loader.

Instructing Days - OTC South Side

The following day, I took up my appointment as a full time instructor at OTC South Side and was booked to take group of trainees out on Class 455 driving instruction and then on Monday 14th August I was booked to conduct my first traction examination. The two trainees that I was booked to examine on traction (Part B and C) were Driver D Tombs from Redhill and Driver P Cardy from Grove Park. Part B was a static exam and because the drivers' main traction types were different, I elected to go to Victoria Carriage Sidings. Both drivers did well recognising all equipment and were completely safe when it came to safety related 750v fuse changing procedures.

The following day I met both trainees at Waterloo for their Part C exam (driving) and travelled to Victoria so that they could work to Orpington and return (using the EP and Westinghouse brake). They then required assessment on other types of EMU, 1963 stock and Class 455. This was conducted over the South Western Division. They were both pleased to find that they had both passed their final exams and were now qualified drivers and I duly issued them both with EP Keys. I couldn't help feeling the same elation that I felt when I was handed my EP key by Bob Phillips some twenty years previously.

The following week I had to help Fred Johnson with a TM (Trainman) examination at Clapham Junction where both trainees passed.

On the Sunday, I was booked to attend OTC South Side to learn CSR (Cab Secure Radio) as this type of radio was now going to be fitted in cabs of all types of EMU on the Southern. Once the radio had been set-up, with the train's unique WTT (Working Timetable number) the following communications could take place:

- Signalman can call and speak to driver
- Driver can call and speak to signalman
- Signalman and driver can exchange preset text messages
- Signalman can send emergency stop messages to a particular train, or all trains in an area
- Driver can make an emergency call to signalman
- Signalman can speak to passengers via the train's public address system
- Signalman can connect driver to the railway telephone network
- Signalman would be notified of a DSD (driver's safety device) alarm (30 seconds after the DSD is released by a driver on the train).

Had CSR Radio been fitted to all cabs the previous year, the Clapham disaster would most probably have been avoided.

Above: Stornophone 6000 CSR Radio.

Photo: Ivor the Driver - Wikipedia.

Below: 1963 Unit 4VEP 7842 passes Clapham Junction with a Waterloo - Guildford stopping service. An ideal train for driver training purposes.

Photo: Stuart Ray.

For the next month I was either assisting courses on static days and driving instruction days except for an exam on 5th September when I passed D Pocock of Slade Green depot and J Ward of Selhurst Depot on Rules.

The following week I was given the day off with pay and in the evening collected my Long Service Award for twenty eight year's service (a Minox 35GT 35mm camera) at the Woking Railway Staff Association Club.

The week commencing 18th September, I was booked road work assisting course BS8 and used routes Waterloo - Portsmouth Harbour and the 09.33 Waterloo - Reading via Ascot. A good friend of mine was travelling on Concorde on the Thursday and I'd noticed previously that its flight path flew straight over Reading station on its way to New York at approximately 11am. When we reached Reading, we quickly changed ends and I stood on the end of the platform waiting for the big moment as I thought this would be a great opportunity to get a good photograph. I heard the plane but couldn't see it as unfortunately, the wind at Heathrow had swung round and planes were taking off in a northerly direction!

For the next three months, I had an assortment of road work with some traction and rules exams thrown in:

- 22nd September: D Bishop, Selhurst - Part 2 Exam
- 13th October: D Bampton, Charing X - Part 3 Exam
- 27th October P Huran, Seaford - Part 3 Exam
- 3rd November G Ward, Gillingham and M Fry, Redhill - Rules Exam
- 17th November: M Lilly, Slade Green and T Powell, Orpington - Part 3 Exam
- 1st December: B Jones, Streatham Hill and Richard Johncock, Norwood - Part 1 Exam
- 15th December: R Dickell and R Taylor, Strawberry Hill - Part 1 Exam
- 22nd December: J Morgan, Streatham Hill - Rules Exam.

Most candidates passed their examinations but unfortunately, four of the candidates failed.

Above: My Long Service Award for 28 year's service - Minox 35GT 35mm Camera.

Photo: The Author's Collection.

Below: British Airways Concorde.

Photo: Eduard Marmet - Wikipedia.

Instructing Days - OTC South Side

Above: Class 455 Driver Instruction on the Central - 'Wall of Death'.

Below: Driver Steve Bull showing his gymnastic skills on a Class 455 Static at Wimbledon Park Depot.

Photos: The Author's Collection.

The Training School was closed over the Christmas period so I had a well earned break as I'd worked several Sundays over the past three months teaching CSR Radio to drivers and signalmen. The time worked was taken as compensatory leave so I didn't go back to work until 2nd January 1990.

I was booked to assist TM20 for the next two weeks which consisted of 1963 and Class 455 road work. I then examined two members of the same course - B Lawrence from Orpington and W Simpson from Charing Cross and this was done at Victoria and Orpington as both candidates were from the South Eastern Division.

For the next three days I was booked a REP course refresher (having already known the type of unit as a driver at Woking).

On the Friday I brought a bit of cheer to two drivers at Charing Cross (P Scott and C Humm) passing them on their Part 2 Exam.

On 25th January, we again braced ourselves against hurricane force winds with sustained wind speeds of 75 mph and wind gusts of 104 mph.

Called the 'Burns' Day Storm', it forced many ports and airports to close in one of the worst storms seen in the UK since 1987, causing overturned lorries blocking motorways, buildings collapsing and power and telecommunication lines blown down. The railway network was again in disarray with trees blocking some lines. During the following two weeks, gale force winds persisted and again interrupted training programmes at OTC South Side.

For the next two months I was booked to assist on various Trainman courses instructing on static days and roadwork. There were also several exam days interspersed; the trainees' names as follows:

- 2nd February: P. O'Brien and B Collins, Charing Cross - Part 2 Exam
- 23rd February: I Matthews, - Part 1 Exam
- 9th March: A Butcher and M Apted, - Part 1 Exam
- 16th March: G Fox and J Honeyman, Slade Green - Part 1 Exam
- 30th March: C Gunn, Selhurst and M Maunsell, Orpington -Part 1 Exam.

In April and May 1990, I was booked to go to Eastleigh Depot to conduct some special 6REP courses with Fred Johnson.

To begin with, 6REP Class 431/1 1903 had been specially commissioned and because there were two extra coaches added to the normal 4REP configuration and there were slight differences in the unit's faults and failures procedure (paddling up), it was deemed necessary that some of the Eastleigh and Bournemouth drivers would need further training. This was conducted over a number of weeks (including weekends) with half-day courses being delivered as morning and afternoon sessions,

By Sunday 13th May, eighty-two drivers had received training and the following day, train services were brought into operation utilising two 6REP units 1903 and 1905.

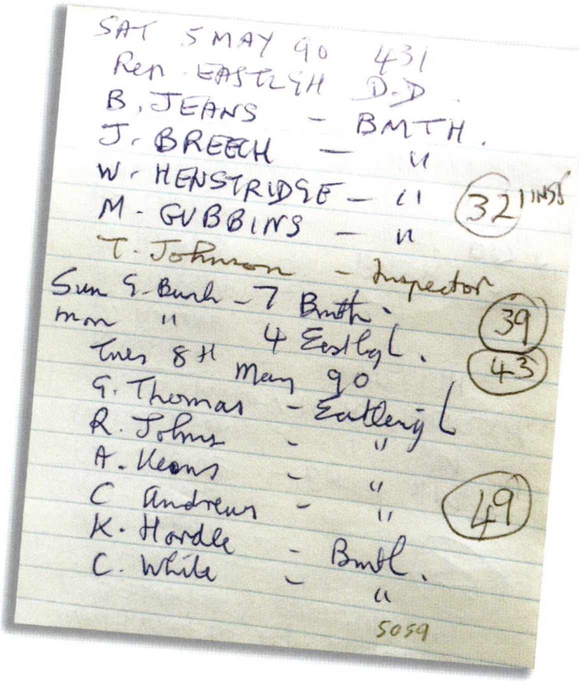
SAT 5 MAY 90 431
Rep EASTLGH D.D
B. JEANS - BMTH.
J. BREECH - "
W. HENSTRIDGE - " (32) INSS
M. GUBBINS - "
T. Johnson - Inspector
Sun G. Burch - 7 Bmth.
mon " 4 Eastlgh. (39) (43)
Tues 8th May 90
G. Thomas - Eastleigh
R. Johns - "
A. Keans - "
C Andrews - " (49)
K. Hordle - Bmth.
C. White - "
5059

Above Right: An extract from Fred Johnson's journal showing names of drivers who had received 6REP training dating from Saturday 5th to Tuesday 8th May 1990. Also shown (circled) are the totals of drivers trained so far.

Courtesy of Fred Johnson.

Below: Fred Johnson attends to the paperwork between the morning and afternoon training sessions.

Photo" The Author's Collection.

Instructing Days - OTC South Side

Following these weekends of REP training, I also worked a further two Saturdays - these were to learn Class 319 units at Selhurst with Brian Cook, which included a trip to Bedford and return. This was the first time that I'd been 'under the wires' and after pressing the 'PAN UP' button (which allowed the pantograph to connect to the 25kV AC overhead current supply), I was astonished at the unit's acceleration.

Above: Instructor David Timothy with Brighton drivers Mick Pullinger and Vic Sexton at Bedford with Class 319 'Thameslink' 319029.

Photo: David Timothy.

Above: Class 319 'Thameslink' 319055 at Blackfriars on 11th September 1990.

Photo: Stuart Ray.

After continuing with TM8, I took my trainees to Victoria Carriage Sidings for a 1957 static.

During the instruction, it was necessary to open the Master Switch to perform control fault diagnosis and although the parking brake was applied in the cab, some movement was felt at the rear of the train. A carriage cleaner came up and spoke to me and asked me if I'd moved the train to which I replied that the rear of the train had moved but this was caused by the train's couplings easing away as the brakes released on the train. I certainly hadn't intentionally moved the train and apologised for any distress this may have caused him. He said that an apology wasn't good enough and that he was going to report the incident to his Supervisor.

I submitted a report and heard no more of the incident.

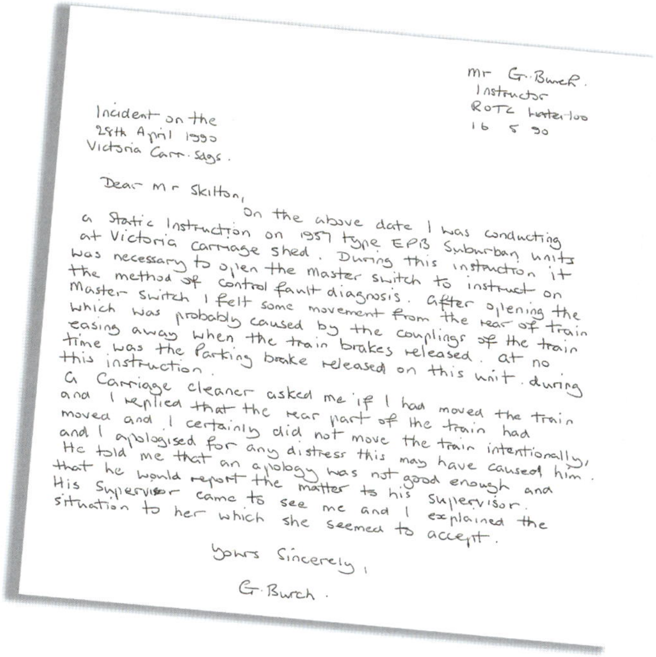

Mr G. Burch.
Instructor
ROTC Waterloo
16 5 90

Incident on the
28th April 1990
Victoria Carr. Sdgs.

Dear Mr Skilton,
On the above date I was conducting
a Static Instruction on 1957 type EPB Suburban units
at Victoria carriage shed. During this instruction it
was necessary to open the master switch to instruct on
the method of control fault diagnosis. After opening the
Master Switch I felt some movement from the rear of train
which was probably caused by the couplings of the train
easing away when the train brakes released. at no
time was the Parking brake released on this unit. during
this instruction.
A Carriage cleaner asked me if I had moved the train
and I replied that the rear part of the train had
moved and I certainly did not move the train intentionally,
and I apologised for any distress this may have caused him.
He told me that an apology was not good enough and
that he would report the matter to his supervisor.
His Supervisor came to see me and I explained the
situation to her which she seemed to accept.

Yours Sincerely,

G. Burch.

Above: The Author's report regarding the incident at Victoria Carriage Sidings.

Below: Class 73 Nos. 73205 and 73141 head the UK Railtours 'A Kentish Odyssey' railtour past Victoria Carriage Sidings with Battersea power station in the background on Saturday 10th August 2013.
This was a favourite place to perform 1951 / 1957 stock static instruction.

Photo: Gary Blyth.

Instructing Days - OTC South Side

Two more of my colleagues at Woking had now joined OTC South Side as instructors - Chris Lemon (in the summer of 1988) and Ian Verrinder in the summer of 1990. I would usually catch the same train as them to Waterloo and as the train was normally packed, we'd occupy a guard's brake van.

We all knew that there were some members of the Training School that were Freemasons so we therefore decided to have our own select 'Lodge'. My brother-in-law had given me several leather aprons (and to this day I don't know in which industry they were used) so Ian, Chris and I decided to conduct an initiation ceremony in the guard's van in front of Acting Instructor Pete Tyler.

Chris had made a ring out of cardboard (depicting the square and compasses symbol) and Ian and I had our aprons on under our jackets to roll down when Chris presented the ring. We were all in hysterics whilst this took place - Pete Tyler looking on in amazement!

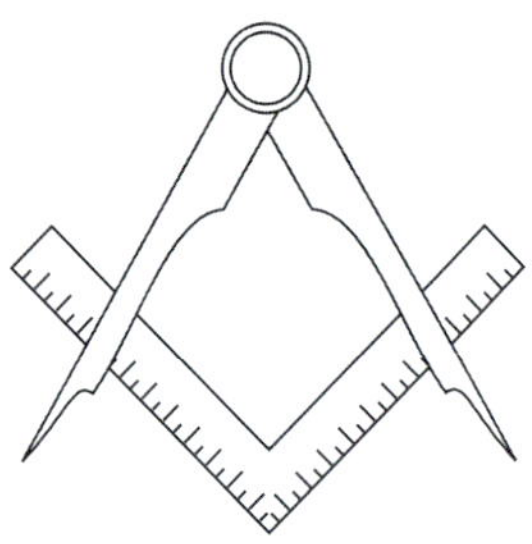

Above: The Square and Compasses is one of the most prominent symbols of Freemasonry.

Below: Our Lodge Initiation Ceremony in the guard's brakevan - looking on is Pete Tyler.

Photo: The Author's Collection.

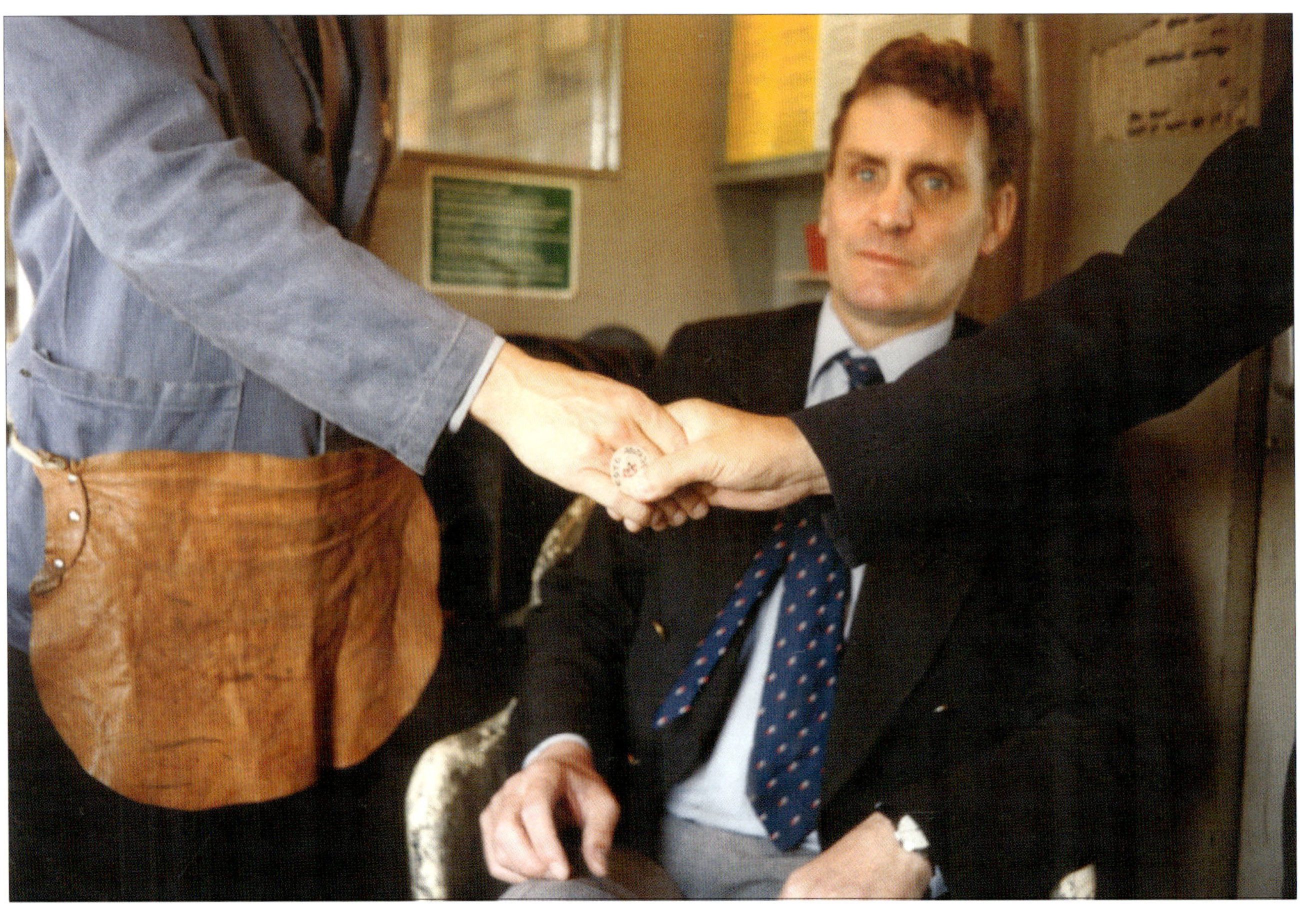

On Monday 30th July 1990, it was decided that I would learn (to instructor standards) Class 73 electro-diesel locomotives with Brian Cook and we were taught schematics by Brian Hobby. This was a dream come true for me as they were my favourite locomotive and I'd been driving them for the past twenty five years. Brian and I went on a number of training trips as well as going down to Stewarts Lane to look round the locomotive in detail.

On 13th September 1990, Brian Cook and I passed our Class 73 electro-diesel schematic examinations; being examined by Cyril Sweet, Bernie Byrne and George Taylor. A couple of weeks before the exam, I remember taking the schematics with me on holiday to revise and sending a post card to the Training School saying that they made excellent beach mats!

David Timothy and I were becoming great pals and were both interested in computers. The Training School possessed a computer system but only had the simplest of word processors (Multimate) and graphic design packages. We both realised that if we didn't start getting to know how they worked we'd be left behind in the IT (Information Technology) world and decided on buying one each. I didn't have a clue at that time what I needed and was guided by him really. We travelled up to Tottenham Court Road and I shelled out £1200 for an Amstrad 1640 setup plus a colour dot matrix printer (it sounded good at the time) and I thought it was the 'bees knees' then with a 40 megabyte hard drive and a 5 1/4 inch floppy disk bay! I was completely hooked and my wife Pauline became a computer widow from then on.

Above: Amstrad 1640 computer with 40 megabyte Hard Drive and a five-and-a-quarter-inch floppy drive.

Below: Whilst working the 10.30 freight train with two Class 73s in multiple from Eastleigh to Three Bridges on 16th August 1990, a lineside fire at Barnham curtailed our training trip and we had to leave the two locomotives and train at Chichester Yard.
Brian Cook (pictured with Class 73/1 electro-diesel No. 73103) and the Author are detained on the end of Bosham platform whilst we wait for the signal.

Photo: The Author's Collection.

Instructing Days - OTC South Side

Above: Copper Strip Fuse that protected 750v power circuits on all 1951 / 1957 / 1963 / 455 stock.
By removing the fuses, the power train line could also be isolated from the conductor rail supply.

Photo: The Author's Collection.

The following week I assisted on course TM18 and met Phil Savage and Sid Hales at Waterloo for two day's driving instruction. They were both Guildford drivers so I decided to take them to Portsmouth Harbour working a stopping service to give them plenty of practice on braking techniques.

On the Wednesday, I was taken off as I was needed for a Class 73 static and met the trainees at Woking as there were several Class 73 locomotives berthed on Hurdles Road siding.

On the Saturday, I had to work as they needed a group of men to be trained on the De-Icer unit and had to travel to Selhurst to perform the instruction.

The following Monday I picked up the TM18 course again and on the Wednesday I was booked a Part 1 exam with Sid Hales and Phil Savage who passed their exam with no problems.

The rest of the week I was booked a variety of work; an EMU static with drivers at Stewarts Lane, a 1951 No. 1 static at Victoria Carriage Sidings and a Part 3 exam on the Friday passing two drivers, S Heard and G Hawkins, both from Streatham Hill depot.

The following week I was booked to take a Brighton driver on 1963 driving instruction all week and on the Saturday, went to Selhurst again to instruct a group of drivers on the De-Icer unit.

On Monday 22nd October, I was booked a Class 73 training trip from Clapham - Weymouth and as the trip was cancelled the following day, we had to change plans and perform the static day at Clapham instead.

The training trip was re-organised on the Wednesday with the trip starting at Eastleigh and running to Wareham and return to Eastleigh consisting of a Class 73/1 locomotive and 2 x 4TC units. On the Thursday we did actually reach Weymouth and on the Friday we worked trips from Victoria to Gatwick and return utilising the Gatwick Express stock.

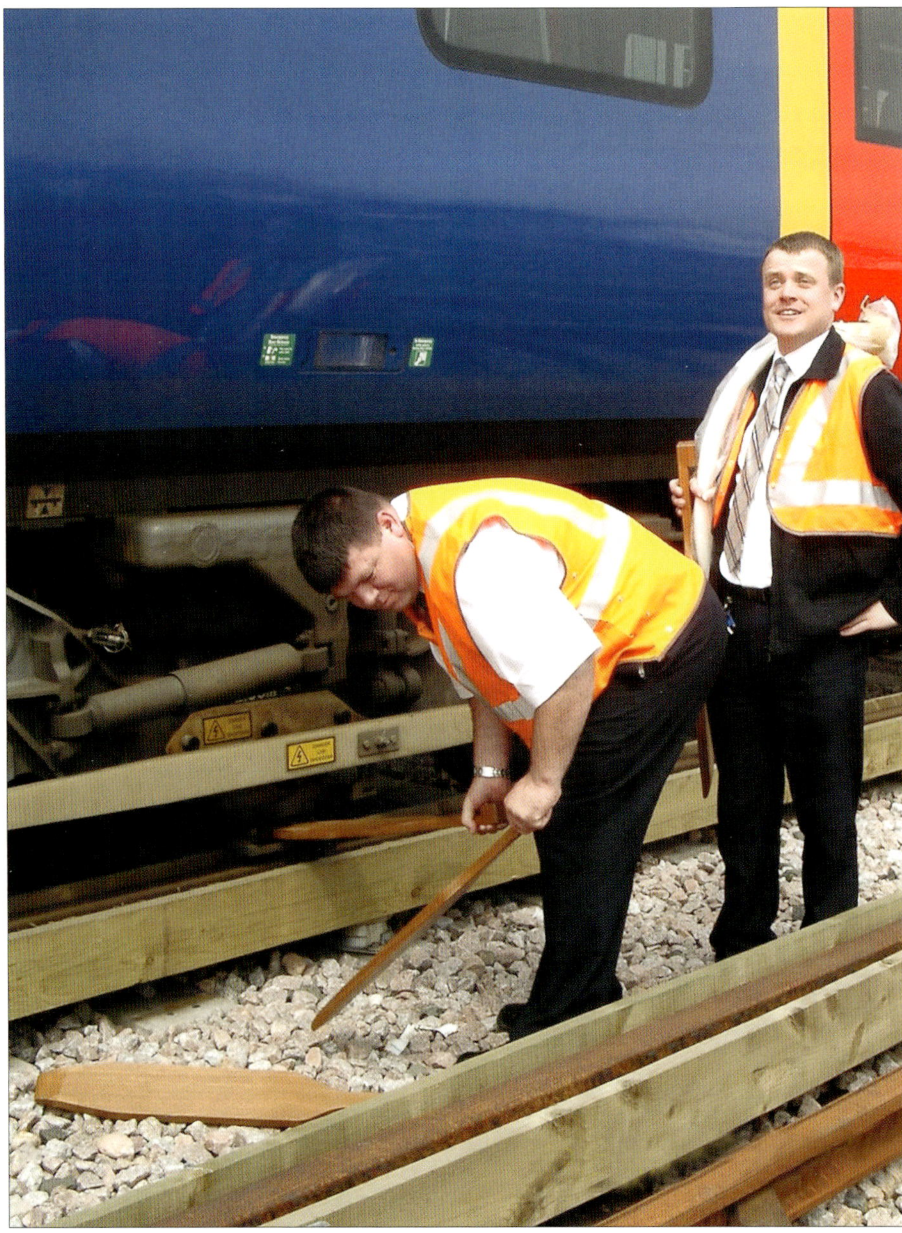

Above: Paddling Up procedure. The trainee is lifting the pickup shoe clear of the conductor rail so he can place another wooden paddle under the pickup shoe to form an insulator. All the unit's shoes that are in contact with the conductor rail must be isolated in this way before replacing or removing a 750v copper strip fuse in the power circuit.

Photo: David Timothy.

Above: Driver Sid Hales using the Westinghouse brake whilst under instruction over the Wimbledon - West Croydon line.

Below: Driver Phil Savage under instruction driving the same 2EPB unit.

Photos: The Author's Collection.

Above: Class 73/2 No. 73235 passes Coulsdon on 12th August 1995 with the 16.15 Victoria to Gatwick Airport service. These 'Gatwick Express' trains operated every 15 minutes.

Below: During 1987 some Class 73s were thrust into the role of long distance express passenger locomotives, when the Class 432 4REP EMUs were withdrawn in order to donate their traction motors to the brand new Class 442 units then under construction. Class 73/1 No. 73136 is pictured racing through Winchfield station on 28th August 1987 with the late running 13.32 Waterloo to Weymouth service.

Photos & Captions: Martin Loader.

In October, I was booked weeks 3 and 4 of a rules course followed by a Part 3 traction exam with I Matthews of Norwood and M Gladman of Selhurst who both passed and again I was booked a De-Icer course at Selhurst on the Saturday.

On the 12th November, I started another Class 73 course; the static instruction days taking place at Stewarts Lane. However, on the second week, instead of running a training trip on the South Western Division, the trip ran on the Central Division, running from New Cross Gate to Brighton most days and from New Cross Gate to Eastbourne on others.

On the following two Sundays I was booked to run two extra REP courses at Eastleigh and in between these dates I assisted Chris Lemon on TM24 course at Victoria Carriage Sidings, conducted driving instruction on 1963 stock and following that, I travelled to Basingstoke Training School on 7th December to conduct a Part 1 rules exam for J Ellery from Wimbledon Park and J Livings from Waterloo (both passed).

The following week I was booked a Part 1 exam with J Thacker from Slade Green (who passed) and assisted on course TM15. On Friday 21st December, I conducted a Part 3 exam for N Butcher and M Evans; (Neil having been a student on my first Traction Trainee course). I'm please to say that both candidates passed which made their Christmas!

Above: Class 73/1 No. 73123 'Gatwick Express' stands at Gatwick Airport with a Gatwick express working to London Victoria on 17th May 1984. This was the original Inter-City livery variation.

Below: Class 73/1 Nos. 73105 and 73142 at Gatwick Airport on Gatwick express workings to London Victoria the same day.

Photos & Captions: Timothy Saunders.

Below: In ex-works condition just after being repainted into Pullman livery to mark the 150th year of the London to Brighton line, Class 73/1 No. 73101 'Brighton Evening Argus' passes Salfords at high speed with a Victoria to Brighton 'Brighton Belle' special composed of Orient Express stock on 21st September 1991.

The vintage VSOE coaches comprised: Zena, Ione, Ibis, Lucille, Vera, Phoenix, Audrey, Minerva and Baggage Car No 7.

Photos & Captions: Martin Loader.

Above: Here Class 73/1 No. 73133 is seen coupled to 4CEP 1581 at Maidstone West. The loco had arrived about 4 hours late with the Postal/Paper train from Victoria and had pushed 1581 from Strood to Maidstone West after it failed on route with the first train of the day. The ensemble returned minus the vans to Strood as the only train of the day heading north from the county town.
After it departed, the line closed for the rest of the day as most signalmen couldn't get to work on the branch.

Photo & Caption: Adrian Nicholls.

Above: Class 73/0 No. 73004 'The Bluebell Railway' (formerly JA Type E6004) at Hastings. This locomotive was the first of its class to be named 'The Bluebell Railway' (the name being transferred later to Class 73/1 No. 73133).

Below: Class 73/0 No. 73002 (formerly JA Type E6002) at Tonbridge West Yard. The loco was delivered new to Stewarts Lane depot on the 12th March 1962 and remained there until withdrawal in May 1993.

Photos: Timothy Saunders.

Instructing Days - OTC South Side

Work at the Training School started on Wednesday 2nd January 1991 and I was booked driving instruction with a driver from Slade Green and another from Victoria Eastern. It made sense to keep to the South Eastern routes so I commandeered a Victoria - Orpington service for the first couple of days taking them over to the South Western Division on the Friday. I also had both of these men on their traction exam the following week and although they passed their driving part, they failed on their traction knowledge. I would always give leeway to a lot of answers given on traction questions but drew the line if it meant that they might be a danger to themselves or others.

On the same morning of their exam (Tuesday 8th January), there was a fatal train crash at Cannon Street station where two people lost their lives and 524 persons were injured.

The 07.58 commuter train from Orpington composed of 1951 and 1957 EPB units failed to stop at platform 3 (a dead-end platform) and collided with the buffer stops at approximately 10 mph.

A report was compiled of the accident by Her Majesty's Railway Inspectorate and no fault could be found in the train's braking system and the driver was held responsible. He was not tested for drugs until three days after the accident, whereupon traces of cannabis were found in his system. However, the public inquiry found that there was insufficient evidence to suggest this had caused the accident.

The inquiry found that the cause of the accident was solely that of driver error. The report also made some of the following observations:

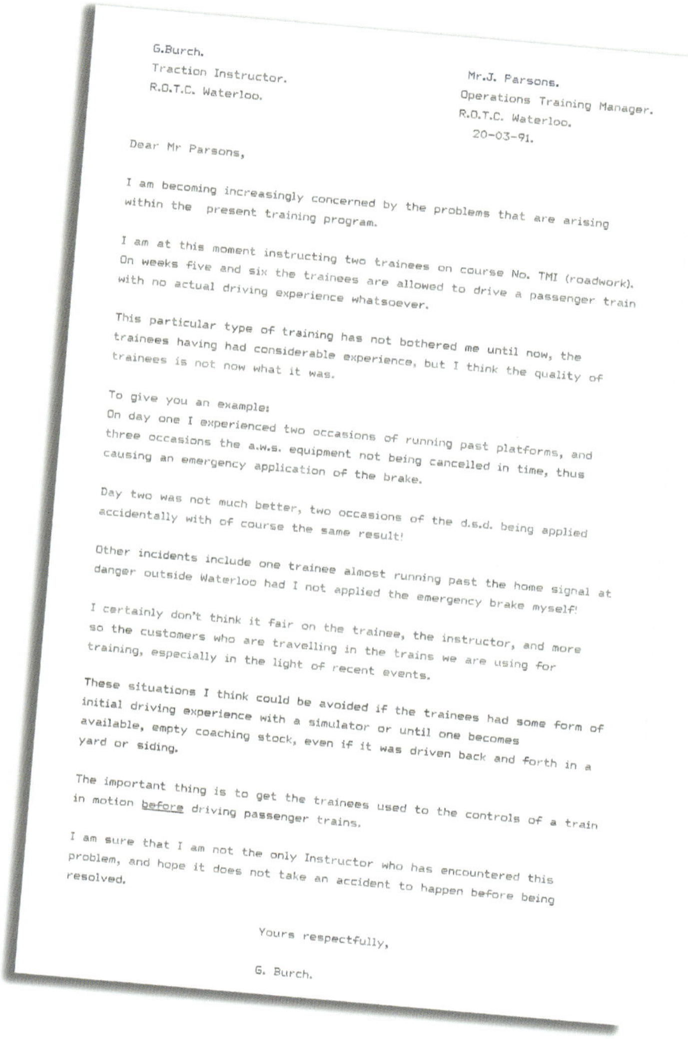

G.Burch.
Traction Instructor.
R.O.T.C. Waterloo.

Mr.J. Parsons.
Operations Training Manager.
R.O.T.C. Waterloo.
20-03-91.

Dear Mr Parsons,

I am becoming increasingly concerned by the problems that are arising within the present training program.

I am at this moment instructing two trainees on course No. TMI (roadwork). On weeks five and six the trainees are allowed to drive a passenger train with no actual driving experience whatsoever.

This particular type of training has not bothered me until now, the trainees having had considerable experience, but I think the quality of trainees is not now what it was.

To give you an example:
On day one I experienced two occasions of running past platforms, and three occasions the a.w.s. equipment not being cancelled in time, thus causing an emergency application of the brake.

Day two was not much better, two occasions of the d.s.d. being applied accidentally with of course the same result!

Other incidents include one trainee almost running past the home signal at danger outside Waterloo had I not applied the emergency brake myself!

I certainly don't think it fair on the trainee, the instructor, and more so the customers who are travelling in the trains we are using for training, especially in the light of recent events.

These situations I think could be avoided if the trainees had some form of initial driving experience with a simulator or until one becomes available, empty coaching stock, even if it was driven back and forth in a yard or siding.

The important thing is to get the trainees used to the controls of a train in motion before driving passenger trains.

I am sure that I am not the only Instructor who has encountered this problem, and hope it does not take an accident to happen before being resolved.

Yours respectfully,

G. Burch.

• Age of the elderly trains increased the effect of the impact. Of the two coaches that suffered the worst damage, one was built on an underbody dating from 1934, having been refitted with a new body in 1953 and involved in a previous collision with a locomotive in 1958; the other was built on an underframe from 1928.

• The interior design of the coaches' fittings and the large number of slam doors could have resulted in weaknesses in the structure of the rolling stock.

• Automatic Train Protection, or ATP, should be installed as quickly as practicably possible

• On-train data recorders would make the finding of evidence easier following railway accidents

• Legislation should be introduced to make it an offence for railway staff with safety responsibilities to be intoxicated while on duty

• Arrangements for the booking-on of staff should be reviewed (a recommendation also made in the report for the Eltham Well Hall rail crash).

Regarding the training of the driver, Gerry Waite (who was a Training Manager at OTC South Side at the time, confirmed that there was no intermediate stage for trainees between learning the controls in a static vehicle and practical experience on a loaded train in service, and I echoed this in a written report to Mr Parsons, the Operations Training Manager on 20th March 1991.

Above: The Author's report to Mr Parsons, the Training Manager of the R.O.T.C. Waterloo.

Below: Duty Manager Fred Johnson and Brian Cook.

Photo: Brian Cook Collection.

The following day after the incident at Cannon Street, I had my first experience of training a female driver - Angela Matthews from Waterloo, (remember that their weren't many female drivers at that time) and found her to be extremely competent. She was accompanied by another driver from Waterloo - Ishmael Deedat and they were with me for the next three days.

I can remember that on one of the Class 455 driving instruction trips, the railhead was particularly greasy and as we ran into Putney station, the wheels picked up. I immediately instructed Angela to place the DBV (Driver's Brake Valve) to the step 3 position and leave it there. She didn't panic and placed the DBV to step 3, the blowdown valves responded and we came to a perfect stop in the station. I commended her on her actions and it taught them both a valuable lesson when confronted with this type of railhead condition.

On the 15th January I was booked TM15 Part 3 exam and both M Couchman from Slade Green and T Lavington from West Worthing passed and I duly handed them both their EP key.

On the 22nd January, I was reunited with Angela and Ishmael conducting their Part 1 exam which they both passed.

I was booked leave until Friday 1st February and because I hadn't been on a Class 319 for a while, I was booked a refresher day before taking a Class 319 course starting on Tuesday 5th February.

Our first day was on a static at Selhurst Depot followed by a driving instruction day when we went to Brighton.

On the Thursday, the weather was bitterly cold and as I drove to Woking station that morning the thermometer in my car was -7 ° c.

It started snowing the following day and we couldn't find a train to use so had to postpone the training and instead, ran the course on the Saturday and Sunday. It was a bit of a struggle getting to Selhurst because of the snow but I eventually made it.

Below: Snowing hard at Clapham Junction whilst waiting for a train to Selhurst.

Photo: The Author's Collection.

Above: Icicles galore on these EPB Units outside the driver's mess room at Selhurst but warmer on the inside looking out!

Below: Thick snow abound as a set of empty coaching stock (the rear unit being 4EPB 5404) passes through Selhurst station.

Photos: The Author's Collection.

Snow still laid on the ground during the following week and it was nice to be in the warmth of the Training Centre conducting revision with TM1 course. On the Thursday though I had to brave the elements and go to Clapham Yard for a Part 3 exam where I'm pleased to say, both of the trainees passed.

On Friday 15th February, Don Ottignon one of the stalwarts of the OTC retired and after work we went to the Red Lion to wish him a happy retirement and say our good-byes. As mentioned, I'd known Don since I joined BR at Guildford Loco in 1961 and had fired to him on steam locomotives on several occasions.

On Saturday 16th February, David Timothy, Ralph Sullivan, Eric Christian and myself went to Selhurst Depot to look at a new Class 456 unit that was going to be introduced onto the Central Division. On the Sunday, we were allowed to take the unit out onto the main line and went all over the place, each of us having a spell in the driving seat.

Right: Fellow Instructor Ralph Sullivan inspecting the driver's sliding door.

Below: The Author on the Class 456 training trip.

Photo: The Author's Collection.

Above Top: Class 456 002 at Selhurst.

Above: Fellow Instructor David Timothy with a Main Reservoir blanking plug carried on the unit for assistance purposes.

Photos: David Timothy Collection.

Right: Class 456 002 at London Bridge.

Photo: The Author's Collection.

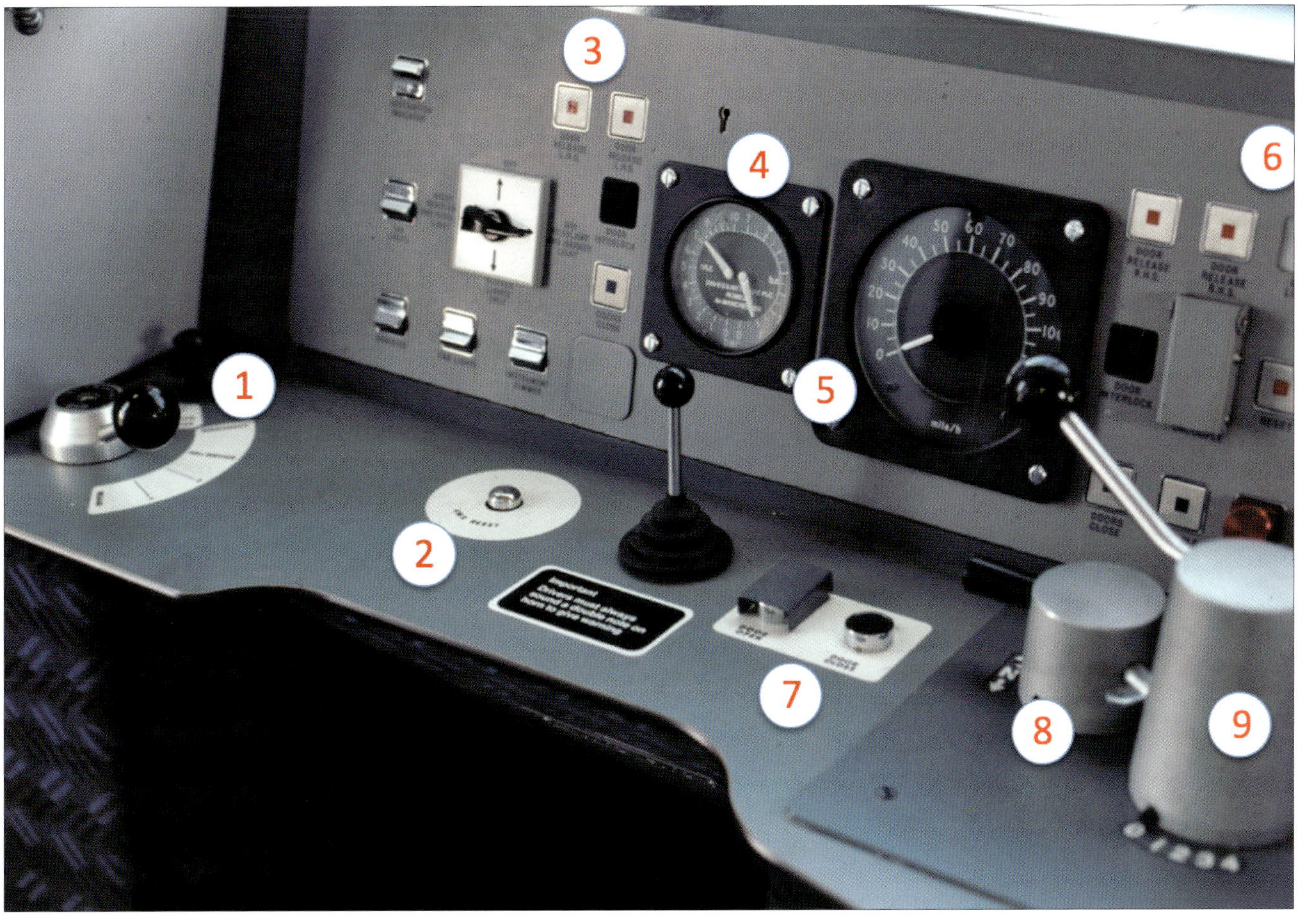

Above: Class 456 desk and driving controls:

1. 3-Step Brake Controller
2. AWS Reset Button
3. Door Release Buttons (left)
4. Main Res. / Brake Cylinder Pressure Gauge
5. Speedometer
6. Door Release Buttons (right)
7. Door Open & Close Buttons
8. Master Switch
9. Power Controller.

Left: Blackbird's nest - how long has this Class 456 unit been stabled here?

Photos: The Author's Collection.

Instructing Days - OTC South Side

On the week commencing 18th February I should have started another Class 73 course but because there was a bomb alert at Victoria station, the train services to London were in complete disarray. Instead, the course started the next day and after reaching a mutual agreement with the drivers on the course, we worked on the Saturday to regain the course element.

Unfortunately, the following Monday's training trip from Eastleigh - Poole and return was cancelled so we were back to being a day short again. The rest of the week went well; the training trip running from Eastleigh to Poole and on the Friday, from Eastleigh - Weymouth and return. On the Saturday and Sunday I was booked a 319 Course at Selhurst with two drivers from Victoria and Three Bridges.

I then continued with the third week of the Class 73 course going to Stewarts Lane for the final static day's training.

For the next three weeks I was booked a variety of work; either assisting on static days or driving instruction; then another 456 course on Sunday 24th February.

I was then booked to take two drivers (D Buddin and H Hassan on 1951 and 1963 driving instruction and worked over the Victoria - Orpington and the Waterloo - Portsmouth routes.

The Training Centre was having a refit the following weekend and this would take up until Tuesday 2nd March so we had to remove all contents from our lockers and desks etc.

We re-occupied the Training Centre on Wednesday 3rd March; moving all of our kit back into new desks and lockers.

For the next two weeks I was kept busy with either driving instruction on 1963 or Class 455 units, varying the suburban routes to include: Waterloo - Chessington, Waterloo - Shepperton, Waterloo - Hampton Court, Waterloo - Guildford (via Cobham) Waterloo M - Waterloo W (via Richmond), Waterloo W - Waterloo W (via Brentford), or Waterloo - Reading via Ascot.

Above: Class 319 'Thameslink' 319176 at Selhurst Depot.

Photo: The Author's Collection.

Below: This 455 was renumbered 5750 following a repaint into NSE colours later in 1990 in connection with a naming ceremony at Wimbledon depot, the number 5750 relates to the number of the British standard for safety systems. Two decades later the name is long gone, as is the NSE livery, but the unit never regained its original number thus making shots of 5743 very scarce. The unit is seen here working a Waterloo to Guildford via Hounslow service, calling at all stations.

Photo & Caption: Matt Taylor.

On 17th April, I was booked 1951 driving instruction with four trainees and met them at Victoria to work to Orpington. The 09.33 service was already being used by another Instructor so we went to the front of the 10.02 service and waited for the driver to appear.

When the driver arrived, I introduced myself and asked him politely if I could use his train for training purposes; the driver normally granting the request. Instead, the driver was quite abrupt and said that I couldn't use his train. I asked him what his name was and the depot he came from (which was normal procedure when a driver declined) and he refused to give me either. I then told my trainees to sit in the train and I said to the driver that I was going to accompany him in the cab to Orpington and showed him my green cab pass. This he agreed to at first but then suddenly changed his mind by shutting the cab down and applying the parking brake. He then disappeared along the platform. After a few minutes, he reappeared and told me to get out and stop 'winding him up'. I repeated to him that I would be riding with him in the cab and that I had authorisation to be there. He then became very abusive and I decided to take him off the train and report to the Train Crew Supervisor. It ended up with the train being cancelled as there wasn't another spare driver at Victoria to work the train. I then reported the incident to my Training Manager.

4 Types of Cab Passes

4.1 Personal "Named" driving cab passes

These are issued on a personal basis to staff who require to ride in driving cabs on a regular basis for the execution of their duty. To assist in the identification of these passes and their respective restrictions, they are colour coded as follows:-

4.1.1 "Green" - Authorised to Instruct

Issued only to those persons who are qualified to advise and instruct Drivers in technical and practical handling skills. Held by Traction Inspectors/Leaders /Instructors etc.

Below: 2EPB 6264 making a shunt move from the up sidings at Orpington. Class 319046 waits for the road into the platform on 2nd September 1991.

Photo & Caption: Timothy Saunders.

Instructing Days - OTC South Side

That weekend I was kept busy conducting Class 456 courses at Selhurst Depot followed by a static instruction at Clapham Yard on the Monday and TM driving instruction the rest of the week using the Waterloo - Portsmouth Harbour and Waterloo - Guildford via Cobham routes finishing up on the Friday working over the Wimbledon - West Croydon line. As mentioned earlier, I liked using this line to get trainees used to using the five-position brake valve and to use the Westinghouse brake.

I worked again the following Saturday with another group on a Class 456 course at Selhurst and following on from that conducted two separate Part 2 traction exams on the Wednesday and Thursday and REP courses at Eastleigh on the following Saturday and Sunday.

Looking forward to a break - travelling in the opposite direction on 13th May as I was booked to learn Class 483 units on the Isle of Wight!

Right: Fellow Instructor Chris Lemon contacts the Signalaman at Victoria Signalling Centre (located at Clapham Junction) via the signalpost telephone at Signal No. VC885 situated just outside Beddington Lane station on the Wimbledon - West Croydon line.

Below: 456015 with the service from Victoria to London Bridge arriving at Wandworth Road.

Photo: Janderk1968 - Wikipedia.

Monday 13th May was a glorious spring day and I was on my way to the IOW, making the crossing from Portsmouth Harbour to Ryde Pier Head. I must admit, I hadn't been across to the island for years and certainly hadn't been on any of the new Class 483 units - introduced a couple of years earlier to replace the ageing Class 485 /486 units. The Class 483 Units had originally been built in 1938 and had already worked for nearly 50 years on London Underground and had been extensively refurbished at Eastleigh Works.

I made my way to Ryde St Johns Road station and met fellow Instructor Martin Sqibb (who was going to show me the ropes). Martin had been born on the IOW and therefore, like anyone else that was born there, was known as a 'Caulkhead'.

Alan Rackett from East Cowes, IOW says: "I was always taught as a child that this term originates from when a ship carrying people from the island along with people from the mainland (overners) sank in the Solent and the only survivors were from the island. However, a better explanation is that 'Caulkheads' were hired at Bucklers Hard in Beaulieu as caulkers in the boat yards. A local myth is to drop a new born baby into the Solent, and if they float unharmed they are true caulkheads."

I spent the next four days on the IOW with Martin, not only learning the unit but also the route between Ryde Pier Head and Shanklin where the line terminated. Most of the route consisted of single line sections with passing loops at various stations.

On the Friday, Gerry Waite came over to Ryde to conduct my static traction exam which I successfully passed and was now ready to take my own course on Class 483 units in the future.

Above: Island Line Trains poster showing the route from Ryde Pier Head to Shanklin. As a child, I often visited these places when on holiday with my parents.

Graphic: Courtesy of South West Trains and Island Line Trains.

Below: The view towards Ryde Esplanade from Ryde Pier Head.

Photo: The Author's Collection.

Instructing Days - OTC South Side

On Monday 20th May I was back in London and conducting a Part 3 exam with two Waterloo drivers, Trudy Thorne and John Cassidy who successfully passed.

The rest of the week I was booked two Class 319 courses running consecutively which finished the week off nicely before a three-week holiday which I was really looking forward to.

On my return to work, I found that I'd been booked to conduct a Class 483 course for two drivers and that John Hartford (another fellow Instructor) was going to accompany me to also learn the unit.

On arrival at Ryde St Johns, we looked round a static unit and then in the afternoon did some practical handling to Shanklin and Ryde Pier Head.

This continued for the rest of the week with another Instructor taking the exam on the Friday.

Right: Ryde Driver John Little on board Class 483 No. 005.

Below: Instructor John Hartford with the same unit.

Photos: The Author's Collection.

On July 8th, I picked up the second and third week of a Class 73 course and again, instead of working a training trip on the South Western Division, ran trips from New Cross Gate to Brighton and one day to Eastbourne with the normal static days being held at Stewarts Lane depot.

Right:* *Trainees on the training trip to Brighton with Class 73/1 No. 73126.

Below:* *Class 73/1 No. 73134 travelling light to New Cross Gate to pick up the training trip stock for Eastbourne.

Photos: The Author's Collection.

Instructing Days - OTC South Side

On Monday 22nd July, I started TM11 course with two other Acting Instructors sitting in to learn the course structure.

One of these men was Jerry Harris and the other was Roger Luckins and they would shadow me for the duration of the course in the classroom and during static instruction on all the types of EMU featured on the course.

During the course on Friday 2nd August, I was waiting on Woking platform to catch a train to Waterloo (and eventually conduct a 1951 static at Victoria Carriage Sidings) and when the west of England train ran into the platform, I noticed that Roger Luckins was in the cab of the Class 50 hauling the train. I was invited into the cab to do the driving (a type of locomotive that I'd never driven before). The number and name of the locomotive was 50002 *'Superb'* and this was to be one of its last trips to Waterloo before being withdrawn from service.

Following the course, I had a mixture of work; assisting various courses on static and driving instruction and then had a further week's holiday booked.

A vacancy for a Senior Instructor (mixed traction) had been advertised and I was encouraged to apply. Other interviews took place but I couldn't have mine until after my holiday so that was another time when I had to take my homework with me! Upon my return, my interview took place, the interview panel being Tim Morgan, Ian Thorpe and Ralph Sullivan and after a couple of hour's deliberation, I was told the job was mine!

As you can imagine, I was ecstatic - I was now a Senior Instructor with an MS1 grade. A manager of a team of six instructors and a dream that I would have never have thought possible when I joined the railway as a 15 year old engine cleaner at Guildford in 1961. This meant another increase in salary but the drawbacks were that I had a lot more work and responsibility.

Above: Class 50 No. 50002 'Superb' arriving at Woking with the 1L08 09.50 Salisbury – Waterloo service on Saturday 20th October 1990.

Photo: Gary Blyth.

Below: Class 50002 'Superb' certainly lives up to its name as it races through Winchfield on 28th August 1987 with the 1V15 15.10 Waterloo to Exeter St Davids Network SouthEast service.

Photo: Martin Loader.

On Monday 17th September I was booked to instruct a group of drivers from Eastleigh and Bournemouth depots on Class 73 roadwork; a course that had been started by Cyril Sweet. The training trip would run all week from Eastleigh to Poole and return to Eastleigh and consisted of a Class 73 locomotive and 2 x 4VEP Units. The 10 point control cut-out switch on both 4VEP units were cut-out so as not to overload the traction current index.

I thoroughly enjoyed the trips as this was my favourite class of locomotive and it was an absolute pleasure to instruct the trainees on the correct way to operate the locomotive on diesel and electric conditions in a variety of ways including driving under auxiliary power using the electric controller. Apart from the EP (electro-pneumatic) brake being utilised, the Westinghouse brake was also practised.

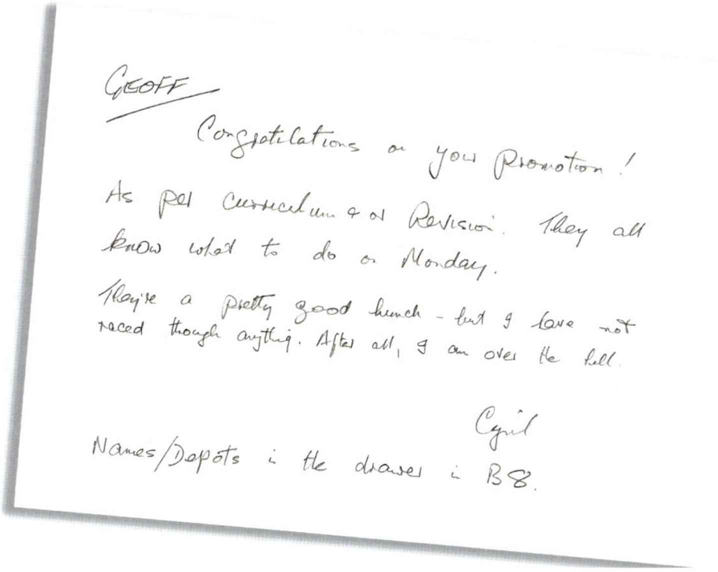
GEOFF

Congratulations on your Promotion!

As per curriculum & or Revision. They all know what to do on Monday.

They're a pretty good bunch - but I have not raced though anything. After all, I am over the hill.

Cyril

Names/Depots in the drawer in B8.

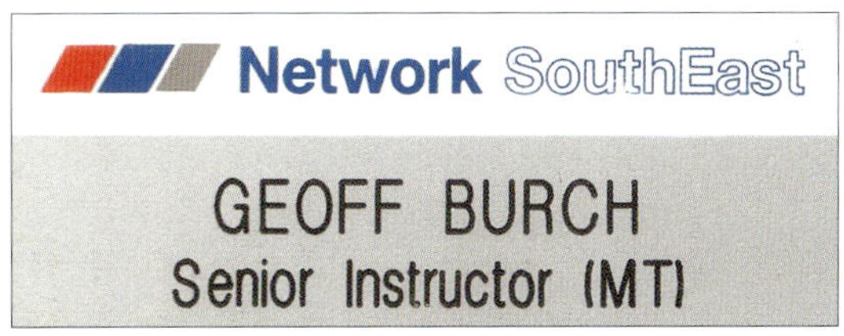

Above Top: Cyril Sweet's message of congratulations on the Author's promotion to Senior Instructor (MT).

Below: The Author at Poole with Class 73/1 No. 73133 'The Bluebell Railway', the locomotive used on the training trip.

Photo: The Author's Collection.

Network SouthEast

SOUTH WEST DIVISION

To: Mr G Burch
Traction Instructor
Southside, Waterloo

From: Training Centre Manager
Southside
Waterloo

Ext: 00-26173

Ref: S2791/28
Date: 17th December 1991

Dear Geoff

VACANCY NO S2791, LIST NO 28
SENIOR INSTRUCTOR (MIXED TRACTION) MS1
OPERATIONS TRAINING CENTRE, WATERLOO

I am pleased to confirm that you have been appointed to the above position at a salary of £15,373 plus £1,415 per annum London Allowance.

As you have been covering this position for some time, your transfer to your new post will be recorded as taking effect from Monday, 7th October 1991, and any arrears due will be paid as soon as they are calculated.

Enclosed are 2 copies of a revised Contract of Employment regarding your appointment to the Management Staff. Please sign and return one copy to the Personnel Services Manager, Room 388, General Offices, Waterloo.

Congratulations and best wishes on your appointment.

Yours sincerely

John Parsons
TRAINING CENTRE MANAGER

Left: The Author's confirmation of appointment to Senior Instructor (Mixed Traction).

Below: Class 73/0 No. 73005 'Mid Hants Watercress Line' passes Millbrook on 30th November 1989 with the 6Y62 08.57 Eastleigh to RAF Dinton MoD stores.
The unusual livery of all over Network SouthEast blue is certainly effective and not far off the original 'Electric Blue' that the class carried in the 1960s.

Photo & Caption: Martin Loader.

On Monday 21st October, I attended a British Railways Board workshop at a hotel in Scarborough for four days.

The driver training programme was changing rapidly and objective writing was the key issue.

The teaching process towards students was that there must be a key objective at the end of each lesson and measures in place to observe that the key objectives had been met.

For the next two weeks that's all I was doing at work; looking through each part of the traction course and writing objectives.

However, I was given a break form this task on some of the days leading up towards Christmas and utilised for a variety of work including 1963 and 455 Class driving instruction with a number of Part 2 and Part 3 traction exams thrown in. I also had to learn how to operate the new Class 465 'Networker' Driver Training Simulators that had been installed.

Right: Gerry Waite and David Timothy in the newly built Class 465 Simulator building at OTC South Side.

Below: Gerry Waite in the hot seat within the Simulator room.

Photos: David Timothy.

Instructing Days - OTC South Side

The new year of 1992 brought a lot of changes to the OTC with the new prospectus and as I needed to hone my computer skills, I decided to enrol in a computer course at Guildford Technical college.

Up until this point, all classrooms had overhead projectors with viewfoils and the occasional slide projector but now instead of DOS based programs, Microsoft Windows (version 3 and then 3.1) had been introduced at the OTC and this meant that it was possible to use scanned digital images in our course material. Apart from that, it was also possible to place digital images into our training literature as up until then, this had all been done using line drawings or pencil sketches.

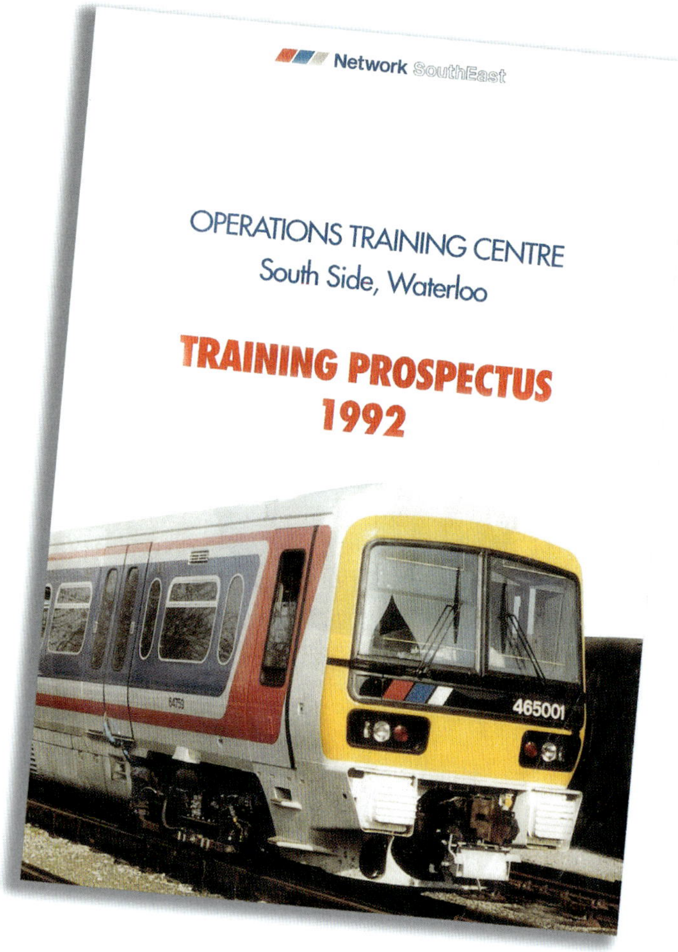

Right: 1992 Training Prospectus at the Operations Training Centre, South Side Waterloo; the front cover showing the new Class 465 unit.

Below: Organisational chart showing the trainers associated with the Operational Training Centre.

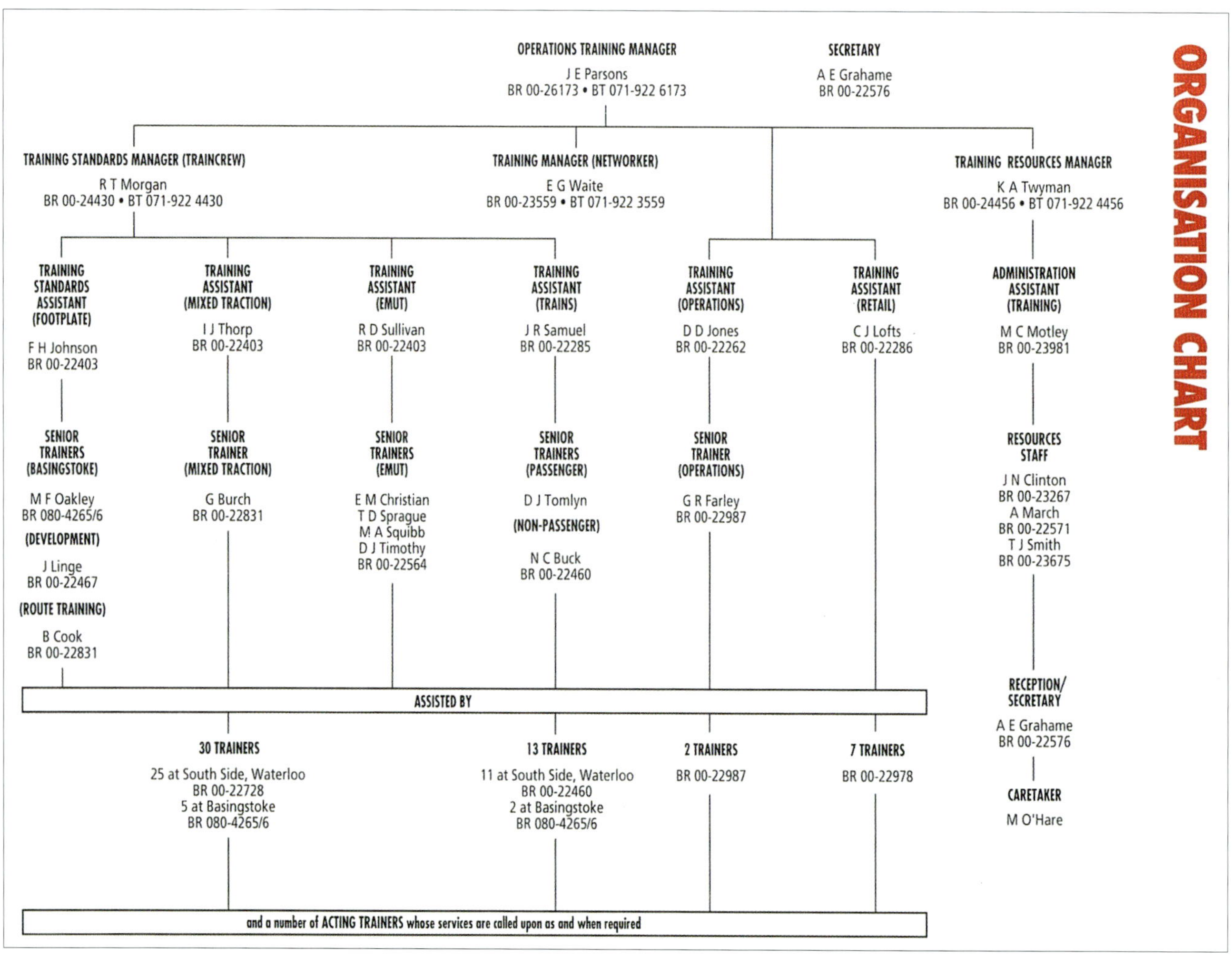

OPERATIONS TRAINING CENTRE • South Side, Waterloo

TRAINING PROSPECTUS 1992

TRAINING PROGRESSION (DIAGRAMMATIC)

Steps in the training process for new entrants or ex-Guards to become Train(wo)men (D), Train(wo)men (G), Conductors or Drivers are shown in diagrammatic form.

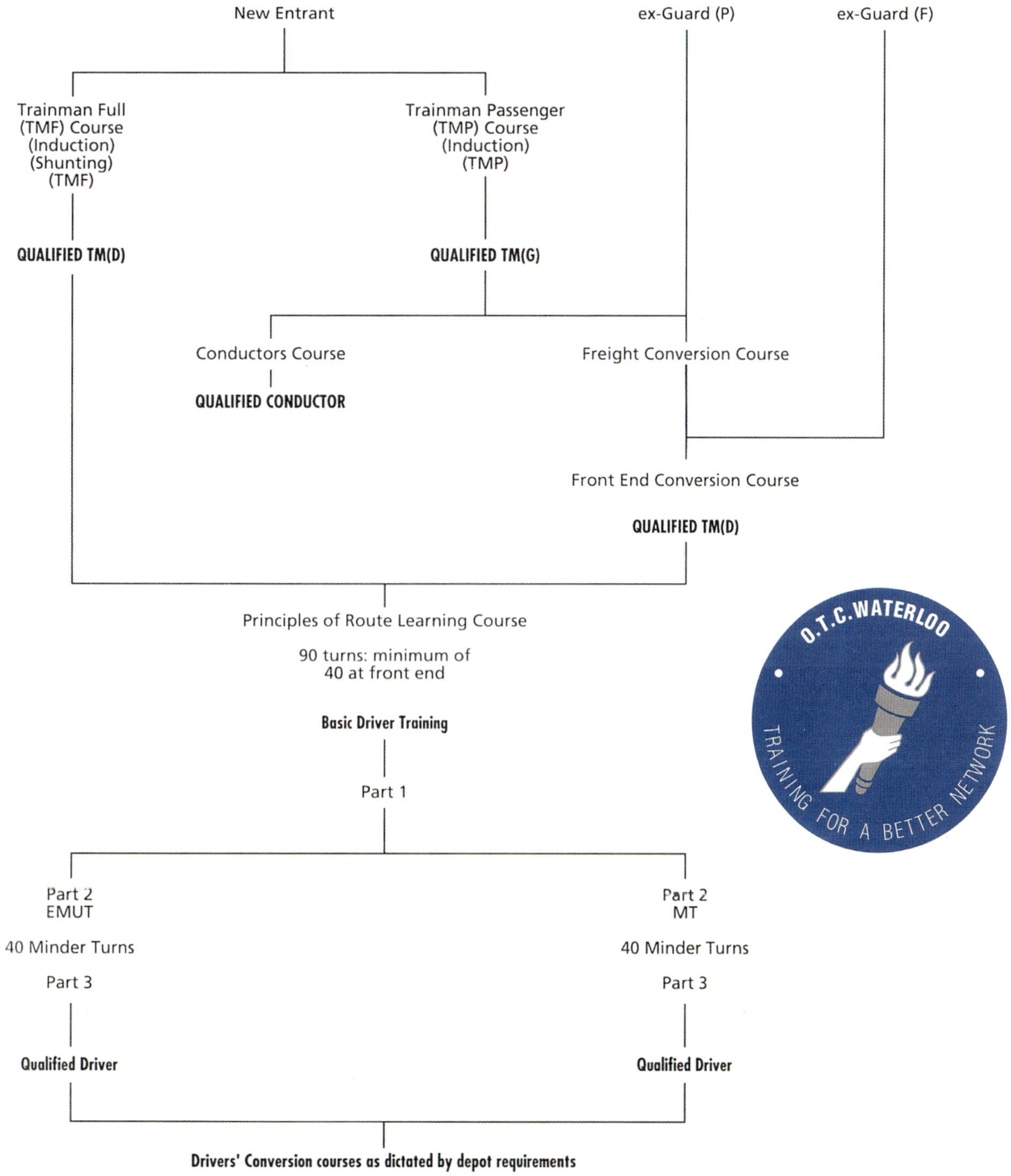

Above: Training progression from new entrant to qualified driver in diagrammatic form.

Instructing Days - OTC South Side

The first couple of months of 1992 saw me running two consecutive Class 73 courses; one of which the driving instruction was with freight trains over the South Eastern Division.

On the first course, we worked a freight train from Tonbridge West Yard to Dover via Canterbury from Monday to Thursday, completing the static instruction at Stewarts Lane Depot on the Friday. However, on the second course, on reaching Ashford, the driver refused to let us use the train for training purposes which meant that we had to try to find another train to use. This was easily accomplished by using Victoria Gatwick services but only having a Class 73 locomotive at one end of the train made things awkward. We were lucky the following day though; the trip running from Tonbridge West Yard and return via the Medway Valley line.

On the 4th March, I had to attend another Management course at Southampton for three days with some of my colleagues from the OTC, namely: Mick Oakley, Trevor Sprague, Tim Morgan, Ralph Sullivan, Brian Cook, Martin Squibb, David Timothy and Gordon Farley. It was my birthday during the course and this was celebrated during the evening of the 5th March with a birthday cake with chocolate nipples on the top!

Above: Quality Through Teamwork Seminar at Southampton.

Back Row - from left to right: Martin Squibb, Gordon Farley, Brian Cook, David Timothy and the Author.
Middle Row - from left to right: Trevor Sprague, Tim Morgan, Ralph Sullivan and kneeling in front: Mick Oakley.

Photo: The Author's Collection.

Below: Class 73/1 No. 73133 resplendent in British Rail's Chief Civil Engineers 'Dutch' livery stands in Tonbridge West Yard on 25th October 1990 having emerged from a heavy overhaul at Selhurst Level 5 Depot the previous month.
After overhaul the locomotive was adorned with the 'Bluebell Railway' nameplates and crest formerly carried by withdrawn sister No. 73004.

Photo & Caption: Adrian Nicholls.

Above: Class 73s galore at Tonbridge West Yard - Nos. 73006 and 73134 wait to leave with engineers trains, while No. 73005 arrives. Also in view are a class 47 and one of the resident 09's on 10th April 1988.

Below: Class 73/1 No. 73117 'University of Surrey' working an engineers train in the Jubilee Sidings, Tonbridge on 24th September 1993.
The locomotive was named at a ceremony at Waterloo on 3rd July 1987.

Photos: Timothy Saunders.

Instructing Days - OTC South Side

My next task was to learn the Class 158 / 159 'Sprinter' units and to start with, I caught a train to Fratton where I picked up a Class 155 'Regional Railways' service to Cardiff with one of my team, Graham Allen. I repeated the journey the following day, doing most of the driving which gave me a flavour of how a 'Sprinter' operated.

Class 158 / 159 units were going to be the mainstay of services from Waterloo to Exeter and a new servicing depot was in the process of being built at Salisbury.

For the rest of the year, I had a lot of work on my hands; apart from covering Class 73 courses I also had to make sure that my team of six trainers were performing to standard and this was measured by assessing their capabilities in the classroom or on static training or driving instruction.

It was also my job to update the Class 73 Faults and Failures book and also produce the Class 159 Instruction Manual that were issued to drivers and this is where my previous computer knowledge learnt at night school came in handy. There wasn't a day went by when I was either working on some project or other and because I'd invested in another home computer, I did a lot of this work at home.

In July, I 'sat in' on a Class 159 Course that Martin Squibb was running at Salisbury and for the next two months, travelled there to either take the course or teach other trainers.

Meanwhile, it was decided that I should lead the project of training all of the South Western drivers (Salisbury and Exeter) on the new class 159 'Sprinter' diesel units that were being delivered. It was during this project that my mother-in-law passed away and I decided to take my wife Pauline on a holiday to Australia for a month to take her mind off it.

Above: The Author with the brand new Class 159 'Sprinter' unit at Bournemouth Depot.

Photo: The Author's Collection.

Below: 155310 passes Sherrington on a bitterly cold January day in 1991 with the 11.29 Cardiff Central to Portsmouth Harbour Regional Railways service. Photo & Caption: Martin Loader.

Above: One of the first groups of Salisbury drivers to learn the Class 158 / 159 Units. From left to right: Annie Winter, Brian Hawes, Alfie Fletcher, the Author and Ted Hooper.

Photo: The Author's Collection.

Below: Class 159 159003 round the curve at Oborne (on the approach to Sherborne) with the 08.35 Waterloo to Exeter St Davids Network SouthEast service on 26th March 1994. The NSE livery now makes this picture historic.

Photo & Caption: Martin Loader.

Instructing Days - OTC South Side

When I returned to work, it transpired that whilst I'd been away, there had been a bit of a change at the OTC and the Class 159 training programme that I'd been running at Salisbury had been given to someone else. An Instructor (who lived at Salisbury) had suggested that it would be a good idea that he should be in charge while I was away and I should be taken off the project. I objected of course, but it fell on deaf ears. I was given another project - this time training drivers on the new Class 465 'Networker' units. In the background though, privatisation was looming its ugly head and the writing was on the wall for the OTC South Side.

The Central part was the first to go under a new franchise and a Training Centre was set up at Croydon taking with it some of the trainers. This left the South Eastern and the South Western sectors being left at OTC South Side. I had even been told that I would be moving to Croydon but I wasn't going to be 'stitched up' again.

By this time though, my computer knowledge had increased a thousand-fold and it was decided that as I'd made a good job of producing the 159 handout for drivers, I would be better utilised in helping to write the 'Networker' training manuals and handouts.

There were two different types of Class 465, one manufactured by BREL and the other by METCAM and at first, they had so many compatibility problems it was untrue and the units were always breaking down. The trains were also DOO (Driver Only Operated) and the new technology was just too much for a lot of the older drivers and as you can imagine, so the sickness record at depots rocketed.

BRITISH RAIL : NETWORK SOUTHEAST.

To: Mr G. Burch.
MS 1,
Operations Training Centre,
Waterloo.

From: J. Parsons.
Training Manager,
Operations Training Centre,
Southside,
Waterloo.

Tel: 26173.
Date: 23rd February 1993.

Operations Training Centre Waterloo; Reorganisation.

Following consultation on the above. I have to advise you that with effect from 29th March 1993 you will be displaced from your present position within the Operations Training Centre.
New Training Organisations are being created at Waterloo and Croydon. So far as is possible you will be accommodated in similar work in the new organisations, in accordance with your stated preference, subject to seniority and post availability.
Will you please return the tear-off portion of this letter below, indicating your order of preference by inserting 1, 2 or 3 against the relevant locations. This document is the "Closed List" in connection with this reorganisation, and should be returned to the Training Manager as soon as possible please, at the latest by midday on Friday 5th March 1993.

J. Parsons.
Training Manager.

To : Mr G Burch
Senior Traction Instructor
Waterloo

From : Training Manager
Operations Training Centre
Waterloo

Date : 31st March 1993

Operations Training Centre : Re-organisation W.E.F. 5.4.93

Further to the above, and my previous letter dated 23.2.93, I am pleased to advise you that due to impending moves within the organisation here it will now be possible to accommodate you within our South East structure as a Senior Traction Instructor in accordance with the option you originally expressed, and your transfer to Croydon will not now be necessary.

This now resolves your displacement as advised in my letter dated 23.2.93. Your seniority date and rate of pay remains unaltered.

J E Parsons

Above Right: Letter of Reorganisation of the Training Centre.

Right: Letter from John Parsons informing me that my move to Croydon would not be necessary.

Below Right: Last Days at Effingham Junction - from left to right: The Author, David Timothy and Ian Verrinder.

Photo & Graphics: The Author's Collection.

I had also been given the task of training all of the Traction Inspectors on the Parizzi data recorders that had been fitted on all new trains, including the 159 type that I had been working on at Salisbury. Apart from that, David Owen and I were also writing the new Driver 2000 competency based curriculum for drivers as well, so it was quite a busy time.

The crunch came when we were told one day that the South Eastern part of the OTC was going to move to London Bridge and that I might have to move there. I wasn't keen on this idea at all as I'd been on the South Western sector all of my working life and not only that, it meant that I'd be working on 'Networkers' which I hated (even typing the words makes me cringe)!

	MON 29/3	TUES 30/3	WED 31/3	THURS 1/4	FRI 2/4	SAT 3/4	SUN 4/4		
T. MORGAN								To	SW
E WAITE								To	SE
F JOHNSON	SPL DUTIES							To	SW
R SULLIVAN	DM →							To	SE
I THORP	CL 56 →				CL 37 EX			To	SW
D TIMOTHY	A/L →			ASSIST ET 9	R7 PT 2 EX			To	SE
E. CHRISTIAN	NW 11A →			NW 11B EX	R7 PT 2 EX			To	SE
T SPRAGUE	ASSIST ET 8	ASSIST BRML →		ASSIST ET 9	R7 PT 2 EX			To	SW
J LINGE	NW 11B →			NW 11A EX	NW COND			To	SE
M SQUIBB	WRC →							To	SW
G. BURCH	ET 9	(INT)	WK 3 & 4 →					To	C
B COOK	BRML →							To	SW
A ROE	R9	WK 2 →						To	SE
J RUTTER	R10	WK 1 →							
L PRICE	R7	WK 4 →			CL 56 EX				
M BOWMAN	D 12	WK 20 →			R7 PT 2 EX				
P WENSLEY	ET 7	PT 1 EX →	ET 8	WK 5 →					
M GEALL	NW COND	ET 10	NW COND		R7 PT 2 EX				
D WEBB	NW 12A	WK 1 →							
C EXLEY	DOO RADIO				CAB SECURE RADIO				
A HARPER	ET 7	PT 1 EX →		ASSIST ET 10	D 12 PT 3 EX				
I VERRINDER	ET 7	PT 1 EX →							
T HARRIS	R8	WK 3 →							
C HAYNES	ET 7	PT 1 EX	ASSIST ET 11	ASSIST ET 10	R7 PT 2 EX			To	C
G PENN	ET 11	WK 1 →							
T REYNOLDS	ET 8	WK 4 & 5 →							
P FLINT	NW 12B	WK 1 →							
D OWEN	ET 7	PT 1 EX →	ET 8	WK 5 →				To	SE
M MEDLEY	NW 11F	SIT IN EX →			D 12 PT 3 EX				
P DELACEY	ET 10	(LEAVE)	WK 1 & 2 →						
D BROWN	DRVS 2	WK 4 →						To	SE
D OTTIGNON		ASSIST ET 9	ASSIST DRVS 2					To	RETIREMENT
M OAKLEY	BASING →							To	SW
G ALLEN	BASING →								
C LEMON	BASING →								
J HARTFORD	BASING →								
R LUCKINS	BASING →							To	SW
C FOOT	BASING →								
C SWEET	CL 37	9 WORKING →						To	RETIREMENT
D ROUSSET	A/L →								
P INGE	ASSIST ET 10	ET 9	ET 8	WK 5 →					
G GILLINGHAM									
I SIMMONDS	ASSIST ET 10	ASSIST ET 9	ET 8	WK 5 →					
A COOK	SAFETY →								
P LEMON	SIMULATOR →								
I GLOVER	ASSIST ET 8		ET 8	WK 5 →					
A SAUNDERS	D 13	WK 19 →							
N HICKMAN	A/L →								

Above: The trainer's roster for week ending 2nd April 1993 showing the Author's interview date at Croydon (30th March) and impending move thereafter!

Graphic: Courtesy of Fred Johnson.

Instructing Days - OTC South Side

Above: 465 Training with David Timothy between Meopham and Sole Street circa 1993.

Above Right: Front Cover of the Class 465 'Networker' Driver's Handout which I helped to produce.

Photo & Graphic: The Author's Collection.

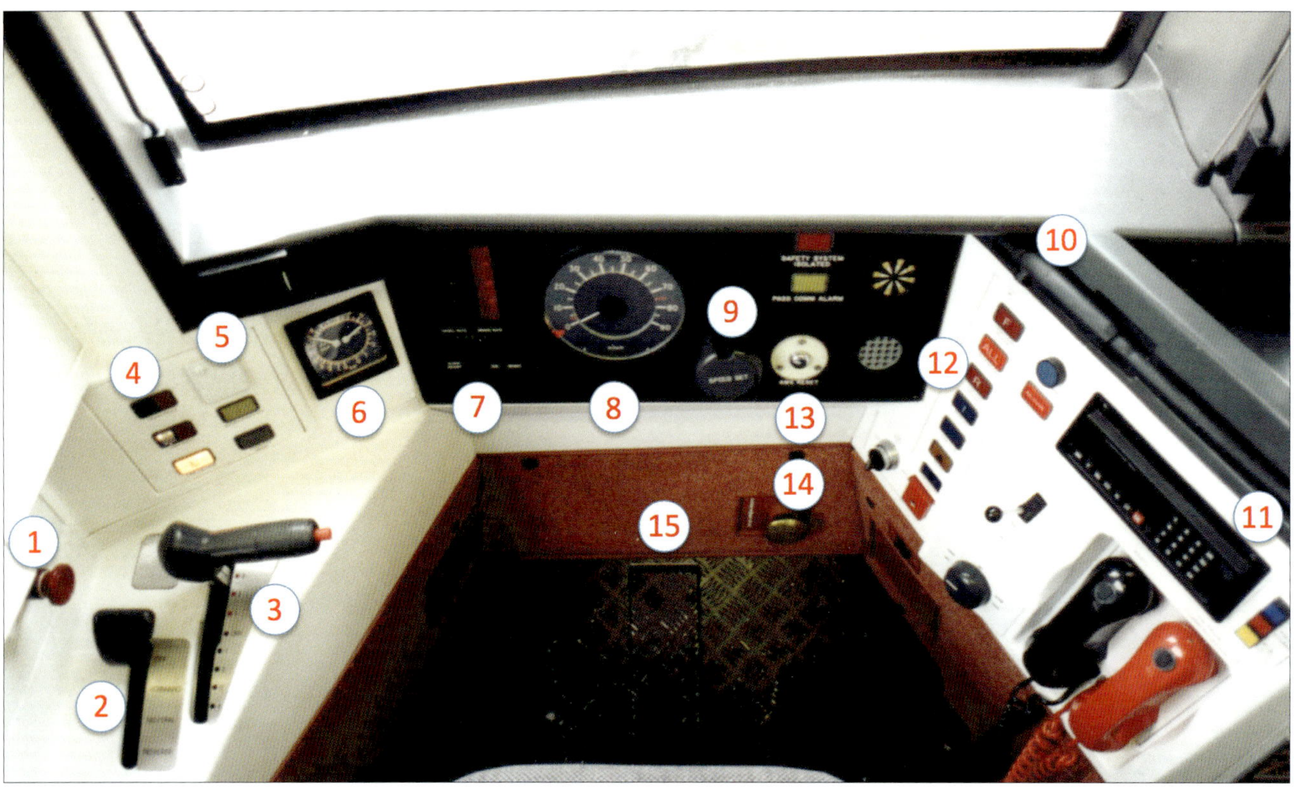

Above: Class 465 'Networker' Cab & Controls:

1. Emergency Brake Button 2. Master Switch 3. Power / Brake Controller 4. Train / Unit Fault Indicators 5. Regen. Brake Button 6. Main Res. Air / Brake Cylinder Pressure Gauge 7. Acceleration / Brake Rate Meter 8. Speedo 9. Speed Set Control 10. Stalk Microphone 11. Radio Console 12. Door Release Buttons (Right) 13. AWS Reset 14. Passcom Holdover Button 15. DSD / Vigilance Treadle.

Photo: The Author's Collection.

Clockwise from Top Left: : David Timothy and the Author with a pair of Class 465 'Networker' units, Bernie Byrne and Trevor 'Chopper Harris, David Timothy at his 'leaving do' with Eric Christian and Ian Simmonds; Dave Brown, David Timothy, John Parsons, Jim Samuel, Mick Oakley, Tony Saunders and Ralph Sullivan; Chris Lemon with a 'mop' of hair and finally, the Author with Brian Cook, Peter Johns, Ian Simmonds and David Timothy.

Photos: The Author's & David Timothy Collection.

Instructing Days - OTC South Side

In January 1994, we all had to have interviews with various bosses and my job was contested with another senior trainer at the OTC. He wasn't exactly a friend of mine (or most of the other trainers for that matter), for reasons far too numerous to mention here.

After my interview, my work colleagues and myself were fairly confident that I'd get the job and it came as a bit of a shock when the other trainer was chosen. I demanded another meeting with the head of the OTC and he tried to fob me off with all sorts of excuses as to why I hadn't been chosen and offered me a job as a 'trouble-shooter' between management and drivers at Victoria. I wasn't interested of course and decided to take the severance package that was on offer. I only attended work for another two weeks as I had also decided to take the time off that I was owed.

Friday 18th February 1994 was my last day on the railway and was quite a sad day for me really. My career within the railway industry had spanned 32 years 11 months but at least I had worked my way up through the ranks rather than by grace or favour. I had also enjoyed the best days of my working life with my colleagues at OTC South Side and it was a shame it had to end the way it did.

Above: The Author writing the Driver 2000 Competency based Curriculum for Drivers at OTC South Side.

Below: Letter confirming my departure from OTC South Side.

Photo & Graphics: The Author's Collection.

Network SouthEast

Mr G Burch
Management Staff
Operations Training Centre
South Side
Waterloo.

Mr M Holden,
Operations Manager (SW),
Floor 6,
General Offices,
Waterloo.

Tel: 00 75616
Date: 8 March 1994.

Dear Mr. Burch

Arrangements are being made for you to leave the service on Saturday 19 March 1994, your actual last working day is still to be confirmed, although it has been agreed to pay you any outstanding 1994 leave which you are unable to clear prior to your discharge. As you appreciate, no payment will be due to you in respect of the period of your personal notice which you have agreed to waive.

I confirm that your lump sum payment will be and this will be paid into your Bank Account, less tax as appropriate, on Friday 18 March 1994.

Your pension will be progressed through the Pension Fund, Stooperdale Offices, Brinkburn Road, Darlington.

You will retain Travel Facilities as for Normal Retired Staff.

I would like to take this opportunity of placing on record my personal appreciation of, and congratulations for, the valued service you have given during your 32 years of service, and especially for all the help and support you have given to the Operations Team.

In the event of you requiring any further information or should you wish for any assistance, please do not hesitate to contact me.

Yours sincerely,

Bernard Melanophy.
for Operations Manager (SW)

Network SouthEast is a business sector of the British Railways Board

Postscript

I recently attended a retirement party of a friend that worked with me at OTC South Side and the person that conducted my last interview was also present.
To satisfy my curiosity, I asked him outright whether he remembered the encounter.
It gave me great satisfaction to hear that my suspicions were correct and that he'd been briefed beforehand to select the 'other trainer' even though I was a more suitable candidate for the job.
I thanked him for his honesty and told him that it was all water under the bridge now and had I not left at that time, I wouldn't have experienced meeting and working with a host of other friends from other walks of life besides the railway industry,

GB

I was now officially out of a job so I signed on the dole on the 21st March 1994. I did a few computer jobs for friends for a couple of weeks and then saw an advert in the Surrey Advertiser for a Computer Based Training Development Officer with Surrey Police. The old proverb came to mind again, so I applied. A couple of weeks later I received a reply asking me to come for an interview on the 18th April and I was asked to bring a presentation (I still have it somewhere). I duly arrived for the interview taking my own computer just in case (I'd had about four by then and were a far cry from my first Amstrad) and set it all up in what was then the basement classroom.

There were three police officers present on the panel: Inspector Brian Russell (who was then head of the training department), Sergeant Steve Wood and PC Ian Parrott. They all sat there with arms crossed and asked me to begin and to be honest, it was quite easy for me as I had learnt my presentation skills at Watford. I think that I realised that I had secured the job when a humorous 'level headed' slide came on and I saw them all smile! A few days later I was told officially that my interview had been successful and I started work at the Surrey Police Headquarters at Mount Browne on the 16th May.

It was strange to start with (working with lots of policemen) but I think that my age was an advantage. Everyone I met thought that I was a retired police officer and I seemed to be accepted by everyone. Ian Parrott and I got along very well as his brother had previously been a fireman at Guildford Loco in the steam days before joining the police force himself and Ian was also dead keen on anything to do with railways.

A couple of weeks went by and the IT (Information Technology) department was in need of a trainer to deliver courses to all police officers and civilian staff on their new network computer system. I was chosen for the job and 'hired out' to the IT department for a year. It meant that I'd have to go to Reading for a couple of weeks to be trained and then to start with, I would begin training staff in a classroom environment at HQ Mount Browne. I'd already booked our holiday to Samos in June, so they had to wait for me to get back but it meant taking homework on holiday yet again!

Once back from leave, I went over to DEC (Digital Equipment Corporation) at Reading to be trained, which was quite enjoyable. I then 'sat in' on a SPINE (Surrey Police Integrated Network Environment) course run by DEC at Mount Browne and then I was all on my own. My boss, Inspector Brian Russell was very pleased with my progress and I had some very good feedback including comments from Superintendents who thought it was a refreshing change to be trained professionally!

After a spell at HQ, I then had to move all the training equipment to Reigate and start on the eastern part of the county.

By Christmas, I was joined by another trainer, and after a few months it was decided to train the rest of the staff utilising a CBT (Computer Based Training) package. Ian Parrott and I started programming the package and I'm very grateful to Ian for teaching me so much and having the patience to work with me for the following six months. We had great fun though and the package turned out to be quite a success.

Above Top: The original advert for a CBT Development Officer that was in the Surrey Advertiser.

Above: The Author training staff on 'SPINE' - (Surrey Police Integrated Network Environment) Computer System at Mount Browne.

Left: Level Headed!

Surrey Police Days

On Sunday 22nd January 1995, Ian Parrott and I went to see A4 Pacific 60009 *'Union of South Africa'* at Woking. It was heading a special charter running from London Waterloo - Staines - Woking - Basingstoke - Salisbury - Romsey - Southampton Central - Basingstoke - Woking and return to London Waterloo.

As I'd parked my car in Woking Down Yard, I also gave Ian a guided tour on a Class 33 'Crompton' that was berthed there.

In March 1995, Woking Borough Council ran a number of steam-hauled services to mark the town's centenary. On Friday 24th, an early morning commuter special *'The Woking Centenarian'* ran from Woking to Waterloo and my good friend Pat Kinsella was the driver. The locomotive booked to haul the train was Rebuilt Merchant Navy Class 35028 *'Clan Line'* and I went up to Woking early in the morning to see the train depart.

Other steam-hauled trips that day included M7 Class 30053 working special 'shuttle' trips to Guildford and Aldershot and return to Woking.

Right & Below: A4 Pacific 60009 'Union of South Africa' pulls out of Woking station with a Special Charter on 22nd January 1995.

Photos: The Author's Collection.

Left: Ian Parrott stands beside a Class 33/0 'Crompton' in Woking Down Yard.

Below: Pat Kinsella leaves Woking Up Yard with Rebuilt Merchant Navy Class 35028 'Clan Line' on Friday 24th March 1995.
This was the first commuter service to Waterloo to be steam hauled since steam finished on the Southern on 9th July 1967.

Photos: The Author's Collection.

Surrey Police Days

On Sunday 25th March 1995, My pal David Timothy and myself and our wives went to Woking to catch a glimpse of the Woking Centenary celebrations. Class M7 tank 30053 was running shuttle services from Woking to Woking (via Guildford and Aldershot) so after seeing the train in the platform, we decided to go to 'Twin Bridges' (by Woking Junction) to get a better view. Woking drivers Albert Wright and Alex 'Mac' McClymont were the crew accompanied by DSM (Driver Standards Manager) Jim Grainger (who had also been a driver at Woking whilst I was there). It was a splendid sight and brought back very happy memories of my days on the footplate.

***Right:** DSM Jim Grainger gives a cheery wave as Driver Albert Wright opens the regulator of M7 Class 30053 as they leave Woking.*
For those of you that read my first book 'The Ramblings of a Railwayman', Jim was the fireman on my memorable trip from Guildford Yard to Reading Yard and return when I was a 15 year old engine cleaner.

***Below:** It's Alex McClymont's turn to do the driving as the train runs into Woking on the return journey from Aldershot.*

Photos: The Author's Collection.

Above: M7 Class 30053 leaves Guildford bound for Woking with 'The Woking Wanderer' - part of the Woking Centenary celebrations on 26th March 1995.

Below: M7 Class 30053 on the shuttle to Aldershot / Guildford as part of the Woking 150 celebrations. The locomotive is now preserved and operates on the Swanage Railway.

Photos: Michael Thorne.

Surrey Police Days

By this time another computer-based trainer had joined our team. She was very ambitious and had an uncanny knack of rubbing everyone up the wrong way. Her ambition was to run the department and she very nearly succeeded. The Training School at Mount Browne was going through a really tough period at this time and a new man had been drafted in to run it. He was Lt. Col. Tony Kennett OBE who had previously been in charge of training at Sandhurst. I got on very well with him; however, the other trainer was beginning to really annoy me with the way she was operating and I told my boss about it. He said to me that his hands were tied and that she had been promised a manager's job by his predecessors and couldn't renege from the issue. I must admit I was disgusted and should have taken it a stage further then. In the end, she was getting me down so much that going to work in the same office with her was becoming unbearable, so I decided to look for an opening back into training within the railway industry.

Mike Geall, one of my fellow trainers at the OTC Waterloo had started his own company 'South Coast Training' (SCT) and was on the lookout for people like myself. He came to see me one day at Mount Browne and convinced me that I'd be doing the right thing if I worked for him. I must admit the thought of only working 2-3 days a week for the same money as I was getting was enough to swing it. I handed in my notice much to everyone's surprise and left the following week, taking my leave as part of the month's notice. I wasn't at all happy though with the way I'd been treated and decided to put a letter of complaint into the Acting Chief Constable, explaining the reason of my departure.

I was now working two-to-three days a week for Mike Geall's South Coast Training company as a consultant providing Cab Secure Radio (CSR) training at Waterloo to signallers from different areas. Dave Webb had also left the railway by this time and came to work with me and it was just like old times. In the end though, the training did become a bit monotonous.

I still kept in touch with Ian Parrott, back at Surrey Police and found out that PC Merv Young had been tasked with assessing control room staff on the Crime Information System (CIS) and the Police National Computer (PNC). They must have said something to Tony Kennett that I'd been a bit bored recently because he phoned me on Friday 13th March asking me if I would do like to do some consultancy work for him back at Surrey Police. Luckily, I had nothing planned that day, as he wanted me to liaise with Merv that afternoon at Addlestone. The following Monday I was back at Mount Browne for ten days and the strange thing was that most people I met didn't even realise I'd gone. I still kept my same Force Identification number (FIN) and I was even able to logon to all my work that was still there after six months.

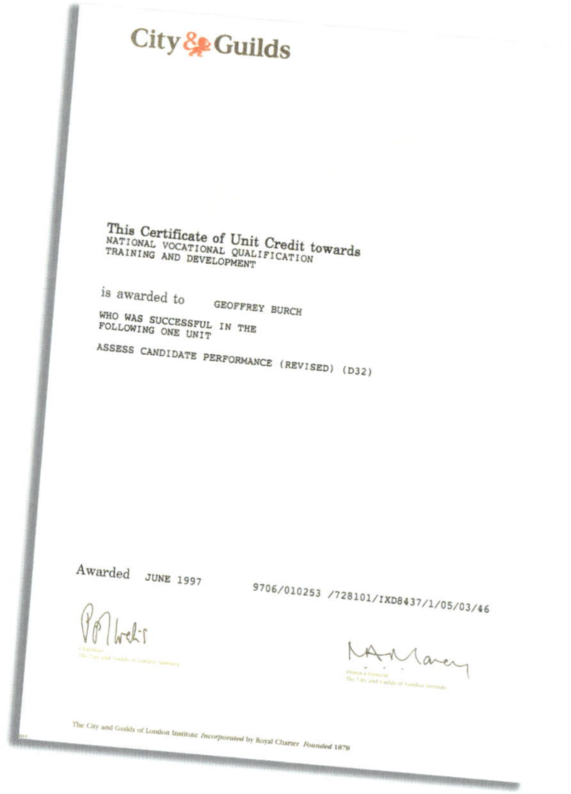
City & Guilds

This Certificate of Unit Credit towards
NATIONAL VOCATIONAL QUALIFICATION
TRAINING AND DEVELOPMENT

is awarded to GEOFFREY BURCH
WHO WAS SUCCESSFUL IN THE
FOLLOWING ONE UNIT

ASSESS CANDIDATE PERFORMANCE (REVISED) (D32)

Awarded JUNE 1997 9706/010253 /728101/IXD8437/1/05/03/46

The City and Guilds of London Institute Incorporated by Royal Charter Founded 1878

My first contract was for three months and it was at this time that Tony Kennett told me that he had felt very guilty about my previous exit and had 'pulled out all the stops' to get me back.

Above: City & Guilds D32 Certificate.

Below Left: South Coast Training Badge.

Below: Rank Structure of Surrey Police.

Graphics: The Author's Collection.

Anyway, I was back and enjoying every minute of it. Mike Geall was also very understanding and it was at this time I decided to further my education and enrolled on an evening City & Guilds course at Mike's SCT venue at Petersfield. I was duly awarded a City & Guilds NVQ D32 qualification that I knew I would need later. After my three-months contract was up, it was renewed again but by this time it had become evident that the whole force needed updating on the CIS system.

Malcolm Shuttleworth had taken over from Tony Kennett by this time and he desperately wanted me as a full-time employee, the job that I was doing on a contract came up and I was advised to apply for it. He had also worded the advertisement stating that only persons with a D32 qualification could apply.

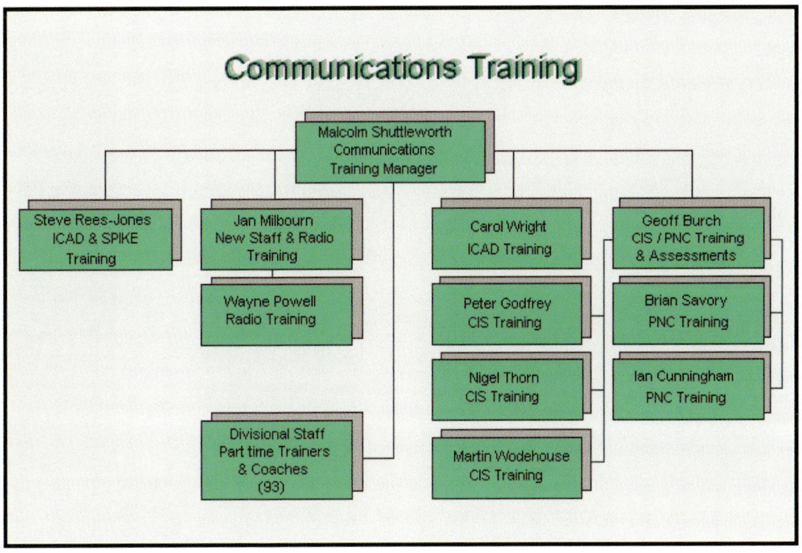

Above: Communications Training Structure.

Left: Jan Milbourn.

Below: Pete Godfrey.

Graphic & Photos: The Author's Collection.

The field was narrowed dramatically and I was invited for interview. I got the job and was back in full-time employment with Surrey Police although my base was now going to be at Addlestone.

It was there that I first met Jan Milbourn who was a student on one of the CIS courses I was running. Jan had been away from Surrey Police for a year on a career break and Malcolm desperately wanted her on his team.

Not long after that, Jan applied for a temporary job with us and shared our office at Addlestone. She was great fun to be with and not at all like the girl I worked with at Mount Browne.

Later on that year it was also decided to expand the department and I was joined by three police officers; Pete Godfrey being one of them. I had also carved a niche for myself at work with my computer skills and Malcolm put me in charge of quite a few projects. I designed and maintained the Human Resources (HR) website and had complete control over the re-certification process. This I did at home and gave me an extra day off a month. Another couple of trainers had now joined me and our department was really taking off.

Surrey Police Days

1st January 2000

The computers and clocks around the country didn't go berserk as predicted and the start of the year 2000 was much like any other year.

In our spare time, Ian Parrott and I had been working on a CBT rules package for train drivers in the hope of selling it to South West Trains, and we both went to a meeting at Basingstoke to meet Jim Rowe who was the Training Manager there.

He was quite impressed with the multiple choice graphics package and I was given the opportunity to have a further meeting with one of the SWT directors at Friars Bridge Court who was also suitably impressed. However, there had been two serious train crashes within the last two years (at Southall and Ladbroke Grove), which could have been prevented with the introduction of ATP (Automatic Train Protection) and because of this, all driver training was going through a strict overhaul. Unfortunately, this meant that our efforts to become future CBT programmers for SWT was in vain.

At work, I'd been given the job of designing and creating an HR intranet with a 'who's who?' element containing photographs of everyone within the HR department. This kept me pretty busy as I also had to take photographs of all of the staff.

I'd also been given the job of being the official photographer at all of the Surrey Police awards and ceremonies plus the Special Constabulary attestations.

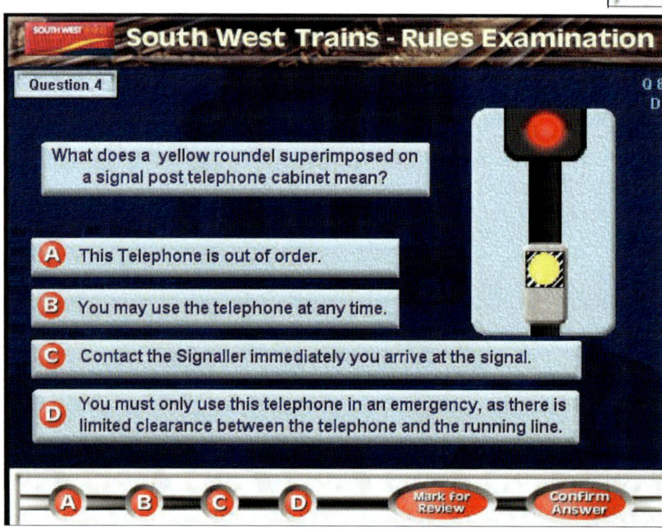

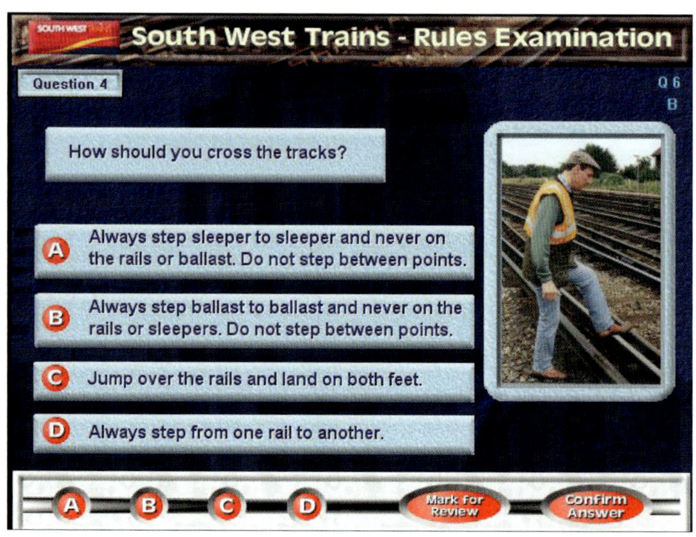

Above & Right: Part of the CBT Rules Examination package that Ian Parrott and I created to hopefully sell to South West Trains.

Graphics: The Author's Collection.

I was chatting to Ian Parrott one morning about training techniques regarding accident prevention, and mentioned that the best examples to give students were incidents that actually happened.

One of these was regarding a train crash at Guildford in 1952 and I'd used this example in the classroom a number of times when working at the OTC South Side.

The incident happened at Guildford involving a 2BIL EMU in a collision with a 700 Class locomotive, adjacent to Guildford Yard signalbox on the evening of Saturday 8th November 1952.

The collision was caused by an Ascot - Guildford service consisting of a 2BIL EMU that had left Wanborough station (its last station stop) and once over the top of the bank at Pinks Hill, ran down the descent to Guildford with insufficient air for the brakes to function properly.

Unable to stop at the outer home and home signal protecting the line ahead, the 2BIL EMU collided with a light engine that was just leaving Guildford for Woking; the impact of the force pushing it back some thirty yards.

There were sixty-five passengers on the train. Sadly, the driver of the EMU and one passenger were killed and a further thirty-seven passengers were hurt or suffered shock, six of whom were detained in hospital. The driver and fireman on the light engine were also slightly injured.

Ian recalled the incident as his father was the last person to see the driver before the fatal crash as he'd been the porter/signalman on duty at Wanborough station that night.

The cause of the accident was blamed on a compressor failure; the compressor governor fuse rupturing, probably before it left Ascot as a 2-car unit. The driver was completely unaware that by the time the train reached Guildford, there was little or no air left in the main reservoir and auxiliary reservoirs for the brakes to function.

One can only imagine the horror of what must have gone through the driver's mind after he had unsuccessfully tried to apply the brake as the train descended the 1 in 100 bank at a speed of 50 to 55 mph and then struck a locomotive coming the other way!

Following the outcome of the inquiry, a Control Circuit Governor (CCG) modification had to be fitted to this type of stock, so designed to ensure that there was sufficient air in the train pipe for brakes to be operative before a train could be moved in a forward direction and would also cut off power should the pressure fall below safe limits. The provision of this additional safeguard ensured that an accident of this type could never happen again.

Above: After its obligatory stop at Wanborough station, an Ascot - Aldershot - Guildford service (headcode 21) comprised of a 2HAL + 2BIL descends the 1 in 100 gradient to Guildford.

Below: X marks the spot of the approximate point of the collision at Guildford.

Photos: Les Mills Collection.

Above: Guildford driver Bill Phillips looks back for the tip from the Guard on 2BIL 2100 at Wokingham with a Reading bound service in June 1969. Bill doesn't have to look far as the guard is riding in the brake van directly behind him! The black inverted triangle on a yellow background gives a visual indication to platform staff which end of the train the guard's van is situated.

Photo: Tony Callaghan.

Below: This photo of hybrid 2-car 2133 was taken at Three Bridges on 25th May 1970; the motor coach was part of the unit involved in the runaway incident at Guildford on 8th November 1952 (as previously explained on previous page). It returned to traffic in 1955.

Photo: John Scrace.

Some six years later, Ian Verrinder (whom I'd worked with at the OTC South Side and was now working as a Traction Inspector for Eurostar) asked me if I was interested in a cab ride from Waterloo to Paris and return. Naturally I jumped at the chance. Brian Cook, who had also worked with me at the OTC South Side came with us that day.

The trip was to be duly sanctioned by Eurostar and we would be accompanied by Ian throughout.

The big day arrived and we both met Ian at Waterloo who guided us through Customs and to the front of the train. As it turned out, the driver who was working the turn was Bernie Knibbs whom I'd worked with in my firing days at Guildford and in my driving days at Woking, so I couldn't have been in better company!

We left Waterloo and just before Queenstown Road branched off the Windsor Line and over the flyover past Stewarts Lane Depot towards Factory Junction. We then continued down the South Eastern main lines towards Tonbridge, Ashford and onwards towards the entrance to the Channel Tunnel. On this part of the journey, the power supplying the traction units was being supplied by the SR conductor rail system, however just before we entered the tunnel, the pantograph was raised and our power was then obtained via the overhead catenary wire.

This was my first trip under the 'chunnel' and I was surprised to find how quickly we arrived on French soil. There are no conventional signals on the High Speed Line and the maximum speed is 300kph (186mph). The timetable is loaded in to the signalling system and if the train is on time the route will open a short time before the train arrives. If the train is running late the signaller will have to set the route themselves. The maximum permitted speed for each section of the route are programmed into the system and so the appropriate speed will be automatically displayed to the driver when the route opens.

Above: Speedometer reading just below 300kph (186mph).

Photos: The Author's Collection.

Above: Driver's view from the front of a Eurostar. The paper directly in front of the driver is the 'Fiche Train' which is a timing sheet. It shows passing times and stations as you would expect. Interestingly, it also shows a recommended average speed between given points. This can be used if the train is running to time and will ensure the train keeps time without using more electricity than is absolutely necessary.

Obviously, the recommended average speed will never be higher than the permissible speed. The sheet also shows coasting points. The folders on the desk are the communications forms that are used between the signaller and driver during out-of-course events. Generally there is one folder for each network through which the train runs. The note pad is to record information that may be required in a report. The screen with the keyboard is the fault-finding computer. The train's speed is just under the maximum permitted speed (300kph) as can be seen by the inset photo.

The Signaller can close the route if they need to and whenever this is done the signalling automatically blocks back. The closer the train is to the stopping point dictates what indication the driver sees. If the train is far enough away (around 7 km) the driver will see a normal stopping sequence, but if the train is within 7 km the driver will get an abnormal indication. If the train is in the closed section then the driver will get the famous 'rouge-cabine' (red indication).

After arriving at Paris Gare-Du-Nord station, we went for a bite to eat in a restaurant in the street outside and then walked to the Square Louise Michel below the Basilique Sacre Coeur which is famous for its street artists. However, our return journey beckoned and we left Paris to return to London Waterloo. A truly excellent day out!

Below: The tunnel portals (French side).

Below Bottom: It's nearly starting time for the return trip and a chance for a group photograph by the side of the Class 373 Eurostar at Paris Gare-Du-Nord station before departure for Waterloo.

Photos: The Author's Collection.

The following year, another trip presented itself - this time from Waterloo to Brussels. On this occasion I was joined by Ian Parrott, only this time with a different Eurostar driver. Bernie Knibbs (the driver on my previous trip in the cab of a Eurostar to Paris) was on a different duty and as we headed towards Lille, Bernie approached us in the other direction at a combined speed of over 450kph! It was another fantastic opportunity for both Ian and I to see France and Belgium from the sharp end of a Eurostar!

Right: Ian Parrott stands alongside Class 373 3223 before leaving Brussels for London Waterloo.

Photo: The Author's Collection.

Above: On my second trip (to Brussels) in 2001, we make a high speed pass at a combined speed of 450-500kph; the driver of the train passing us is Bernie Knibbs (the driver that I was with on the previous year's trip to Paris).
The photograph clearly shows the zigzag pattern of the overhead wire. As the contact wire makes contact with the pantograph, the carbon insert on top of the pantograph is worn down. Going around a curve, the 'straight' wire between supports will cause the contact wire to cross over the whole surface of the pantograph as the train travels around the curve, causing uniform wear and avoiding any notches. Therefore on straight track the contact wire is zigzagged slightly to the left and right of centre at each successive support so that the pantograph wears evenly.

Photo: The Author's Collection.

Surrey Police Days

During my eleven years with Surrey Police, I'd moved around the county, training at Banstead, Dorking, Godstone, Guildford, Godalming, Staines, Camberley, Farnham, Woking, Addlestone and Headquarters at Mount Browne and had moved offices seven times. I'd also had ten different job titles in that time and was at the limit of my salary band. Unfortunately, I can't divulge most of my work within Surrey Police as I'm bound by the Official Secrets Act but can honestly say that I enjoyed the time that I worked there.

However, although I enjoyed my job, I still had a passion for railways and still kept in touch with some of my old railway colleagues. One of these was David Timothy who had been a fellow Instructor at the OTC South Side. He'd had a number of jobs within the railway industry and was now working for South West Trains at their Training Centre at Basingstoke.

He asked me if I'd be interested in joining him there as there was a vacancy for a trainer. The temptation was too great so I visited the Training Centre and met Roger Luckins (who was then the Operations Training Manager). I'd also worked with Roger when he was a trainer at the OTC South Side. I was extremely tempted by his offer - the salary was far more than I was receiving from Surrey Police and it also offered free first-class travel on SWT for myself and my wife. Over the following weekend, I created my CV and sent it in with the application form. A couple of weeks went by and I was invited to attend an interview (which was more of a screening process) and I was offered the job.

I was working at Addlestone Police station at the time and with some reluctance, tendered my resignation. I had to work a month's notice but some of this time was used up as annual leave.

It was a sad day when I left as I'd made a lot of friends in the police service. I'd also gained a tremendous amount of knowledge regarding computer systems and how to interrogate databases; held certificates for Module 1 & Module 2 courses on PNC & IT Training and had been Secretary of the Surrey Police Fly Fishing Team and Chairman of the Clay Target Shooting Team. It seemed really strange walking past Woking police station to the railway station to start my first day at work for South West Trains.

Above: Ten Surrey Police job titles in eleven years!

Below: Surrey Police Support Services staff (of which I was part) at a conference at Barnett Hill, Wonersh.

Photo: The Author's Collection.

Above: Class 73/2 electro-diesel No. 73201, one of South West Trains' rescue locomotives, berthed on Hurdles Road Siding, Woking. Previously numbered 73142 and named 'Broadlands' this locomotive hauled the Royal Train carrying Prince Charles and Princess Diana from Waterloo - Romsey for their honeymoon at Broadlands in 1981.

Photo: Mike Knell - Wikipedia.

Below: Train Protection & Warning System (TPWS) panel and below that the Driver's Reminder Appliance (DRA) button. The button, when set, will ensure that a driver is unable to move the train (or in this case locomotive) until the button is reset. Drivers are instructed to always use the device when stopped at a signal at danger to prevent a SPAD (signal passed at danger).

Photo: Courtesy of South West Trains.

I started working for South West Trains at the Operations Training Centre at Basingstoke on Monday 5th September 2005 and this began with a week's Induction at Basingstoke station. There were several other people on the course coming from all walks of life and completely unfamiliar with the railway industry.

The following week I had a 'crash course' on Rules and Regulations but was able to get this under my belt quite quickly because of my previous knowledge.

One of the 'hooks' to make me join SWT was Roger Luckins' promise that I would be involved in training drivers on Class 73 locomotives. SWT had three of these locomotives and were used as 'Thunderbirds' based at various locations should there be a problem with trains and assistance being required. They were also used by drivers at Wimbledon Park and Bournemouth depot for shunting purposes.

On 15th September I revised on the subject ready to 'sit in' on a Class 73 course the following week. At the start of the course, the trainer who should have been running the course was off sick so I had conduct the course myself!

As there were only minor changes to the cab layout - Driver's Reminder Appliance (DRA) and Train Protection & Warning System TPWS) plus slight differences to the braking system, this wasn't a problem and I continued running the course with my old pal Chris Lemon (from earlier instructing days at OTC South Side) running the driving instruction part of the course.

The Train Protection & Warning System (TPWS) is a train protection system throughout the two UK passenger main-line railway networks. It automatically activates brakes on a train that has passed a signal at danger or is overspeeding.

Unlike Automatic Train Protection (ATP), it does not aim to stop trains at or before a signal that is at danger - it aims to stop the train before the point at which a collision with another train could occur, excluding rear-end collision with a train in front. According to the Health and Safety Executive, it is estimated to prevent between 65% and 80% of fatalities that would be stopped by a full ATP system.

Training Days - South West Trains

The following week, Brian Cook (who was then in charge of Operational Standards at Friars Bridge Court), came down to Woking and assessed my knowledge of the Class 73 locomotive that was berthed on Hurdles Road siding and for the next month I was booked to learn routes to London, Bournemouth and Poole and from Basingstoke to Salisbury.

On 31st October, I travelled to Wimbledon Park depot with another of my old pals whom I worked with at OTC South Side, Dave Webb, and he assessed me on my knowledge of Class 455 units. This also wasn't a problem for me as I had kept all of my training notes when I left the OTC South Side back in 1994.

My next job was to train some of the depot drivers at Wimbledon Park and the driving instruction was performed in the sidings at Durnsford Road.

This was followed by a further course for Wimbledon and Bournemouth drivers at Basingstoke for the classroom instruction followed by practical instruction with booked training trips from Bournemouth depot - Poole - Eastleigh and return utilising 4VEP 3417 *'Gordon Pettitt'* (named after former General Manager of the Southern Region of British Rail) as part of the train.

As part of my ongoing personal development, I was given the task of updating the Class 73 Faults & Failures book and Handout for drivers which I completed in December 2005.

Above: Class 73 training trip with Driver Chris Randall from Wimbledon at the controls.

Below: Driver Neil Larby from Woking gets ready to apply the brake as we approach Bournemouth on the training trip.

Photos: The Author's Collection.

The first week in January saw me return to Bournemouth to train two depot drivers only to find that the locomotive had been left on a non-electrified siding and the batteries were flat. They didn't have any other means of towing the locomotive over a siding with a conductor rail (had this been possible, I could have pumped the shoes down onto the conductor rail and re-charged the battery). Instead, we had to delay the start of the course until the following day.

On the 16th January, I again worked with Dave Webb helping him with a Class 455 course which was particularly enjoyable being back with my old workmate.

On the 23rd January, I sat in on a ten-day Class 159 course at Salisbury and because of the logistics of the static instruction, a meeting room at the back of the Train Crew Supervisor's office was utilised for the classroom training. The static instruction was carried out in the Traincare depot and driving instruction was carried out utilising a service train from Salisbury - Waterloo and return to Salisbury. This was repeated with a further course conducted by myself two weeks later. For my 60th birthday, I had planned a holiday to New Zealand so I didn't return to work until 13th March where I picked up another Class 73 Course.

Roger Luckins and I had a meeting to discuss my concerns regarding the quality of training at the Operations and Safety Training Centre at Basingstoke so it was agreed that I should run a 'Core Trainers Skills' course for some of the Trainers. This was similar to the one that I'd been on at the Management Training Centre at Watford some years previously, and this was completed at the end of March with considerable success.

Phil Eke (who also worked within Operational Standards, Friars Bridge Court then taught me all that was needed to know regarding the four simulators that had been installed at the Operations and Safety Training Centre which were used for extensive driver training. The Simulators had been built by Krauss-Maffei Wegmann (KMW) a German company and simulated the driving controls of the new SWT fleet of Desiro units. It was also agreed that I take on the role of being the O&STC's representative of the Simulator User Group that met at various location around the country.

The first meeting that I attended was at Ashford where I met Mark Medley who had also been a trainer at OTC South Side whilst I was there.

Above Right: Class 73/2 electro-diesel shoegear showing the shoes on the conductor rail.

Below: Bournemouth DSM Richard Trellis arrives at Poole station with the training trip for Eastleigh and return.

Photos: Courtesy of South West Trains and the Author's Collection.

Above: After instruction, Bournemouth DSM Richard Trellis demonstrates the dual control capabilities of the Class 73/2 electro-diesel locomotive to fellow DSM Steve Smith during the training trip to Eastleigh. A button on the end of the electric controller would have to be depressed to allow access to the 'Run-Up' positions on the controller (SER (Series) PAR (Parallel) WF (Weak Field) which would provide current to the traction motors under the control of the CLR (Current Limit Relay).

Access to these 'Run Up' positions could only be gained from the driver's side. A more detailed explanation of the controls can be found further on page 258.

Photo: The Author's Collection.

Training Days - South West Trains

In March 2007, David Timothy had to travel over to the Isle of Wight to assess a Driver Instructor. As I'd been involved in Class 483 training before (as mentioned in a previous chapter), I accompanied him.

The aged Class 483 units (originally built in 1938 for London Underground) were extensively refurbished between 1989 and 1992 at Eastleigh Works, nonetheless the seventy-odd year-old units remain the oldest trains operating in service in Great Britain! Note the copious use of gaffer tape in this photo of the Author at the controls!

These units are equipped with two braking systems - Electro-Pneumatic (EP) and a Westinghouse Automatic Air Brake (should the EP system fail).

The 'deadman' must be held down with a constant pressure at all times that the train is moving. Should the driver become incapacitated at any time, the automatic air brake will apply the brakes and power to the traction motors will be cut thus bringing the train to a stop. The duplex gauge to the left of the cab indicates brake pipe and main reservoir pressures and the gauge above shows brake cylinder pressure (up to 50psi) when the brakes are applied. Apart from having different liveries, they hadn't really changed.

Above: The approach to Shanklin station.

Left: Class 483 in original livery passes through Smallbrook Junction station on its way to Shanklin.

Below: The other end of the line at Ryde Pier Head on a wet and windy day.

Photos: The Author's Collection.

Opposite Page: The Author driving from Shanklin to Ryde Pier Head.

Photo: David Timothy.

David Timothy under instruction from the Driver Instructor.

David Timothy about to board Class 483 008 at Ryde Pier Head for the return trip.

Photos: The Author's Collection.

Training Days - South West Trains

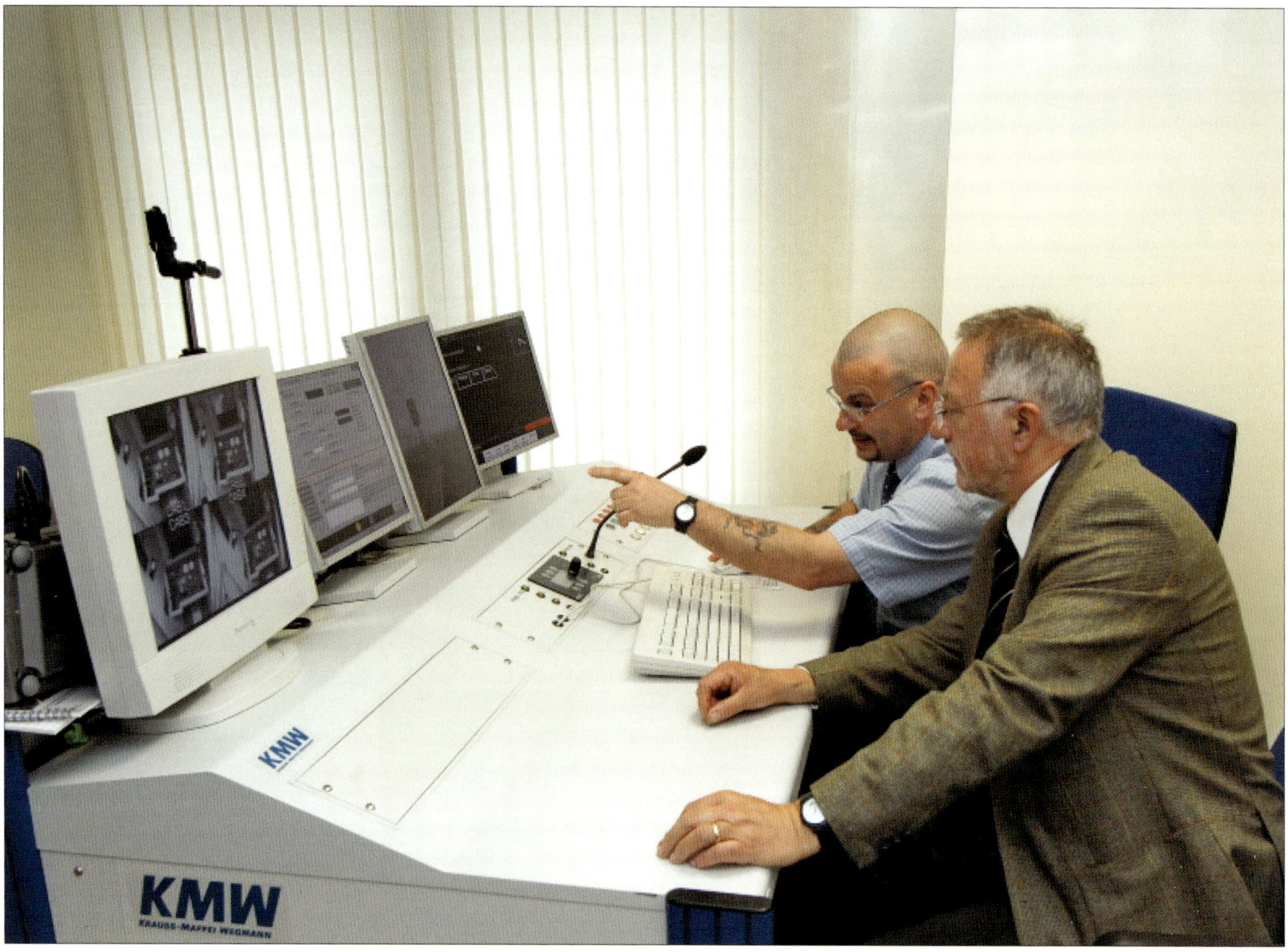

Above: Trainer Dave Webb and Senior Trainer Chris Lemon at one of the two KMW simulator consoles at the Operations & Safety Training Centre, Spring Park House, Basingstoke.

Below: A trainee in one of the four 'Desiro' simulator cabs that can be run simultaneously with four separate trainees. Apart from driving technique, a whole range of faults could be simulated to test the trainee's reactions.

Safety Critical Communication

Correct Cab Procedures

Above: Correct cab procedures and safety critical radio communication in action.

Below: One of four 'Desiro' simulator cabs that can be run simultaneously.

Photos: The Author's Collection.

Training Days - South West Trains

Above: A trio of Class 159 'Sprinters' outside Salisbury Traincare Depot.

Below: Class 159/1 'Sprinter' 159102 inside Salisbury Traincare Depot.

Photos: The Author's Collection.

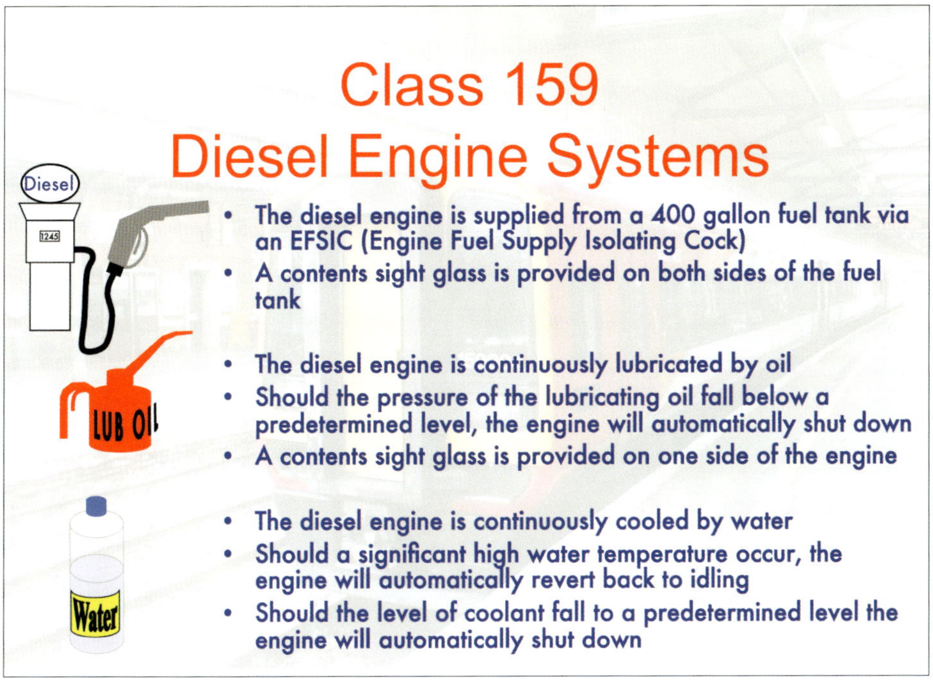

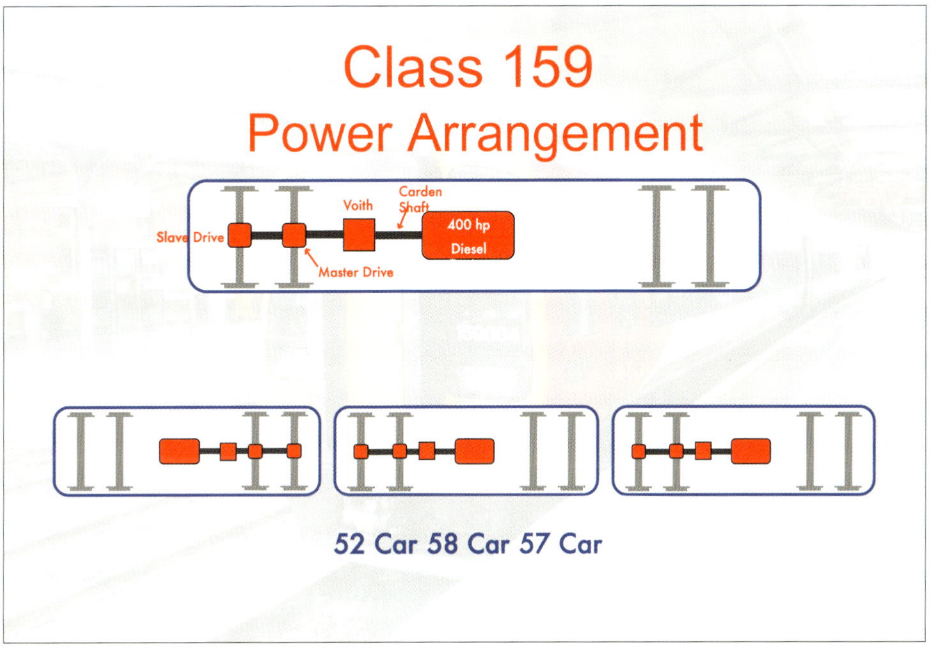

Above: Fuel, Oil and Water.

Right: Diagram of Class 159 power arrangement.

Below: Diagram of Class 159 Hydrostatic system.

Graphics: Courtesy of South West Trains.

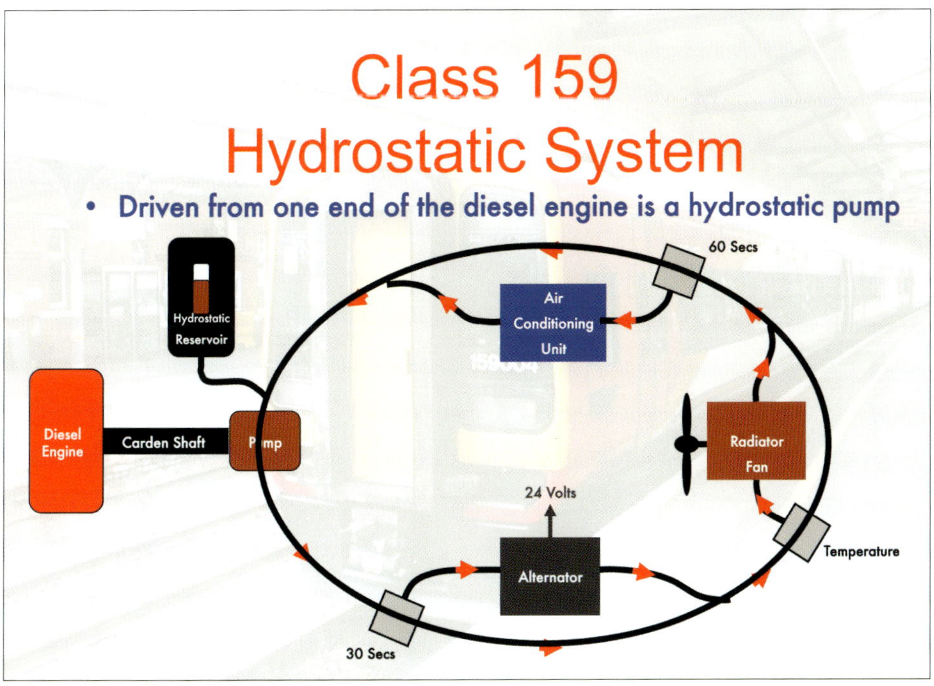

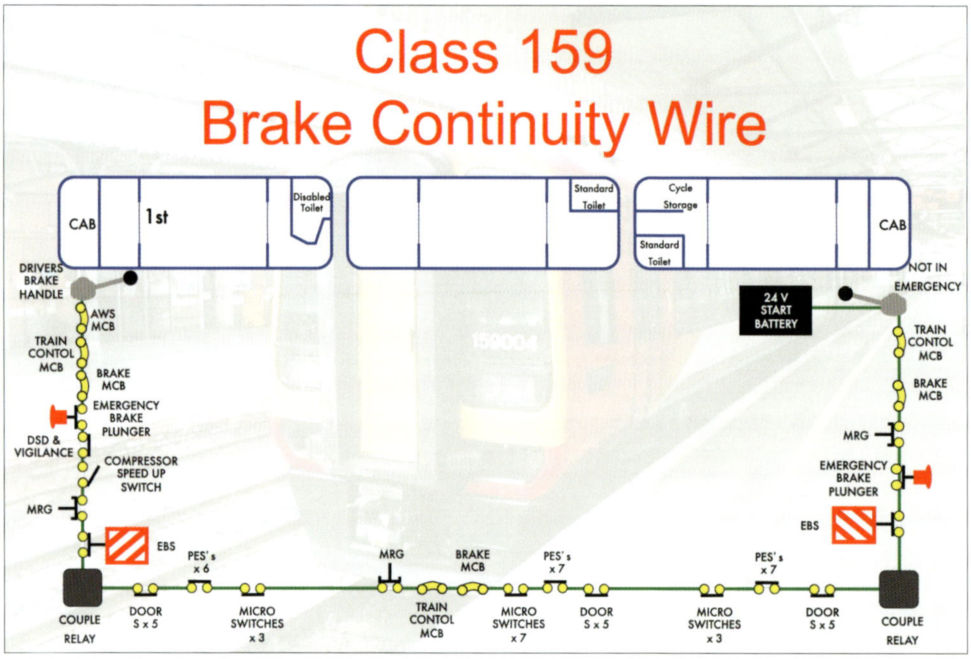

Above: Diagram of Class 159 Continuity Wire.

Right: Diagram of Class 159 Exterior Identification.

Below: Diagram of Class 159 Traction Interlock.

Graphics: Courtesy of South West Trains.

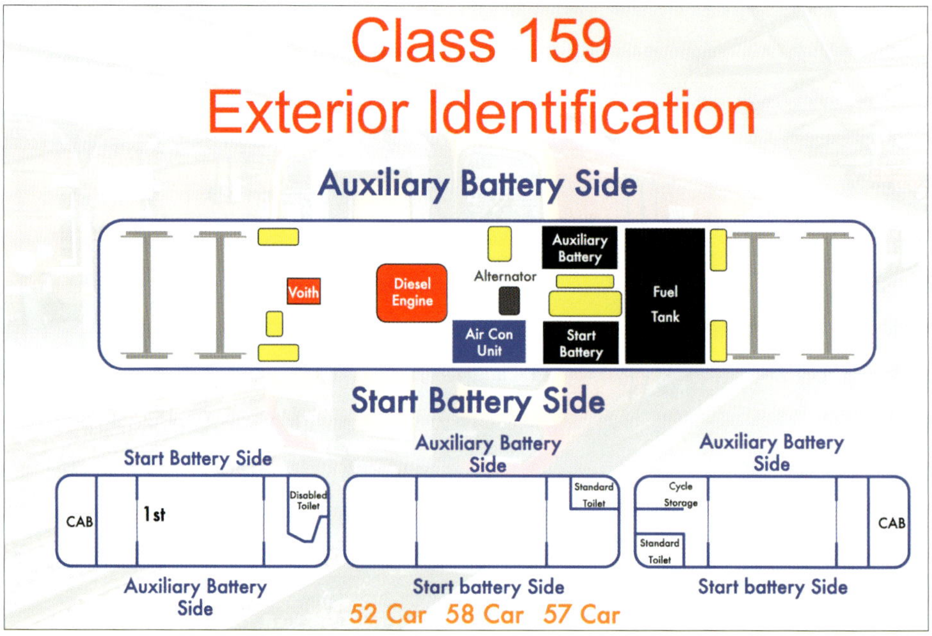

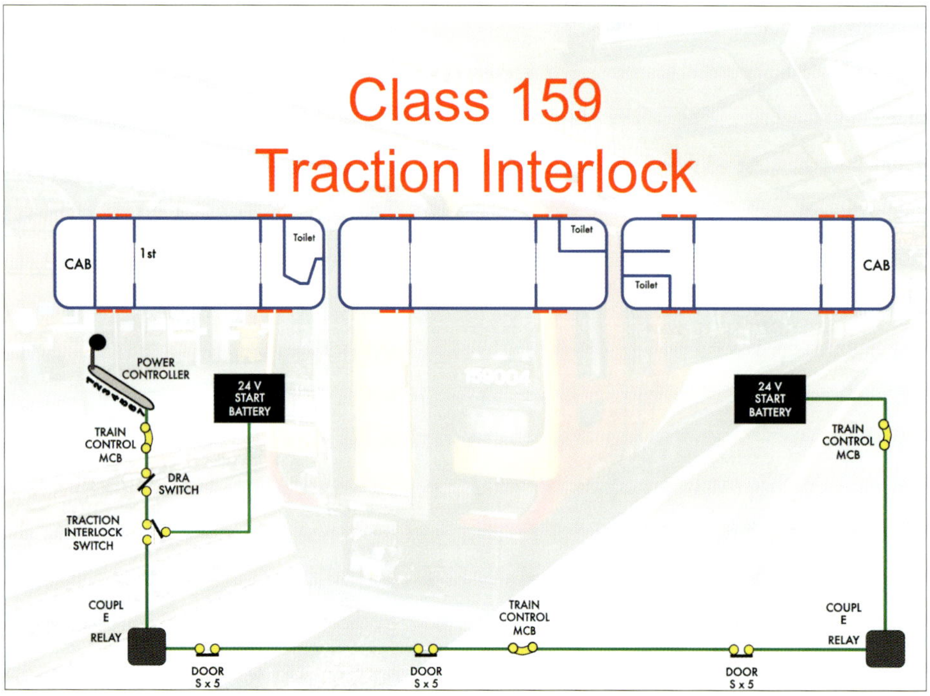

Above: Class 159/1 'Sprinter' 159007 leaves Waterloo with an Salisbury service in July 2008.

Below: Class 159 'Sprinter' 159011 runs into Basingstoke with a Salisbury - Waterloo service in September 2008.

Photos: The Author's Collection.

Above: Class 73/1 No. 73109 'Battle of Britain' passes Campbell Road Bridge with the 5Z99 12.48 Eastleigh to Bournemouth Depot.

The stock comprising 3CIG 1498 'Farringford' and 3CIG 1497 'Freshwater' were being turned via Fareham to help preserve the wheel life and even out the wear.

Photo: Richard Sulzmann.

Class 455 Identification.

Above: Class 455 (57xx).

Left: Class 455 (58xx).

Below: Class 455 (59xx).

Photos: Courtesy of South West Trains and the Author's Collection.

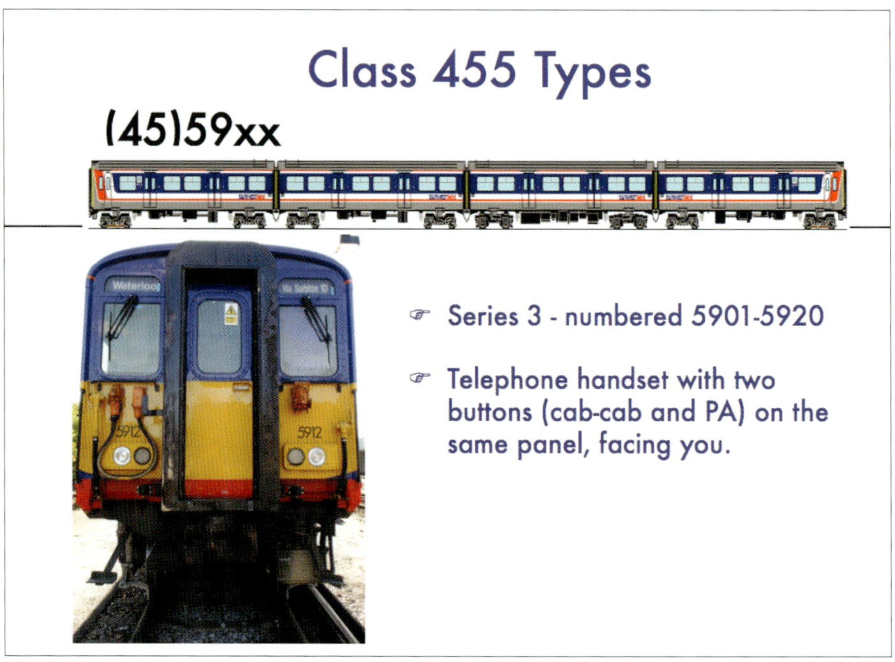

During June, South West Trains drivers called for industrial action which meant that as managers, my colleagues and I were expected to take on the role of driver or guard during the time the drivers were on strike. By this time it had been realised that I'd not received a full medical examination so I had to visit the SWT Medical Centre at Friars Bridge Court.

Three of us went for a medical that day and imagine my surprise when my cardiogram results came back as having an irregular heartbeat! I was put in the restricted category which meant that I couldn't drive trains until I'd been passed fit.

A week later, I attended a cardiology appointment at Harley Street and saw Dr Foale, a Consultant Cardiologist. I was wired up and put on a 'treadmill' for 30 minutes to perform checks on my heart. The following week I had to return and was fitted with a heart monitor for 24 hours taking the results back to Harley Street the following day. The following week, my wife Pauline and I went into the surgery again and Dr Foale said "There's nothing wrong - you've got the heart of an athlete" to which Pauline replied "shame he hasn't got the body of one." This amused everyone except myself!

Above: Connections between 455 units: control jumper, main reservoir air pipes and tightlock coupler.

Photo: The Author's Collection.

Below: Class 455 desk and driving controls:

1. Train Protection & Warning System (TPWS) Panel 2. 3-Step Brake Controller 3. Drivers' Reminder Appliance (DRA) 4. Emergency Bypass Switch (EBS) 5. Main Res. / Brake Cylinder Pressure Gauge 6. Emergency Brake Button 7. Speedo 8. Line Indicator 9. Automatic Warning System (AWS) Indicator 10. Motor Alternator(MA) Indicator 11. Uncouple Button (with safety flap) 12. Power Controller 13. Master Switch.

Photo: The Author's Collection.

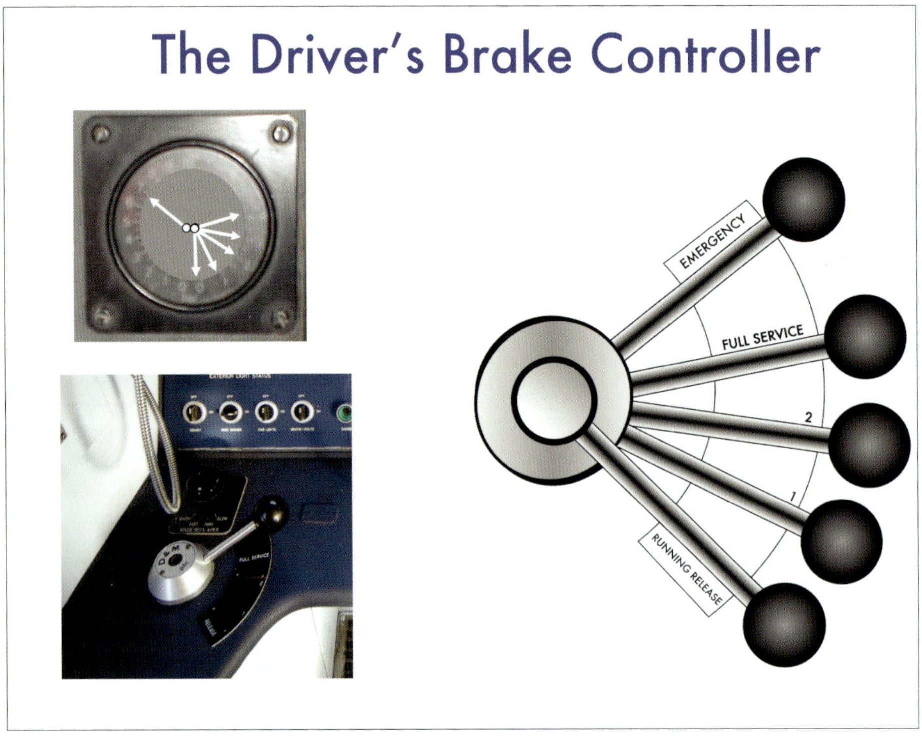

Above: Positions of the 3-Step brake and its relative bar pressure in the brake cylinders.

Below: Class 455 Brake Continuity Wire.

Photos and Graphics: David Timothy.

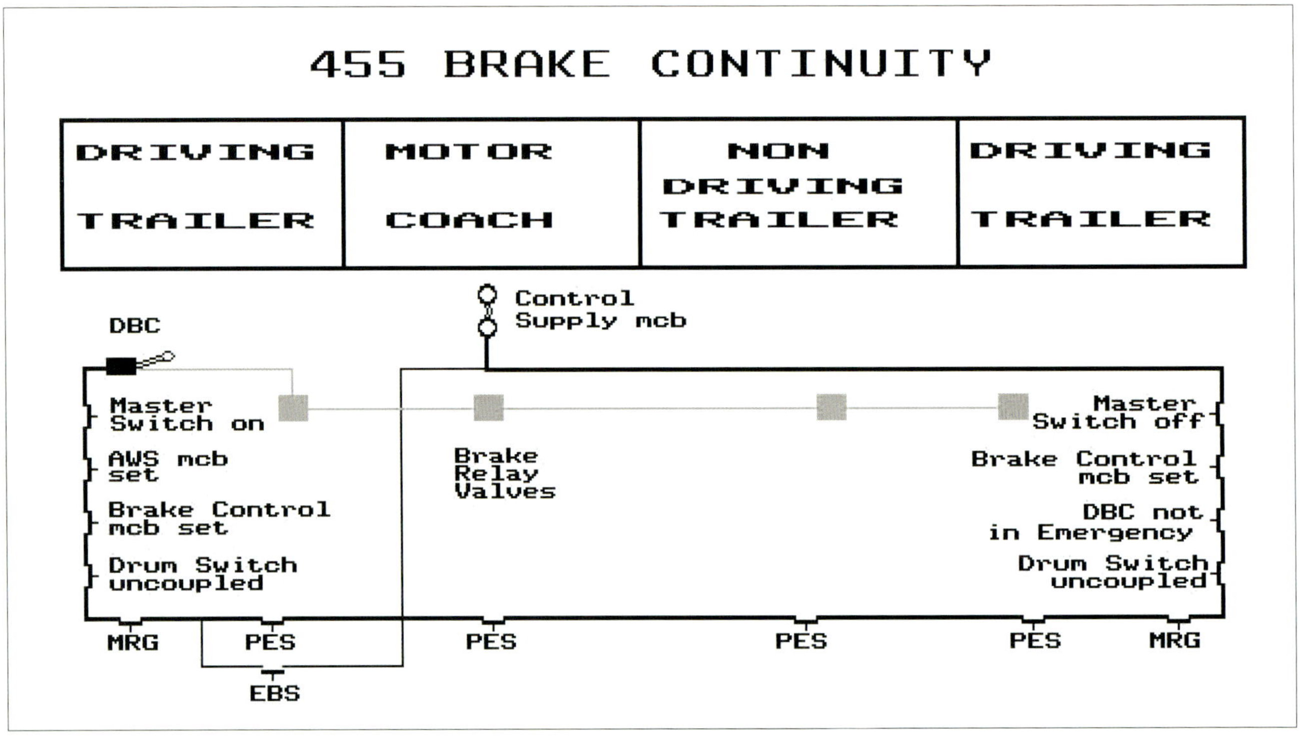

Above: Unlike the Electro-pneumatic brake fitted to slam-door stock (that failed to apply should there not be an electrical supply), the Brake Continuity Wire works in the opposite way in the fact that an electrical supply is required throughout the train to allow the brake to be released.
The supply is fed from Control Supply mcb to the rear of the train's rear cab and through a series of equipment that must be set in the correct position e.g. in the rear cab: Master switch at OFF, Brake Control mcb set, Driver's Brake Controller (DBC) not in Emergency, Drum Switch in the Uncoupled position. All Passenger Emergency Switches (PES) must be in their correct positions throughout the train.
Front Cab: Emergency Bypass Switch (EBS) at normal, Main Reservoir Governor (MRG) set, Drum Switch in the Uncoupled position, Brake Control mcb set, AWS mcb set, Master Switch at ON and the Driver's Brake Controller (DBC) at any position other than Emergency. Any one of these safety devices not being in their correct position will keep the brake applied throughout the train.

Left: Motor Alternator providing a 3-Phase output - 415 volts (AC) for heating fans (including cab fans) - 240 volts for main lighting - 110 volts (DC) for control circuits and battery charging.

Right: MA Indicator on the cab panel. Should the MA fault light extinguish in the cab, a 110 volt supply will still remain available from the battery (or another unit if in multiple).

Below: Class 455 Control Supply circuit providing a 110 volt supply via the Control Supply mcb to each cab for Control, AWS, Brake Supply, Door Control and Compressor Control.

Photos and Graphic: Courtesy of South West Trains and David Timothy.

MA Fault Light

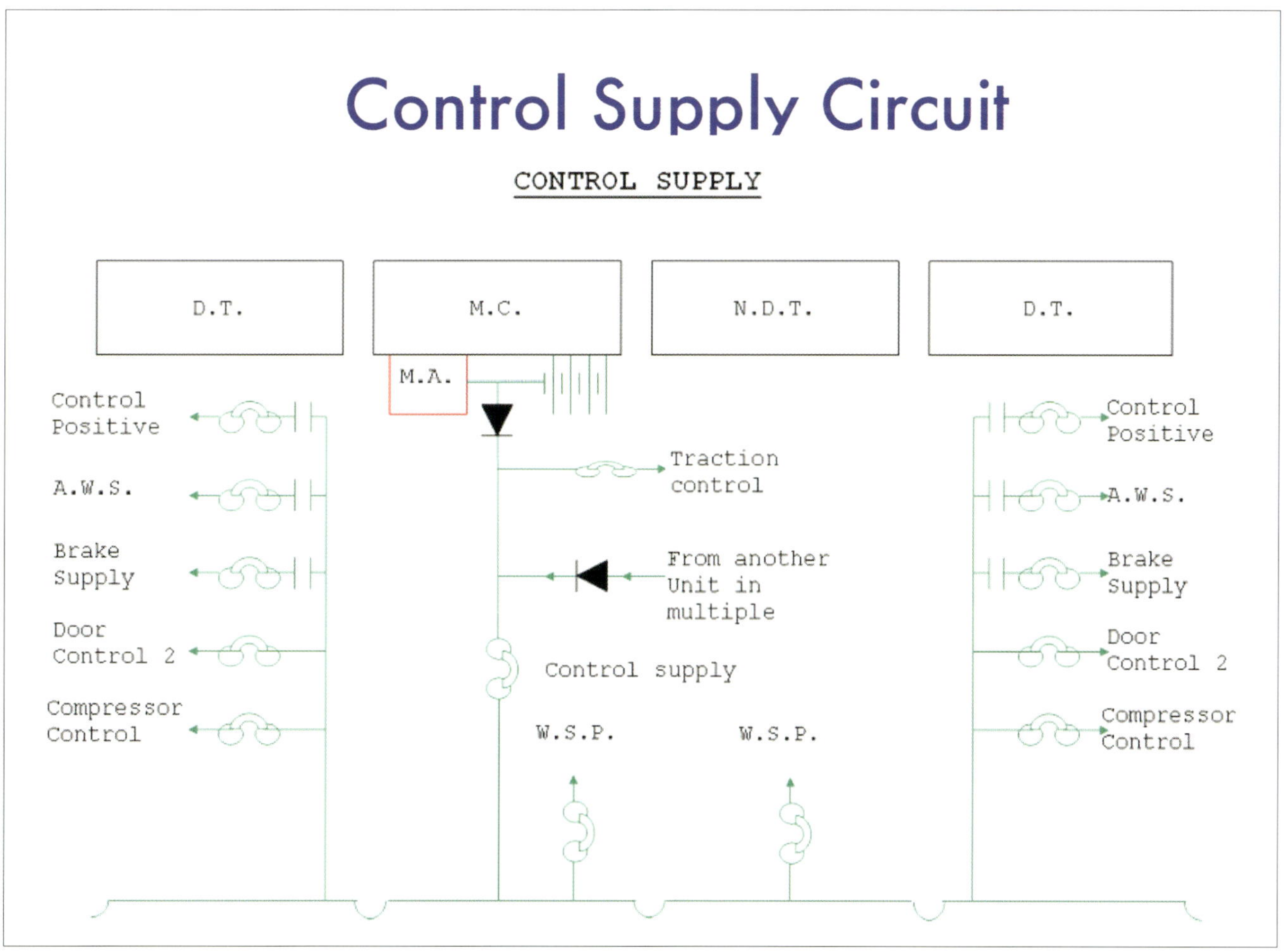

Training Days - South West Trains

By the end of the month I was pronounced A1 and fit for driving again and on the 29th August when SWT drivers had another day's strike, I worked my first train as a driver - this being on my own in a driving cab since I was an Acting Instructor back in 1986. I was booked four trips from Waterloo - Hampton Court and return with a Class 455 but didn't have to work the last trip as it would have necessitated a taxi home.

For the rest of the year I was kept busy assisting other trainers on various courses or on the Simulator and attending the occasional Simulator User Group meetings, one of which was held at Virgin Trains at Crewe.

During my 'one to one' meeting with Roger Luckins, he informed me that he had been offered a position with the RSSB (Rail Safety & Standards Board) and asked me if I'd like to take on the temporary role of Assistant Operations & Training Manager which I gladly accepted. This again meant that I had to take on a lot more responsibility not only for the running of the Training Centre but also the staff within.

During January 2007, I was booked to conduct another Class 159 course at Salisbury and attended another SUG meeting at Ashford. Some of the items under discussion were as follows:

- Global System for Mobile Communication (GSMR) Changeover - when?
- Who is paying?
- What contingency plans are in place?
- Energy Efficiency presentation from the Association of Train Operating Companies (ATOC) - £400m - 500m traction energy bill and 25% energy bill needs to be saved.
- Economy Driving technique
- Hybrid Drives
- Regenerative Braking
- Intelligent engine control
- Fuel additives

The User Group endorsed the ECO driving approach and should champion this cause.

I had to attend quite a lot of other meetings at Friars Bridge Court regarding training and also resource planning meetings every month with the Head of drivers held at the O&STC at

Basingstoke.

Following Roger's secondment to the RSSB, it became apparent that he wouldn't be returning so it was decided that Chris Lemon and I should jointly run the O&STC (Chris being in charge of the trainer's competencies) and that I should be in charge of the everyday running of the establishment. However, we would both have responsibility for conducting performance reviews on staff at the O&TSC and on 12th February, we both moved into what was Roger's office.

Apart from Chris and myself, there were thirteen other trainers at Springpark House, some of which I'd worked with at OTC South Side - namely: Chris Foot, Tim Reynolds, Dave Webb and David Timothy.

The other trainers were: Jerry Bond, Pat Gray, Nicky Harris, Paul Wallis, Lionel Stevenson, Dennis Birch, Jez Morgan, Andy Nash, Nigel Trower and Peter Connolly.

Above: Chris Lemon - the blind leading the blind!

Left: Trainer Jez Morgan updating his course notes.

Photos: The Author's Collection.

OPERATIONS & SAFETY TRAINING ROSTER SPRINGPARK HOUSE BASINGSTOKE

AMENDED ROSTER CHANGES IN RED	20-May-07	21-May-07	22-May-07	23-May-07	24-May-07	25-May-07	26-May-07
Senior Trainer							
Geoff Burch		FBC	Duty Manager	Duty Manager	FBC	Team Brief	
Chris Lemon		Duty Manager	Dave Webb Rules/Regs	Office	FBC	Team Brief	
Duty Manager							
Geoff Burch		Office	Office	Office	See below	Team Brief	
Operational Training							
Jerry Bond		Sit in/Assist BGC2	Driver Final P Fenn Wim pk	Driver Final P Fenn Wim pk	Driver Final P Fenn Wim pk	Team Brief	
Dennis Birch		DI Course 6	DI Course 7	DI Course 8	Duty Manager	Team Brief	
Chris Foot		BGC3 1	BGC3 2	BGC3 3*	BGC3 4	Team Brief	
Pat Gray			BGC 2 Guard's 458	BGC 2 Guard's 458	PTS Ref	Team Brief	
Nicky Harris		Dvrs CL458 (2)	Dvrs CL458 (2)	Dvrs CL458 (2)	Dvrs CL458 (2)	Assess CL458 (1)	
Andy Nash		Dvrs CL458 (1)	Dvrs CL458 (1)	Dvrs CL458 (1)	Dvrs CL458 (1)	Assess CL458 (2)	
Tim Reynolds		Meeting with Phil Eke	DI Rides	DI Rides	DI Rides	Team Brief	
David Timothy		Dave Webb Rules/Regs	FBC	AL	FBC	AL	
Paul Wallis		AL	AL	AL	AL	AL	
Dave Webb		Rules/Regs	Rules/Regs	DI Rides	Assess DI Course	Medical 09:00 + Team Brief	
Safety Training							
Peter Connolly		PTS 1	PTS 2	Induction	Safety Induction	Team Brief	
Jez Morgan		Stn Mngr Familiarisation	E-Learning Mtg	Station Managers Safety Refresher	E-Learning Mtg	Team Brief	
Route Manager							
Nigel Trower		BGC2 28*	Assist PTS	BGC 2 Guard's 458	BGC 2 Guard's 458	Team Brief	
Room Allocation							
Avon (12)			<---DSM Presentation Skills Sharon-->		DSM Course	DSM Course	
Hamble (12)			Dvr Company Day	Dvr Company Day	DSM Course	DSM Course	
Itchen (12)		PTS	PTS	Station Managers Safety Refresher	PTS Ref		
Kennett (14)		BGC3	BGC3	Induction	BGC3	Team Brief	
Lymington (12)		Jez Mtg	Jez Mtg		Safety Induction		
Stour (8/16 Mtg)			Gds Company Day	Gds Company Day	Gds Company Day		
Thames (10)			Gds Company Day	Gds Company Day	Gds Company Day	DI Course (L12)	<---(Buffet for 4)
East Wing							
Nadder (1)							
Wandle (1)							
Wey - Sims (12)			Mary Stevens		Jez Mtg		
Wylye Sims - (10)			D Webb/Jiffy Rules/Regs		John Allan		

Above: Operations & Safety Training Roster - May 2007.

Right: Chris Lemon practises his dentistry skills on Chris Foot as we couldn't give Chris any time off to visit the dentist!

Photos: The Author's Collection.

I had also been given the job of updating the 159/1 driver handout as some of the fleet were being refurbished and I subsequently went to Derby to take photographs of the changes made.

In April, David Timothy and I attended a course at Petersfield to attain our L9 and L10 qualifications which form part of the Level 3 NVQ process, and in May, Chris Lemon and I carried out assessments on each other to ensure our driving and guards' competencies were up to the standard required. We did this by taking over a stopping service from Woking - Waterloo (Class 455), working another service from Waterloo M - Waterloo W (via Kingston) to keep our route knowledge up to date and finally working another stopping service from Waterloo - Woking (taking it in turns to perform the driver and guards' duties).

Training Days - South West Trains

Tim Reynolds

Andy Nash

Chris Foot

Dave Webb

Jerry Bond

Nigel Trower

Jez Morgan

Lionel Stevenson

Paul Wallis

Above and on Opposite Page: Trainers at the Operations & Safety Training Centre in 2007.

Opposite Page: Christmas graphic displayed on the students' lounge's plasma screen with Roger Luckins shown as Santa with his willing helpers at the time - Kevin, Paul, Andy, Codge, Julian, Beverley, Peter, Jerry, David, Chris, Dennis, Nigel, Geoff, Nicky, Chris, Pat and Dave.

Graphic: The Author's Collection.

Nicky Harris *Pat Gray* *Peter Connolly*

Chris Lemon *Dennis Birch* *David Timothy*

Training Days - South West Trains

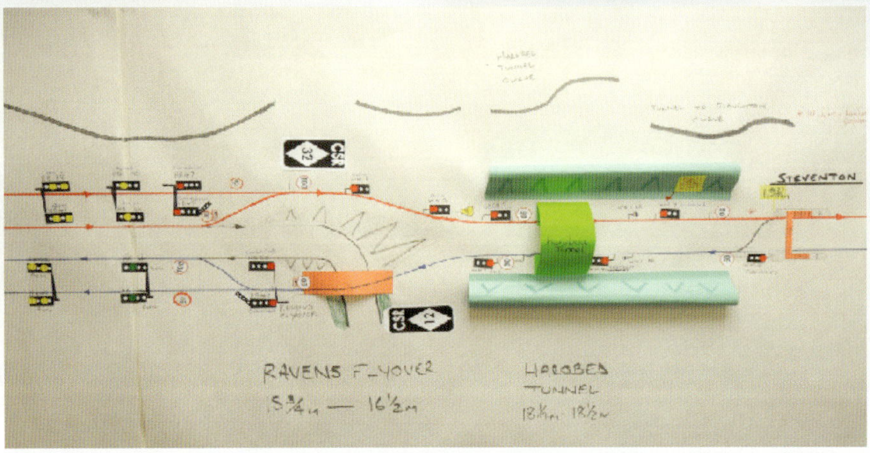

Above: Principles of Route Learning - course students create their own map of a particular simulator route.

Below: Every student is invited to participate in the creation of the route map.

Photos: The Author's Collection.

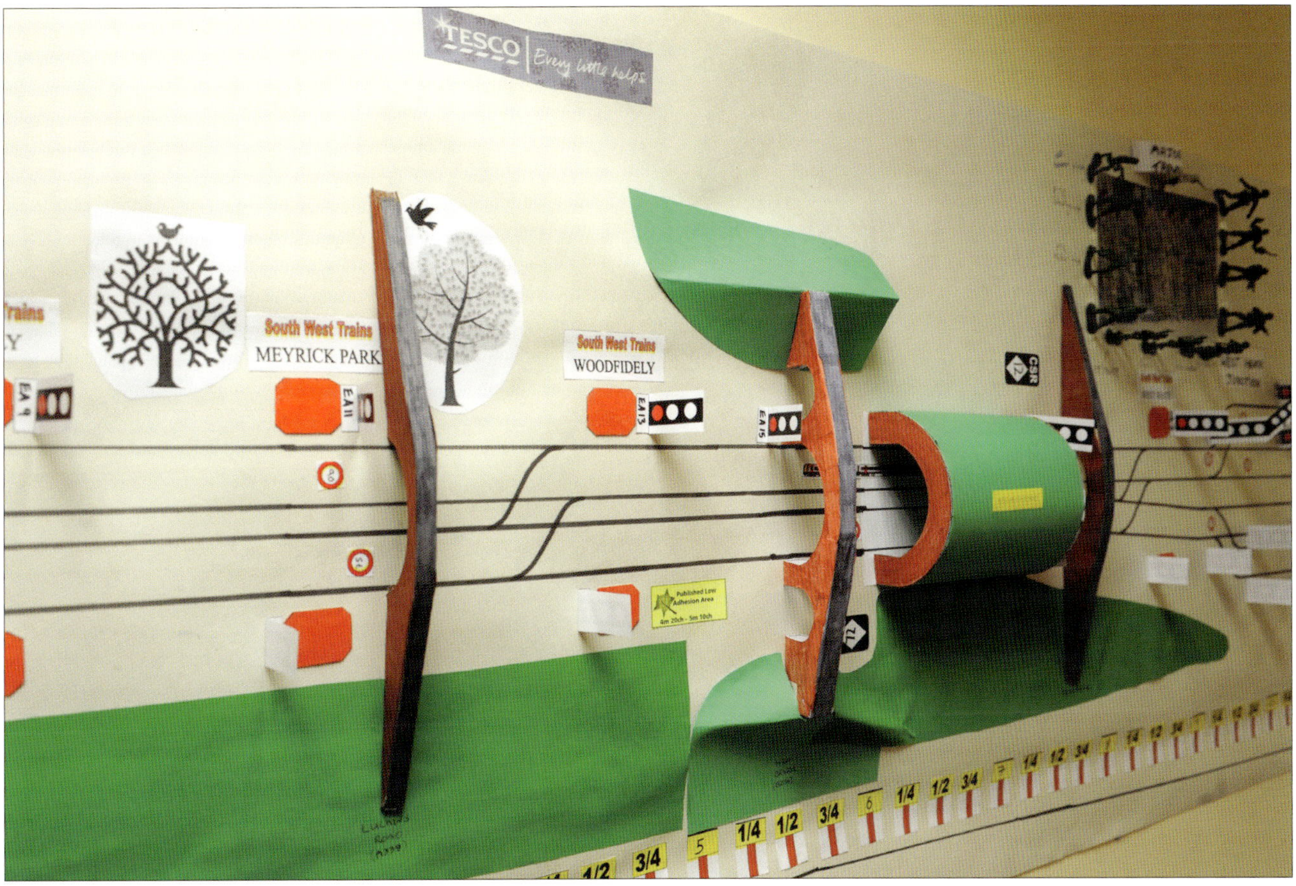

Above: A further version of a route map.

Below: Basic driver course flanked by their trainers - Jez Morgan and Jerry Bond.

Photos: The Author's Collection.

Above: Discovery Learning - David Pinkstone, one of Senior Trainer Chris Lemon's students, explains the rules regarding Temporary Block working.

Below and Opposite page: More flipchart creations from the students.

Photos: The Author's Collection.

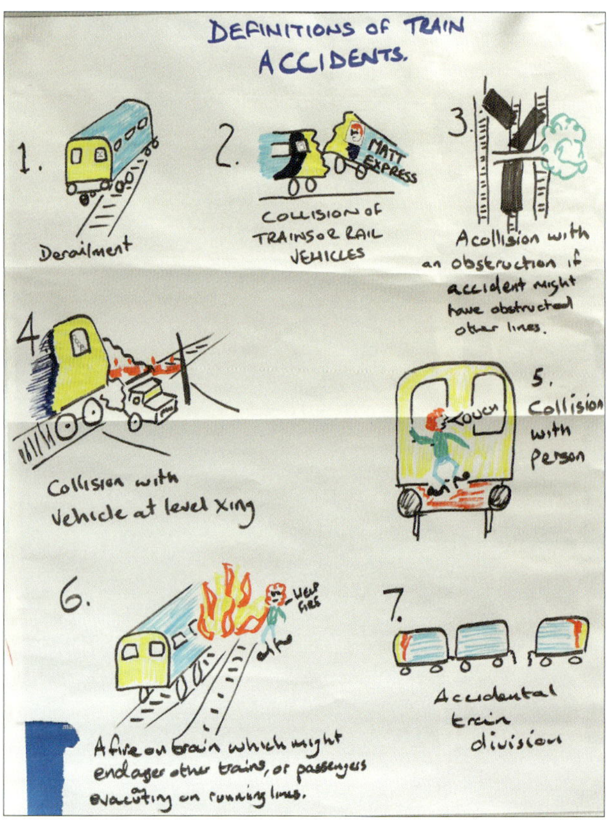

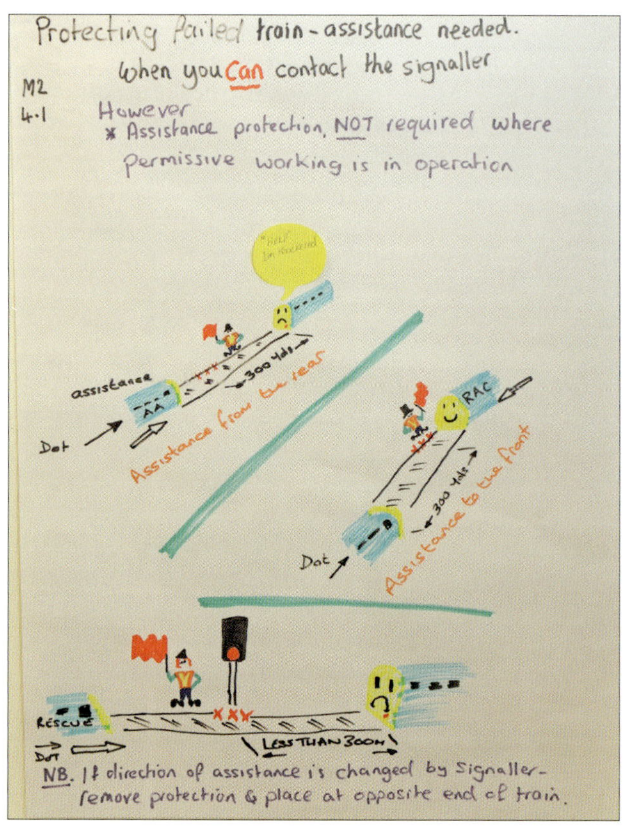

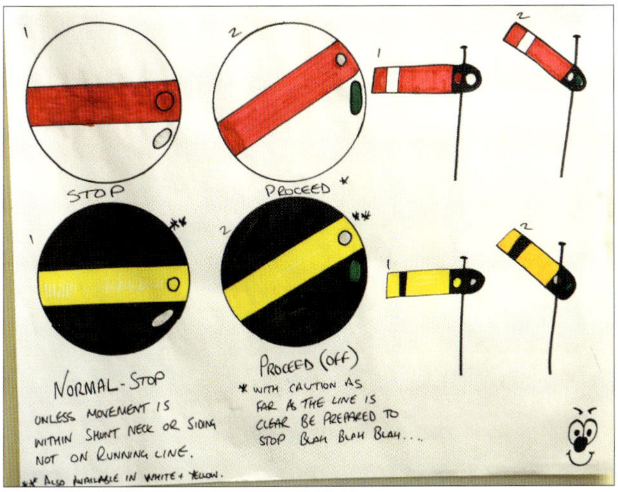
STOP
PROCEED *
NORMAL - STOP
UNLESS MOVEMENT IS WITHIN SHUNT NECK OR SIDING NOT ON RUNNING LINE.
PROCEED (OFF)
* WITH CAUTION AS FAR AS THE LINE IS CLEAR BE PREPARED TO STOP BLAH BLAH BLAH...
** ALSO AVAILABLE IN WHITE + YELLOW.

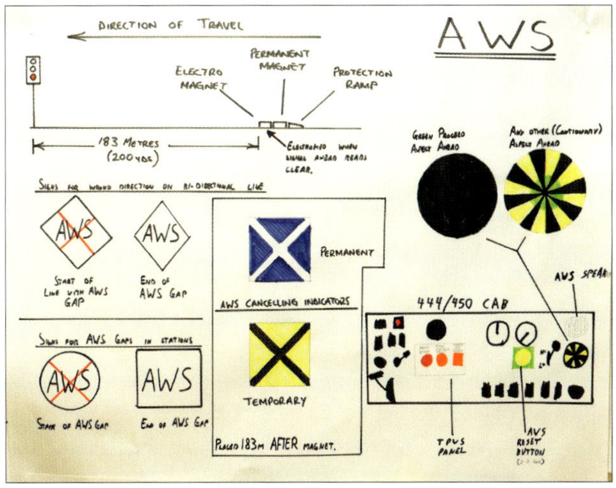
AWS
DIRECTION OF TRAVEL
ELECTRO MAGNET
PERMANENT MAGNET
PROTECTION RAMP
183 METRES (200 YDS)
SIGNS FOR WRONG DIRECTION ON BI-DIRECTIONAL LINE
AWS
START OF LINE WITH AWS GAP
AWS
END OF AWS GAP
SIGNS FOR AWS GAPS IN STATIONS
AWS
START OF AWS GAP
AWS
END OF AWS GAP
PERMANENT
AWS CANCELLING INDICATORS
TEMPORARY
PLACED 183M AFTER MAGNET.
GREEN PROCEED ASPECT AHEAD
ANY OTHER (CAUTIONARY) ASPECT AHEAD
AWS SPEAK
444/450 CAB
TPWS PANEL
AWS RESET BUTTON

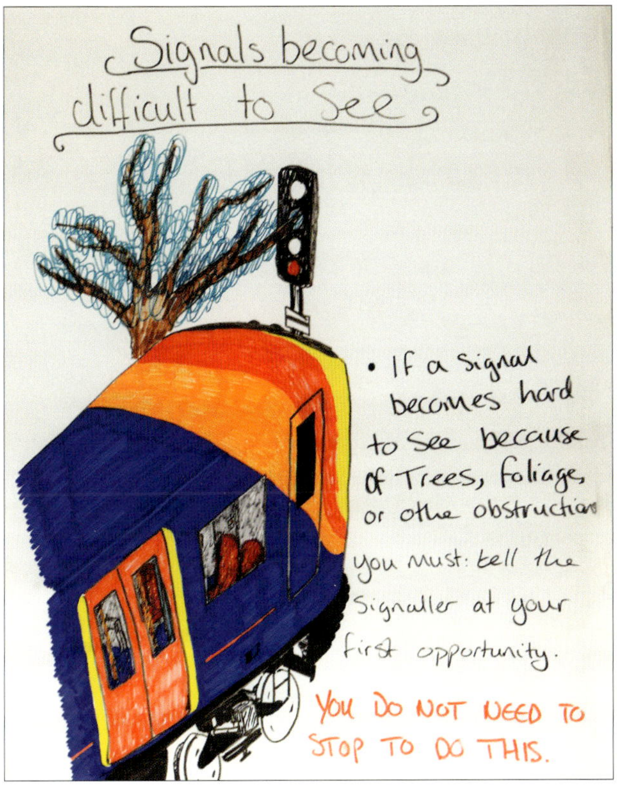
Signals becoming difficult to See
• If a signal becomes hard to See because of Trees, foliage, or othe obstruction
you must: tell the Signaller at your first opportunity.
YOU DO NOT NEED TO STOP TO DO THIS.

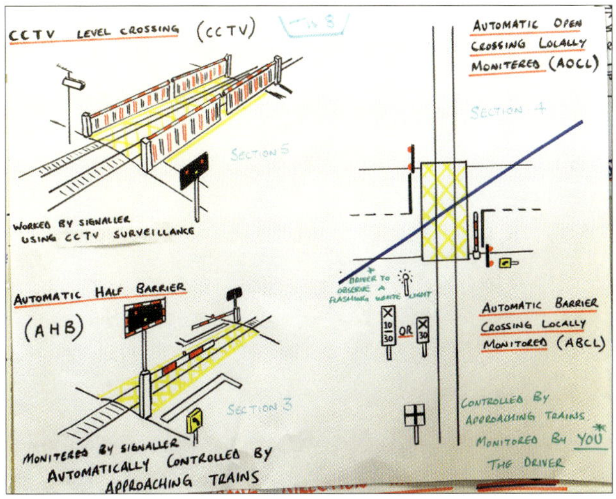
CCTV LEVEL CROSSING (CCTV)
SECTION 5
WORKED BY SIGNALLER USING CCTV SURVEILLANCE
AUTOMATIC HALF BARRIER
(AHB)
SECTION 3
MONITERED BY SIGNALLER
AUTOMATICALLY CONTROLLED BY APPROACHING TRAINS
AUTOMATIC OPEN CROSSING LOCALLY MONITERED (AOCL)
SECTION 4
* DRIVER TO OBSERVE A FLASHING WHITE LIGHT
10
30
OR
30
AUTOMATIC BARRIER CROSSING LOCALLY MONITORED (ABCL)
CONTROLLED BY APPROACHING TRAINS.
MONITORED BY YOU * THE DRIVER

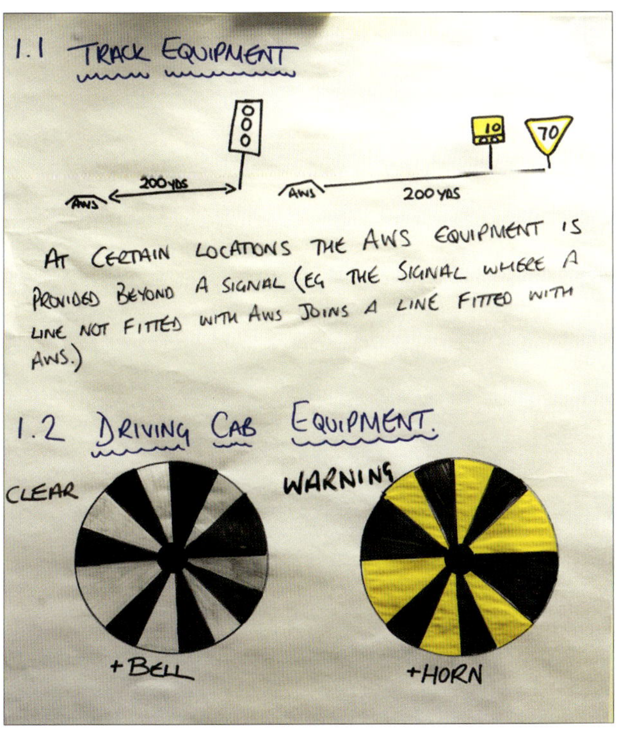
1.1 TRACK EQUIPMENT
10
70
AWS
200 YDS
AWS
200 YDS
AT CERTAIN LOCATIONS THE AWS EQUIPMENT IS PROVIDED BEYOND A SIGNAL (EG THE SIGNAL WHERE A LINE NOT FITTED WITH AWS JOINS A LINE FITTED WITH AWS.)
1.2 DRIVING CAB EQUIPMENT.
CLEAR
WARNING
+ BELL
+ HORN

IF YOU SEE SOMETHING WHICH COULD COMPROMISE YOUR TRAINS SAFETY,* TRY TO AVOID STOPPING ....
- ON VIADUCTS
I DON'T LIKE HEIGHTS!
- IN TUNNELS
BUGGER!
OR ANY PLACE WHERE ITS DIFFICULT TO DEAL WITH THE INCIDENT, OR RECEIVE EMERGENCY AID
* STEEP EMBANKMENTS, ETC
* STOP IMMEDIATELY NORMALLY

Training Days - South West Trains

Because I'd had previous experience with programming software whilst I'd been employed by Surrey Police, I offered my services to put together some Computer Based Training (CBT) packages to supplement the training already in place. The program used to 'author' the packages was made by Macromedia and called 'Authorware'; a licence being granted for me to use. I also programmed a 'Welcome Introduction' package for the plasma screen in the students' lounge. This gave students (and anyone else visiting the building) clear instructions on where everything was situated within the Training Centre plus safety procedures should there be a fire. It also displayed all of the trainers' names and photos and in which room their course would take place.

Several other CBT programs were introduced into the training sessions (using a drag and drop principle) which allowed student participation and prevented boredom. These CBT programs were also available for students to use during their leisure time.

SWT drivers were also visiting the Operations and Safety Training Centre (O&STC) for their driver competency assessment with scenarios being carried out using the simulator.

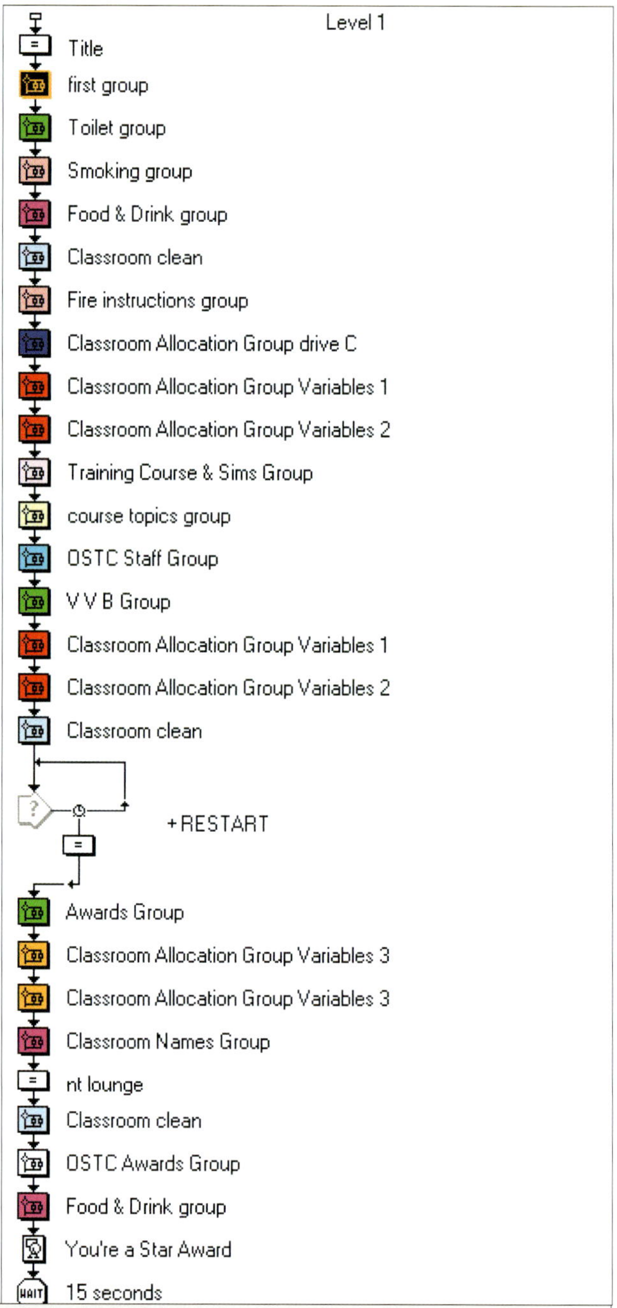

Right: Macromedia Authorware programming showing the path it will travel before returning to the start to repeat.

Below: South West Trains' Vision, Values and Behaviours expected from its staff.

Graphics: The Author's Collection.

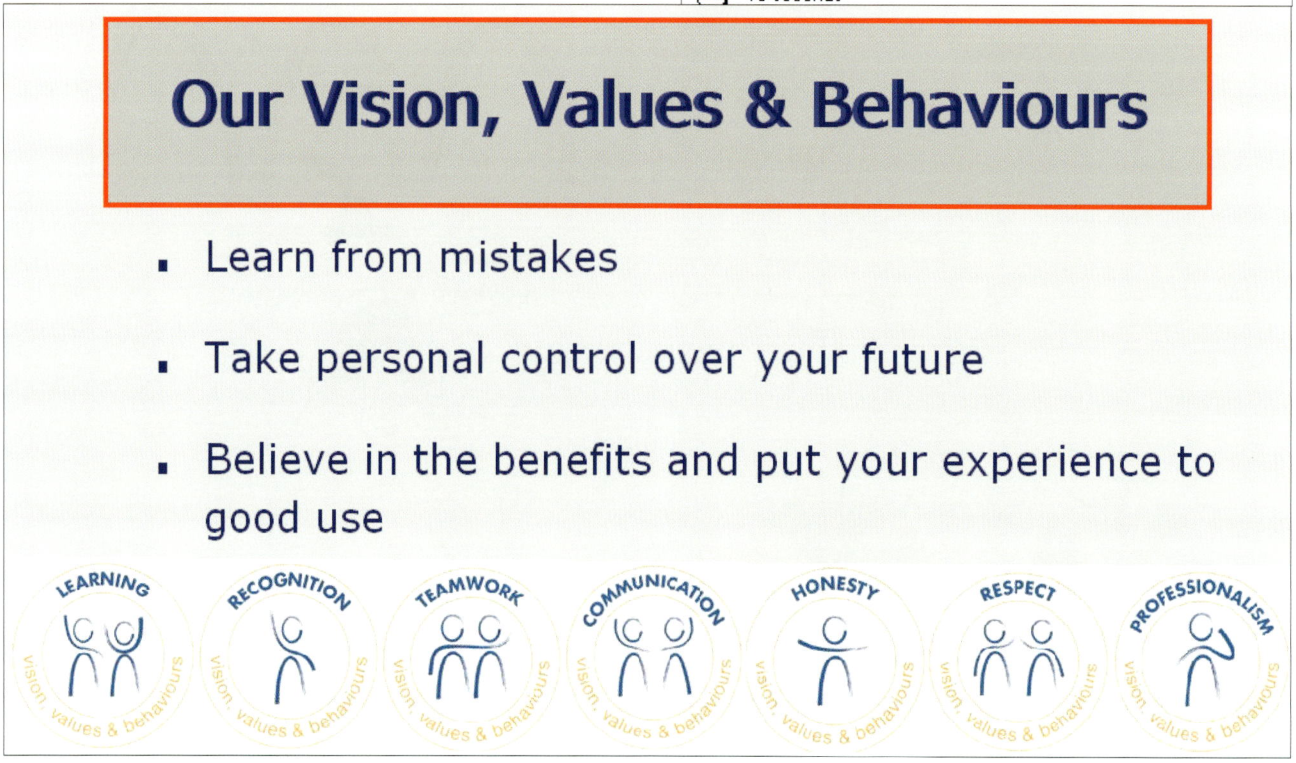

Above and Below: Two screen shots that were shown to students on the plasma screen in the students' lounge.

Photos: Courtesy of South West Trains and the Author's Collection.

Training Days - South West Trains

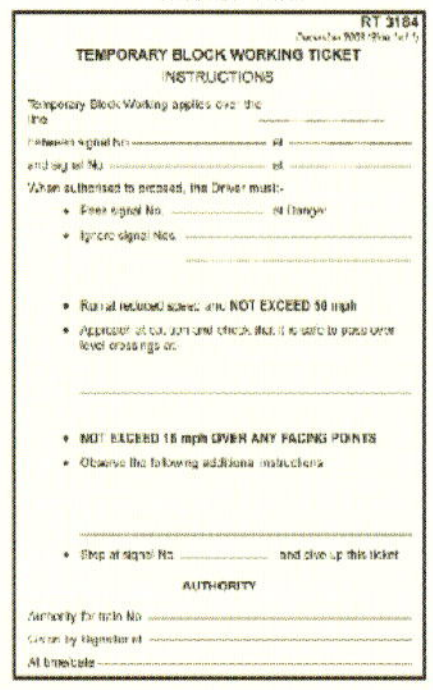

RT 3184

TEMPORARY BLOCK WORKING TICKET

INSTRUCTIONS

NOT EXCEED 15 mph OVER ANY FACING POINTS

AUTHORITY

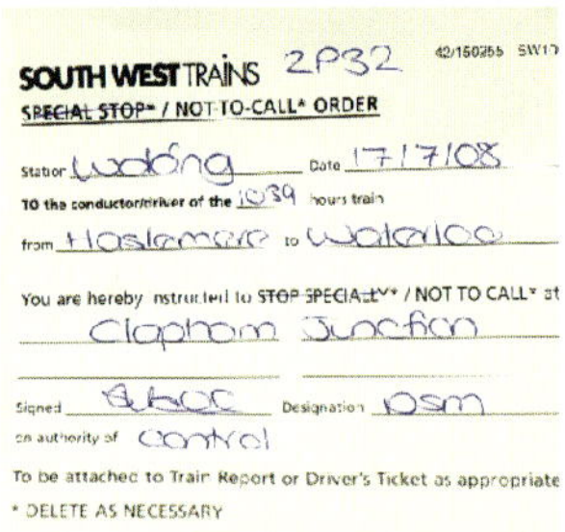

SOUTH WEST TRAINS 2P32

SPECIAL STOP* / NOT-TO-CALL* ORDER

Station Woking Date 17/7/08

To the conductor/driver of the 10/39 hours train

from Haslemere to Waterloo

You are hereby instructed to STOP SPECIALLY* / NOT TO CALL* at Clapham Junction

Signed Designation DSM

on authority of Control

To be attached to Train Report or Driver's Ticket as appropriate

* DELETE AS NECESSARY

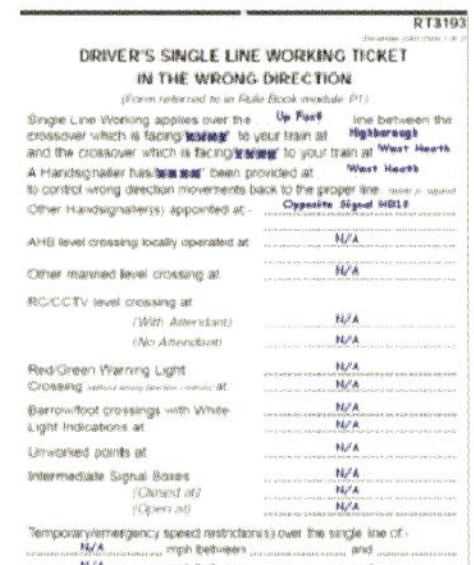

RT3193

DRIVER'S SINGLE LINE WORKING TICKET IN THE WRONG DIRECTION

Above: Driver's Competency Simulator Assessment (4 year cycle). Drivers had commented that whilst undertaking their rules assessments, they have found that some types of 'degraded working' and 'out of course' situations were difficult to comprehend. They say that "a picture paints a thousand words" and situations would be much simpler if they were demonstrated by use of scenarios as shown. Therefore, the driver's competency cycle assessment was designed to incorporate these concerns by re-enacting these events by the use of simulators. From top left:

Passing signals at danger (with authority)
Giving and Receiving Cab Secure Radio messages
Special Stop Orders
Rectification of minor faults
Temporary Block Working
Safety communications protocol
Assisting a failed train
Single Line Working

Below: Trainee Guard Charlie Cook receiving his award from South West Trains' Managing Director Stewart Palmer.

Photos: Courtesy of South West Trains.

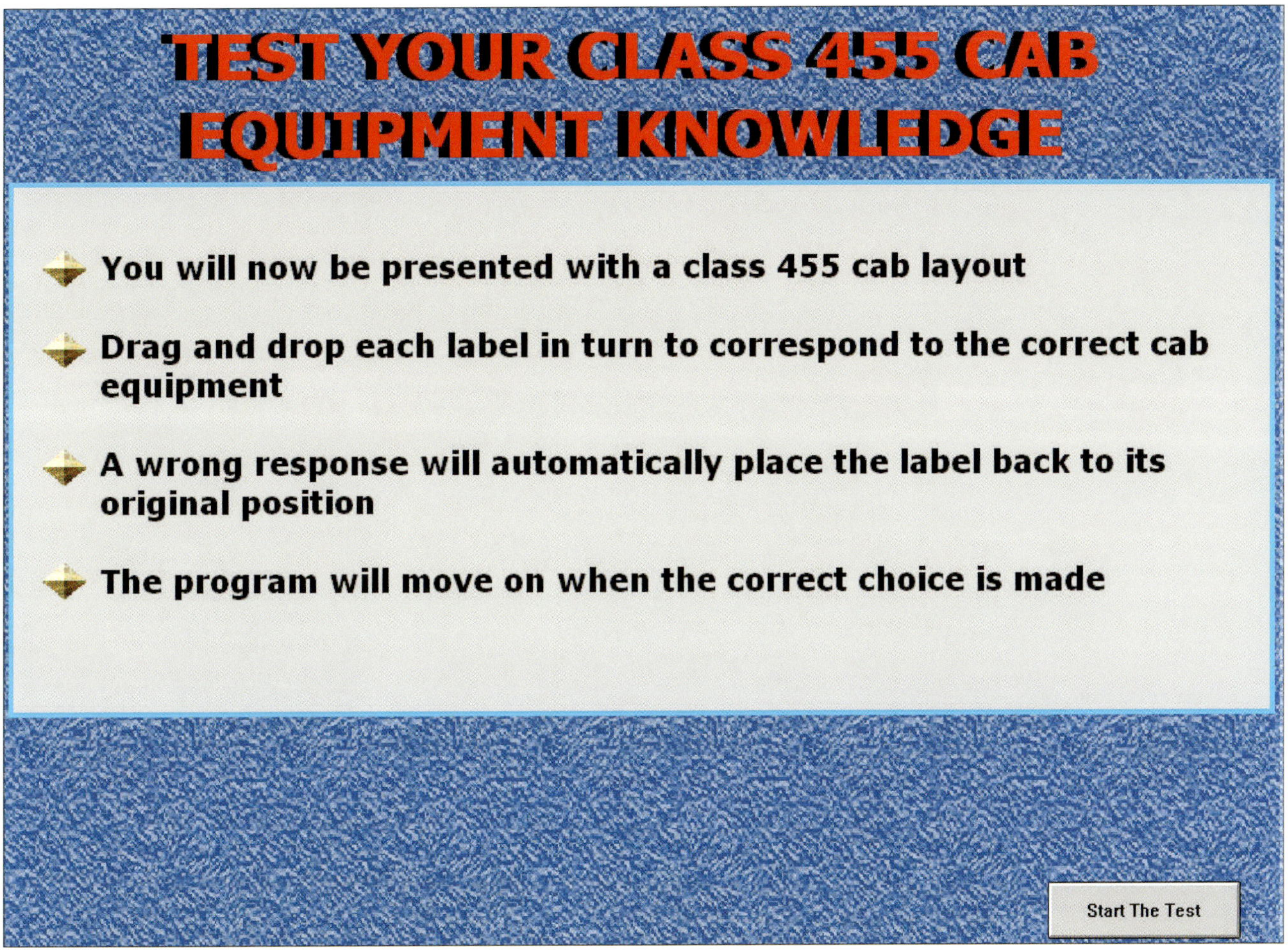

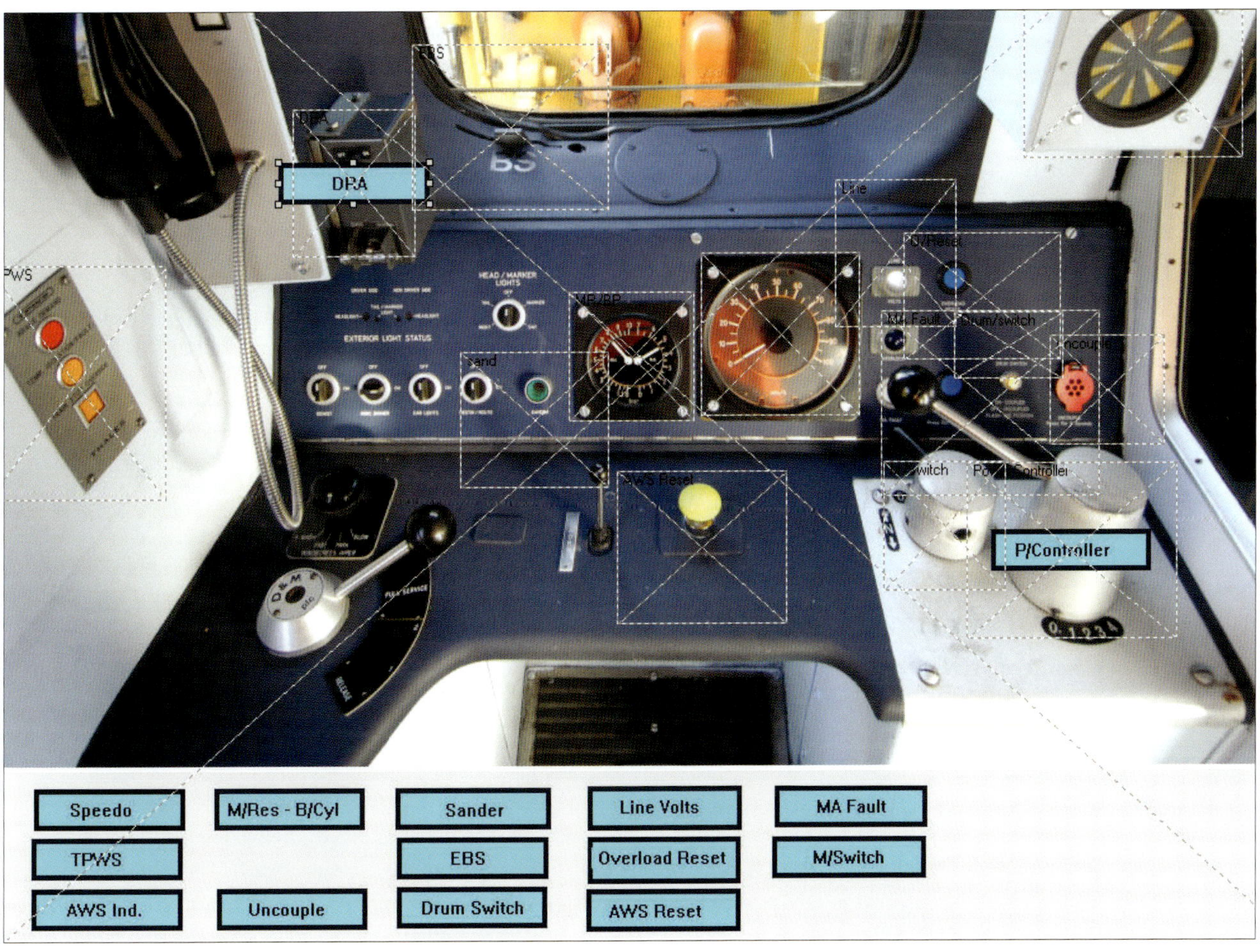

Above: CBT 'Drag and Drop' routine where a label is 'dragged and dropped' onto the correct equipment in a Class 455 cab. An incorrect response will automatically place the label back to its original position. The program will move on when the correct choice has been made. Catchment areas are shown in this graphic for clarity. Photo: The Author's Collection.

The Class 73 electro-diesel locomotive was designed to work from the electric conductor rail or over non-electrified lines. It will operate as a 1600 HP electric locomotive when the conductor rail supply is available, or a 600 HP diesel-electric locomotive when the conductor rail supply is not available.

The power is then provided by an auxiliary diesel engine and main generator. This view of the cab shows both driver and secondman positions. As you can see, the controls are duplicated on both sides for shunting purposes but the controllers can only be changed from the driver's side. A button has to be depressed on either controller to place them to the LOCK OFF positions to enable the other controller to be opened to a power position. The electro-diesel was designed to conduct shunting operations and haul trains in and out of marshalling yards where no electrified lines were present utilising a powerful 600hp 4-cylinder diesel engine with excellent torque. Control of current to the traction motors is governed by the speed of the diesel engine under the control of a load regulator, which in turn is governed by opening and closing of the diesel controller (**W**).

Once the locomotive had left the yard and over the conductor rail, the collector shoes would be lowered (with compressed air), the diesel controller closed to the LOCK OFF position and the electric controller opened to any position of power: i.e. HOLD or any of the RUN UP positions.

Once this was done, the diesel engine would be switched off by pressing and releasing the engine stop switch (**X**).

Other cab equipment shown above and not in the previous photograph are:

(**Y**)Auto Engine Start Switch.

(**1**) Aux Power Off Switch; terminates auxiliary power, collector shoes will lower.

(**2**) Aux Power On switch; to allow the use of the electric controller to work diesel conditions and any other electric unit's power that might be coupled in multiple). Collector shoes will raise.

(**3**) Train Protection & Warning System (TPWS) which will initiate an emergency brake application when a signal is passed at danger, and in most cases when a train approaches a danger aspect or speed restriction at too high a speed. TPWS aims to stop the train before it reaches the first point beyond the signal where a conflict (that falls within the scope of TPWS protection) could occur. This is called the 'clearance point' and the distance from the signal to the clearance point is known as the 'safe overrun distance' (SOD).

(**4**) Route indicator cupboard.

(**5**) Pre-Heat trip switch; turns off pre-heating.

(**6**) Pre-Heat ON switch; cab can be set-up to pre-heat a train without the master key being present, (power for pre-heat coming from the conductor rail). The compressor control wires will remain energised to ensure sufficient air is present to hold shoes down on the conductor rail and to ensure the heating contactor remains closed.

(7) Cab Heat (either side).

(8) Fire Alarm Test; tests fire alarm circuit and fuse - diesel compartment only.

(9) Reset Switch; resets traction motor overloads - controller must be at OFF to reset.

(10) Cab Secure Radio System; once radio is set-up, it allows communication between driver and signaller and vice-versa. As the locomotive passes between different areas, the changes are made automatically. Should there be an Emergency, a STOP message can be flashed to the driver and acknowledged once the driver has stopped.

(11) Brake Cylinder Gauge.

(12) Main Reservoir Air / Brake pipe pressure.

The non-operational items (indicated by the red numbers on a yellow background) are as follows:

(1) Vacuum Brake Gauge; blanked off as South West Trains no longer had any vacuum fitted trains.

(2) Fitted/Unfitted switch; when originally built, these locomotives hauled fully-fitted and unfitted braked trains (unfitted with a guard in a brakevan at the rear of the train). The Driver's Safety Device (DSD) on these locomotives had a delay of 6 to 7 seconds before the brakes were applied (so the driver had time to swap positions in the cab). When working 'fully fitted trains, the switch would stay in the 'Fitted' position and if the driver was incapacitated at any time, the emergency brake would apply fully after the 6-7 seconds. When working unfitted braked trains, it was important to place the switch to the 'Unfitted' position. This feature would initiate a partial application of the brake and a time delay before the emergency brake was applied so as to 'buffer' the train together to avoid possible derailment, locked buffers or even causing injury to the guard riding in the brake van at the rear of the train.

(3) Interlock Cut-Out Switch; heating of passenger trains is normally worked by a 'double-pole' system where the heating jumpers are connected on both sides of the train to initiate a negative return feed to the conductor rail. The Interlock Cut-Out Switch was utilised for one train only, '*The Night Ferry*' which ran from Victoria to Dover Marine and had a 'single-pole' heating system. Until the Eurostar service began on 14th November 1994, the Night Ferry had been the only through passenger train between Great Britain and Continental Europe. The service was withdrawn on 31st October 1980.

Above: Train Heat ON / OFF indication.

The electric train heat supply can only be provided from the conductor rail and will be energised when the Master Switch is moved away from Off. It is therefore known as an automatic train supply.
The white E.T.H. light in each driving cab will extinguish and the red light will illuminate.
To switch off E.T.H, the Master Switch must be moved to Off. The red light will extinguish and the white light will illuminate.

THE WHITE LIGHT MUST ALWAYS BE ILLUMINATED BEFORE ANY MEMBER OF STAFF IS ALLOWED TO APPROACH ANY E.T.H. EQUIPMENT.

Below: A view inside the diesel engine room showing the main and auxiliary generators.
Whilst working under diesel conditions or auxiliary power conditions, the traction current is supplied by the engine-driven main generator. The output of the generator is controlled by increasing or decreasing the engine speed and therefore the speed at which the main generator turns. This is governed by the position of the power controller and the amount of regulating air flowing to the engine speed governor.

The auxiliary generator is coupled directly to the crankshaft of the diesel engine. When the engine is running, the generator produces a 110 volts DC supply.
If the motor generator set is not running, the auxiliary generator will supply the circuits listed above plus the radiator fan motor and the main generator field.

The motor generator is situated outside the locomotive. With the Auxiliary Isolating Switch (AIS) closed and a conductor rail supply available, the motor of this set will run off of the conductor rail supply. Coupled to the motor via a shaft is the generator which will produce a constant 110 volts DC supply. Equipment supplied at 110 volts are: control, compressor, lighting, cab heat and battery charging circuits.

Photos: Courtesy of South West Trains.

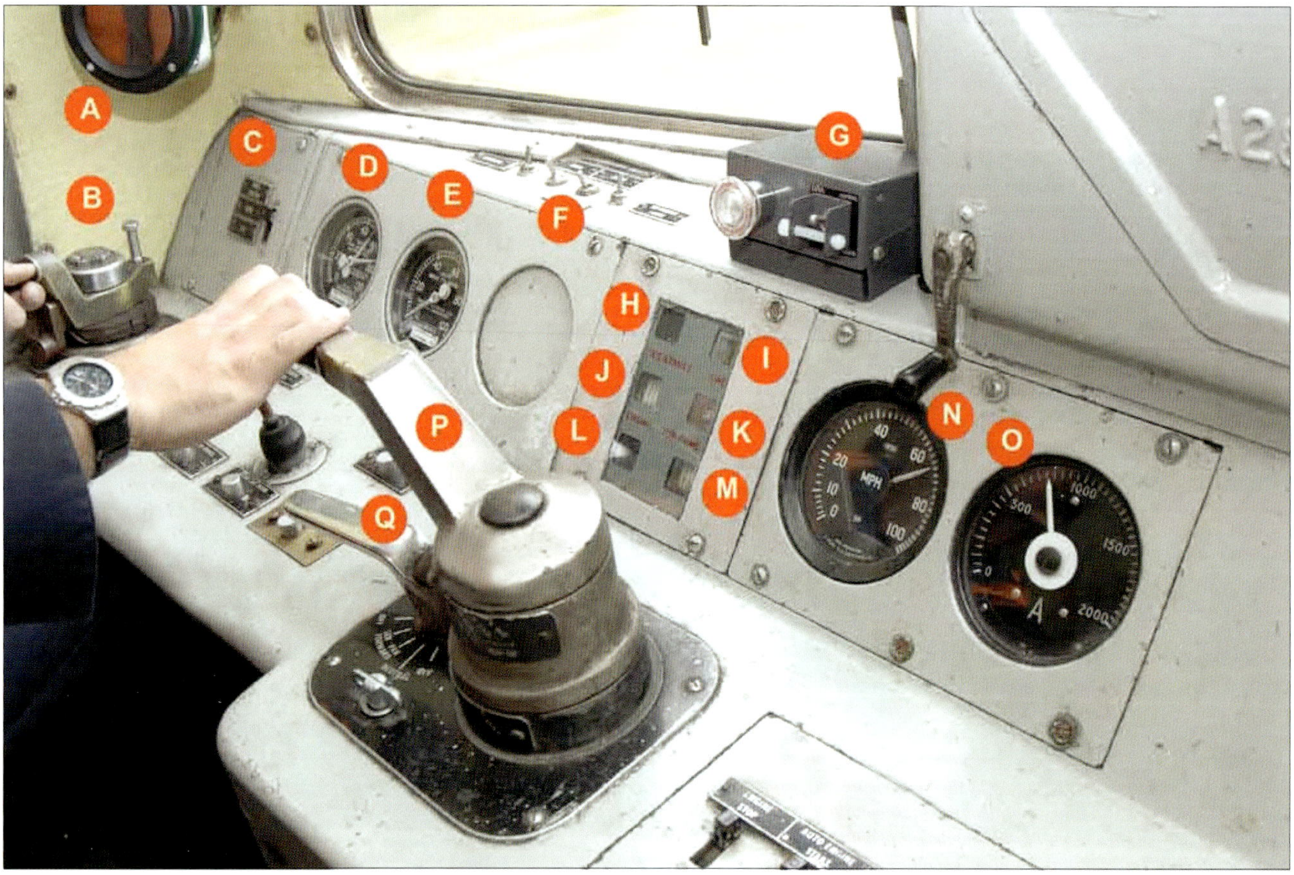

A general view of the cab layout of Class 73/1 showing the various instruments on the desk in alphabetical order:

(A) Automatic Warning System (AWS) indicator. Sunflower segments will turn to yellow and black on cancellation of the horn when approaching a RED or caution signal (one yellow or two yellows) or any emergency, permanent or temporary speed restriction AWS magnet. If the horn sound is not cancelled within 3 seconds, the emergency brakes will apply.

(B) Driver's Brake Valve (DBV); will apply automatic air brakes on locomotive and train (if coupled).

(C) Auto-Air/EP brake selector switch (normally left in Auto-Air position).

(D) Main reservoir/brake pipe pressure gauge; main-res air 90-105 psi, brake-pipe pressure 72.5psi.

(E) Brake cylinder pressure gauge; max pressure 60psi.

(F) Demister/Route indicator/ headlight/instrument light switches.

(G) Driver's Reminder Appliance (DRA) and isolating switch (sealed). The DRA is an additional safeguard to prevent drivers from passing signals at danger. It must be applied when the locomotive has stopped at a RED signal (by pressing in the red plunger provided) which will disable power being applied to the traction motors. Once the signal has cleared, the plunger can be released thus restoring the control circuit to the traction motors.

Above Top: General view of Class 73/1 cab layout.

Above: The six Dowty indicator flags (H) Resistances, (I) Line Indicator, (J) Engine priming / starting or stopped, (L) Wheelslip and (M) Fault.

Photos: The Author's Collection.

(H) Resistance Indicator Flag [R] will show in the window when resistances are introduced in the motor circuit (when first taking power for instance).

To understand the sequence of events on electric operation, it must be remembered that it would be impossible to apply full line voltage to stationary traction motors without introducing resistances into the motor circuit to reduce the flow of current. Upon starting, three power contactors are closed in sequence to allow current to flow through the traction motors with all resistances in circuit. To gain further acceleration, the resistance camshaft must now progress to close the 'R' switches R1, R2, R3, R4 and so on to progressively short out the resistances. As the locomotive gathers speed, the 'back electro-motive force' (back EMF) of the traction motors tends to oppose the applied voltage and so gradually dispenses with the need for resistances until finally, R19 and R20 contactors close to short out all resistances in circuit. The traction motors are now running in full-series with no resistances in circuit.

If more power is required, the electric controller (**P**) is moved to NOTCH UP or SER RUN UP and JR contactor will close to allow the first step to transition from series to parallel working. To meet the sudden increase in current when paralleling the motors, all the resistances are again put back into the traction motor circuit. This time, resistances are removed in pairs, R1 and R2 together, R3 and R4 together, and so on until ten steps have been taken to short out all resistances. The locomotive's motors are now running in full parallel with no resistances in circuit.

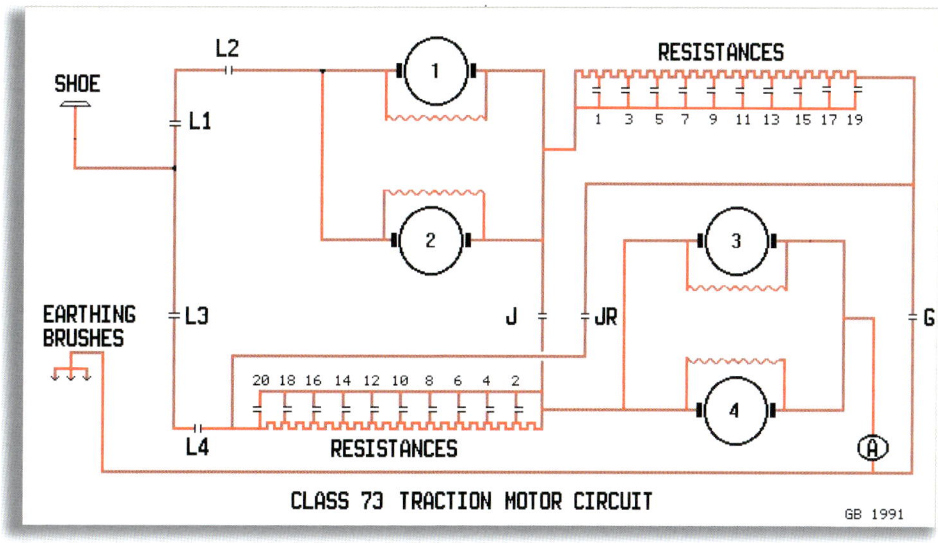

Further acceleration can be obtained by the weak fielding camshaft (WF) introducing field diversion switches in four stages which effectively reduce the traction motor's 'back EMF', thereby increasing the applied voltage to attain more power.

With this type of control of power to the traction motors, the locomotive's versatility comes into its own and speed of trains can be adjusted accordingly to the range of power positions at hand.

The locomotive can even be worked in the series/ weak field position by moving the Master Switch (**Q**) to FORWARD SER; then a further range of power can be applied to the traction motors.

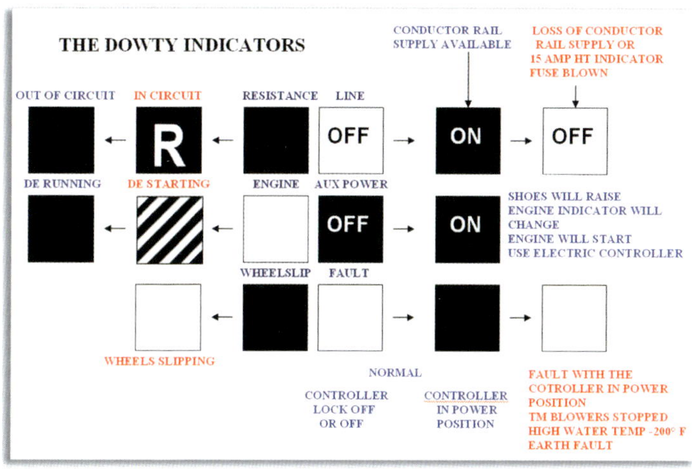

Above Top: Class 73 Traction Motor Circuit.

Above: Dowty indicator flags showing sequences of resistances in circuit, fault, engine priming/ starting/stopped, auxiliary power ON or OFF, Line indicator ON or OFF.

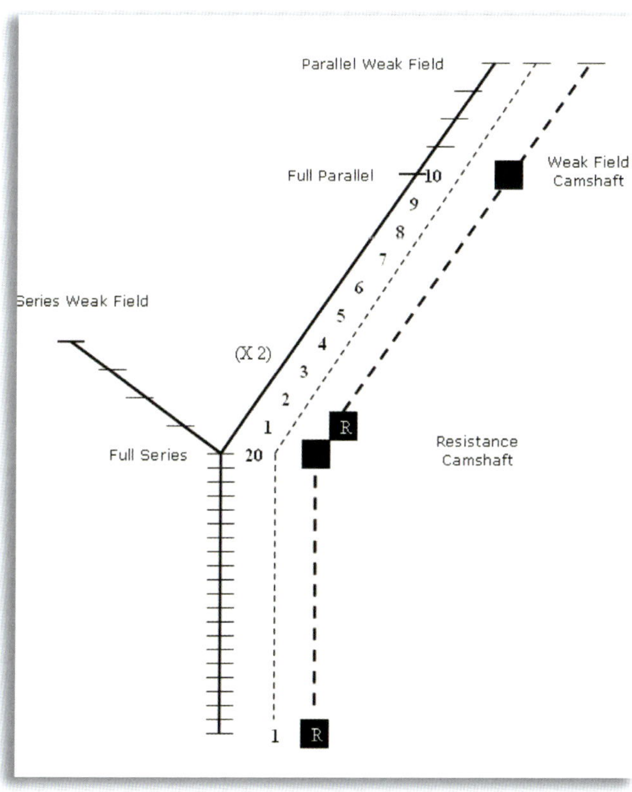

Left: Camshaft positions from Notch 1 to 20 to reach Full Series and Full Series to Parallel Weak Field or Series Weak Field (depending on the position of the Master Switch).

Graphics: The Author's Collection.

Other positions of the Electric Controller (P) are HOLD (the power position required can be held constant); RUN BACK (the resistances can be run out of the power circuit to reduce the flow of amps to the traction circuit). OFF (power is removed completely from the traction motor circuit and LOCK OFF (this position would require the push button on the end of the controller being utilised and would allow the diesel controller to be opened to the OFF position). However, this can only be attained if the master switch was at FORWARD PAR.

It was always taught that to avoid snatches to attached trains, the ammeter should not register more than 500 amps when passing through conductor rail gaps. High amps being drawn (especially at low speed) could also introduce the risk of severe arcing from the conductor shoes when leaving the conductor rail which could result in a fire. Note: should the locomotive shoes go into a gap in the conductor rail, the loss of power would be detected by the No Volt Relay (NVR) and the camshafts will automatically start running back. Once the shoes make contact with the conductor rail again, power is regained and the camshaft will stop in the position it has reached. The resistances will again have to be removed, either by notching or placing the Electric controller to a 'Run Up' position.

(I) Line Indicator Flag [ON] when shoes are in contact with the third rail and [OFF] if shoes are raised or there is no supply to the conductor rail from the sub-station, i.e. a current isolation.

(J) Engine Flag; three possible indications: engine stopped (white flag), engine running (black flag) and black and white diagonal stripes (engine priming prior to starting).

(K) Aux Power (Auxiliary Power); two possible indications [OFF] or [ON] when it is possible to work under diesel conditions utilising the electric controller. If Auxiliary Power is selected and the 27-way EMU control jumper is connected between locomotives in multiple (or similar EMU types), it is possible to drive the locomotive under diesel conditions and control the unit under electric conditions (using the Westcode Valves).

(L) Wheelslip Indicator Flag: indicates wheelslip. The flag changes from black to white erratically. Wheelslip can be corrected by any of the following methods: reducing power by placing electric controller to the Run Back position, applying air to the brake cylinders by pressing the wheelslip button ([S] on diagram) or pressing the sand button on desk (not shown).

(M) Fault Flag; normally a white indication; black if a fault occurs on diesel or electric conditions: i.e. earth on control fault or high water temperature conditions under diesel power.

(N) Speedometer.

(O) Ammeter: measurement supplied to the traction motors under diesel or electric conditions. Amps must be 'run back' to under 500 Amps before running into conductor rail gaps or shutting off power.

Above Top: Detailed view of controls.

Left: Dowty indicator flags.

Below: Detailed view of controller positions.

Photos: Courtesy of South West Trains.

(P) Electric controller; can also be utilised to control the diesel power under Auxiliary Power conditions.

(Q) Master Switch; released by inserting EP Key.

(R) Positions of Electric Controller; Lock Off / Off / Hold / Notch Up / Run Up positions /SER/ PAR/WF.

(S) Anti-Slip Brake push button; releases 20psi air into the brake cylinders to arrest wheel slip.

(T) Rear Cab Horn button; sound the horn at the other end of locomotive.

(U) Automatic Warning System (AWS) horn cancel button. Should the AWS warning sound when running over the AWS magnet in the track, the cancel button must be operated within three seconds or the emergency brake will apply.

(V) Master Switch positions; Off / Neutral / Forward-PAR / Forward-SER and REV.

(W) Diesel controller.

(X) Engine stop toggle switch.

(Y) Auto Engine Start toggle switch; to start engine: with master switch at Neutral, press and release the Auto-Engine start switch (engine flag will turn to black/white diagonal stripes) engine will prime for approximately thirty seconds, crank, fire and run. Engine flag (J) will change to black and the air compressor will run to charge the main reservoir tank to a pressure of 105psi.

***Above:** Engine Stop, Auto Engine Start, Aux Power OFF and Aux Power ON toggle switches.*

***Below:** Class 73/2 electro-diesel No. 73235 at Bournemouth Depot.*

***Photos:** Courtesy of South West Trains and the Author's Collection.*

Inset Right: Close up of the Straight Air Brake. There are two straight air brake valves in each cab. All four work independently, with double-check valves fitted to prevent air pressure exhausting from the other valves when applying the brake. The straight air brake is used for stopping the locomotive when running light engine.

Inset Below: An AUTO/EP brake selector switch is situated on the driving desk to the left of the driving position. It must be placed in the EP position during brake testing and for working with the Class 400 EMU stock fitted with the conventional type of EP brake system. There is no separate EP brake valve handle so the automatic brake valve handle is utilised and the air brake pipe pressure is maintained at 72.5 psi by energising a Cut-Off and Recharging Valve the moment the brake handle is moved. As its name implies, it will 'cut off' the brake valve from the air brake pipe and will 'recharge' (maintain) the brake pipe at 72.5 psi. (the air coming from the control reservoir instead of the normal main reservoir supply). Because there is no fall in air brake pipe pressure and therefore no automatic brake applied in EP, great care must be taken to ensure that the selector switch is not at EP unless the locomotive is coupled to coaching stock with a compatible EP brake system. The brake is electrically controlled to give a simultaneous and uniform application and release of the brakes on the locomotive and all coaches of the train.

The correct method of applying the brake is to move the brake handle toward Full Service and immediately the brake cylinder pressure registers on the brake cylinder gauge, return the brake handle back to an intermediate position needed to reduce the speed of the train, (unless a full service application is required).

Inset Right Below: A photo showing the Driver's Brake Valve in the release position. The automatic brake valve has five positions:

1. NEUTRAL. The brake valve is out of use. Although provided with a locking pin it is not locked securely as on other classes of locomotive, so care must be taken to ensure it is not inadvertently left at Emergency when vacating the cab. Before moving the brake handle from Neutral, the main reservoir air supply must me at least 90 psi., the Brake Selector Switch (BSS) is at 'AIR', the EP/Auto selector switch is at 'AUTO' and the Master Switch is away from Off.

Moving the Master Switch away from Off will cause the electrically operated feed cut off valve to energise (and open) and allow main reservoir air to feed to the brake valve. The DSD EP valve is also energised with the Master Switch at Off or Neutral, and the DSD foot button will need to be depressed before moving the Master Switch to either the Forward or Reverse positions.

2. RELEASE OR RUNNING. A cam on the sleeve of the brake valve will open a sealing valve when the brake handle is moved to 'Running' which will connect the brake valve to the Air brake pipe and will now charge to 72.5 psi.

3. INITIAL APPLICATION. The Air brake pipe pressure will now be reduced to 65/66 psi. The locomotive distributor mounted on the brake frame will react to the lowering of the brake pipe and will cause approximately 18/20 psi. brake cylinder pressure to be applied.

4. FULL SERVICE. The events are the same as those described under Initial Application except that the air brake pipe pressure will be reduced to 50.5 psi. The distributor will respond to this lower pressure and will cause the full 60 psi. brake cylinder pressure to be applied. Understandably, any intermediate position of the brake valve handle selected between Initial and Full Service will give a corresponding amount of brake cylinder pressure. Although the brake valve and distributor are self-lapping in application and release the brakes can be applied and released at will, However, care must be taken not to 'fan' the brake handle. Not only does this have a detrimental effect on the brake equipment, it can also prove potentially dangerous if the train being worked is an EMU fitted with triple valves that do not have a partial release facility. The brake valve and the distributor will react to any minor leak on the system and will maintain the amount of brake cylinder pressure that has been applied.

5. EMERGENCY. When the brake valve handle is moved to Emergency, a second cam on the brake valve sleeve will open a quick-action valve. The valve will connect the brake system directly to atmosphere and the air brake pipe pressure will rapidly fall to zero. At the same time, if the EP brake system is in use, the holding and application valves will again be energised and the EP Brake will also apply. A safety valve is provided on the brake cylinders to vent excess pressure.

Inset Right Below: The Driver's Brake Valve in the shutdown position.

Inset Right: Photo of foot press buttons for the Driver's Safety Device (DSD).

It is arranged for the DSD EP Valve and its Feed Cut-Off Valve to be energised with the Master Switch at Off and at Neutral. To select a power position with the Master Switch either one of the two pedal buttons situated at floor level beneath each driving position must be depressed. Should the pedal button be released with the Master Switch in a powered position, the automatic brakes will be applied after a delay of 6 to 8 seconds. A Speed Sensing Device (SSF) is fitted to apply the automatic brakes via the DSD if the Master Switch is inadvertently moved from a powered position into Neutral when the locomotive is moving.

Left: DSD Foot Press Buttons.
Fitted on the Driver's and Non-Driver's side. Should the button be released with the Master Switch at a powered position, the automatic brakes will be applied after a delay of 6-8 seconds.

Below: Motor Generator Set.

Photos: Courtesy of South West Trains.

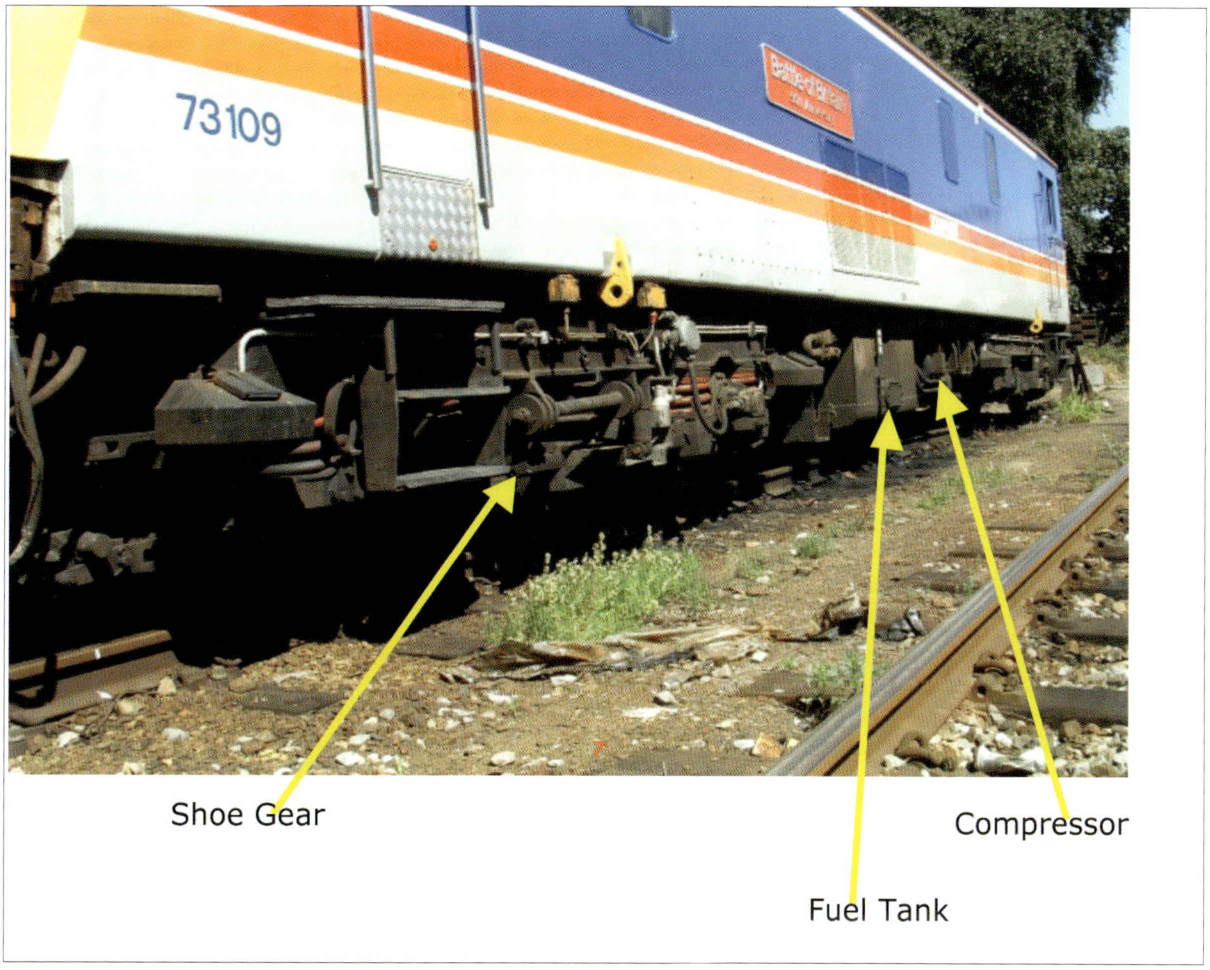

Above: Class 73/1 electro-diesel No. 73109 'Battle of Britain' at Woking Hurdles Road siding.
Outside equipment showing shoe gear, compressor and fuel tank - the motor generator (inset above) being situated on the other side of the locomotive.

Photos: Courtesy of South West Trains.

Training Days - South West Trains

THE DIESEL ENGINE COMPARTMENT

This is adjacent to No. 1 cab and houses an English Electric 4-cylinder diesel engine coupled to main and auxiliary generators. Mounted above the generators is a turbo charger.

Situated at the cab end of the engine room and housed in an enclosed compartment are the radiators and motor-driven cooling fan. Other engine room equipment found adjacent to the cab door include:

Photo Right: Traction motor blower to cool the two motors of Bogie 1.

Photo Left: Motor-driven lubricating oil priming pump

An emergency coupling and four paddles plus additional rescue equipment.

On the other side of the engine room walkway, equipment includes:

Photo Right and Below: A cooling water header tank and gauge glass and a hand pump for replenishing the header tank

Photo Below: Panel containing Local Start and Stop buttons and a fuel transfer pump test switch.

Photo Below: The motor-driven fuel transfer pump with strainer and filter.

Photo Right: Two main Carbon Dioxide fire bottles.

An engine over-speed device which will operate should the engine speed exceed its maximum.

Note:

The engine and governor must be examined for possible damage before resetting.

A governor over-ride handle with three positions: Run, Start and Stop. The handle must be at its uppermost 'Run' position for normal working.

A Westcode unit for Auxiliary Power conditions using the electric controller.

At the far end there is a connecting door to the electrical compartment which must be kept closed at all times.

The lubricating oil system has several functions.

Left: On preparation, three things must be checked on the fire bottles.

Pins secured.

Electrical plugs connected.

Clips connected.

1. Lubricates and reduces friction in the moving parts.
2. Absorbs and removes heat from the moving parts.
3. Provides time operating fluid for the engine speed governor to control the opening of the fuel racks.
4. Operates the two oil pressure switches known as OPS1 and OPS2. (See below).

The sump has a capacity of 40 gallons and a dipstick is provided to check the contents.

Photo Opposite Page: A motor driven priming pump will enable the system to be primed prior to starting the engine. The pump is protected by a 30 amp fuse situated inside the Low Tension (LT) cubicle. The pump will start immediately an engine start switch is pressed and stop once the engine has started.

Photo Left: If the motor driven pump fails, a hand pump is provided to prime the system. When used, the engine can be started with the local engine start switch situated in the engine room.

With the diesel engine running, engine driven pumps will maintain the lubricating oil at the correct pressures according to the speed of the engine. Normal working pressure is approximately 60 psi.

OPS.2 The switch will close when the oil pressure rises to 7 psi. enabling the engine start sequence to commence. The engine will crank over.

OPS.1 When the oil pressure rises above 27 psi., the switch will close in the retaining circuits of the diesel engine. Should the pressure fall below 20 psi., due to a fault, the switch will open and the engine will shut down to prevent damage.

To ensure the oil temperature is kept within working limits, the oil is cooled by passing it through parts of the radiators. A differential valve is fitted to prevent the oil going through the radiator at low temperatures thus ensuring a rapid warm-up to the normal working temperature.

Below: 1. Fire bottles in the engine room compartment only.

Also shown are:

2. Screw coupling, brake pipe and main reservoir extension hoses and the 27-way control jumper

3. Oil temperature and oil pressure gauges

4. Four cylinder SRKT 600hp Diesel Engine

5. Engine governor override handle.

Photos: Courtesy of South West Trains.

Inset Opposite Page: The engine can be started by using the local engine start switch in the engine room. The fuel system can also be primed by holding down the Fuel transfer pump test switch prior to starting the engine.

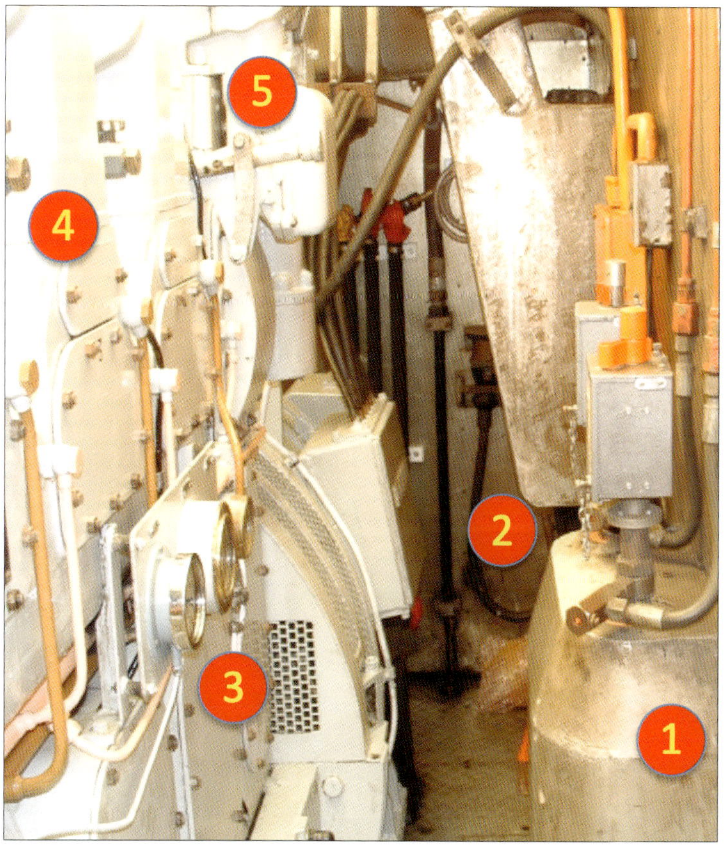

Training Days - South West Trains

THE ELECTRIC COMPARTMENT

On each side of the central walkway from the engine room are the control frames containing the Low Tension (LT) cubicle on the left and the High Tension (HT) cubicle on the right.

Photo Opposite Page: Mounted externally on the LT cubicle is a switch panel with an Auxiliary Isolating Switch (A.I.S.).

To the left of the centrally-positioned door to cab 2 is the brake frame containing brake system equipment including release buttons, gauges, governors and isolating cocks.

Photo Right: The traction motor blower to cool traction motors of bogie 2.

Photos Below: Low tension and high tension cupboards. It must be emphasised that all electrical equipment especially high tension is potentially dangerous.

Maintenance Staff are the only persons permitted behind the electrical cubicles.

Photo Bottom: A foot pump for use with collector shoe control.

Left: Foot pump normally stowed away beneath the traction motor blower.

Only used when the engine cannot be started due to a flat battery. After operating the relevant shoegear isolating cocks, the footpump will provide air to lower the shoes onto the conductor rail. Once shoes are down and 750v power is available, the compressor will supply control air required to keep shoes down.

The shoegear isolating cocks must then be returned to their normal positions.

Photos: Courtesy of South West Trains.

Left: Electric Compartment.
Low Tension (LT) Cupboard with associated switches:
Brake System Selector Switch (BSSS) Air or Vacuum
Test Switch (for testing fuses)
Traction Motor Cut-Out Switch; (cuts out TM's 1 & 2 or TM's 3 & 4.

It is not possible to isolate traction motors under diesel conditions.

Speed Sensing Feature (SSF); this device applies the brakes should the driver select 'Neutral' or 'Off' on the direction selector when the locomotive is moving. Should the loco run away unattended, this same device detects this and applies the brakes.

AIS (Auxiliary Isolation Switch)
When the switch is lifted, it is closed and securely latched.
This connects the motor generator to the conductor rail supply when the collector shoes are lowered.
When the AIS is closed, battery current at 110 volts becomes available to the control and engine starting circuits and to various auxiliary equipment.
Low tension supply will also be available from the motor generator set under electric conditions, or from the auxiliary generator set under diesel conditions.

Photo: Courtesy of South West Trains.

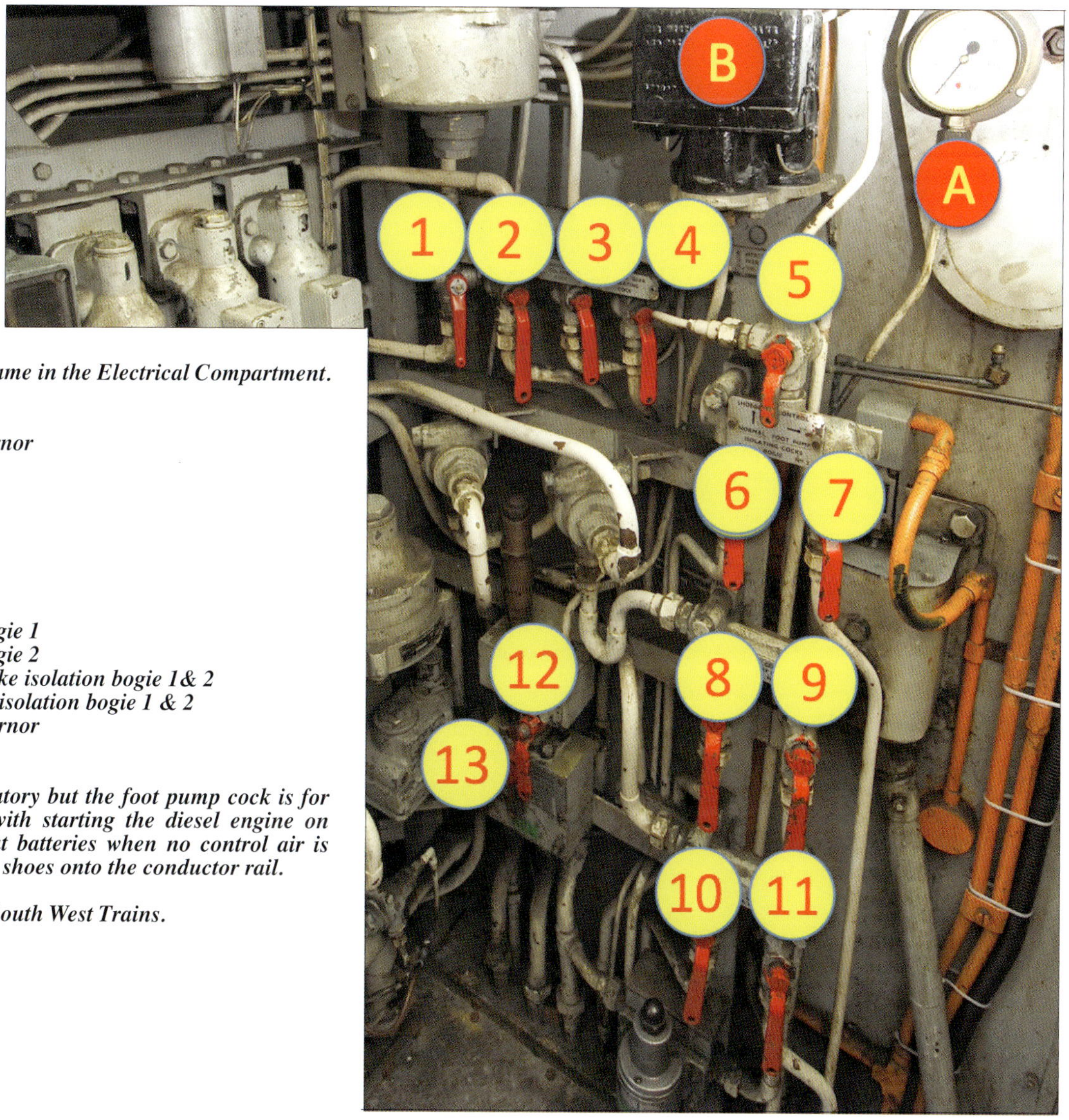

Right: The Brake Frame in the Electrical Compartment.

A. Control Air gauge
B. Compressor Governor

Isolating Cocks:
1. DSD
2. Control Air
3. Shoe gear
4. Sanding gear
5. Foot pump
6. Shoe isolation - bogie 1
7. Shoe isolation - bogie 2
8 & 9. Non-Auto brake isolation bogie 1& 2
10 & 11. Auto-brake isolation bogie 1 & 2
12. Compressor Governor
13. Main Reservoir

Most are self-explanatory but the foot pump cock is for use in conjunction with starting the diesel engine on a locomotive with flat batteries when no control air is available to lower the shoes onto the conductor rail.

Photos: Courtesy of South West Trains.

Training Days - South West Trains

On 25th June, Chris Lemon and I trained two Bournemouth depot drivers on the Class 73 locomotive and Pat Gray needed a refresher and assessment so we all went to Bournemouth depot for the day.

In July, I had to conduct an assessment on Pat Gray for Class 159s as he'd recently learnt the traction. Pat worked the train from Basingstoke to Salisbury and relayed to me his route knowledge on the way. We then visited the Traincare depot and looked around a Class 159 unit, Pat showing and proving to me his knowledge of the unit and his training capabilities.

The Training Centre had a lot going on at the time and more work was coming our way insofar that the Bournemouth depot drivers needed to be trained on Class 458s as the depot had just been awarded a heavy maintenance contract.

Above: *Chris Lemon practising his dentistry skills again; this time on Pat Gray's molars!*

Left: *Chris explaining the low-tension cupboard layout on the Class 73 locomotive.*

Below: *Pat Gray inspecting the water level in the header tank whilst in the engine room of a Class 73 locomotive.*

Photos: The Author's Collection.

Above: The Author in the driver's seat of a Class 73/1 locomotive at Bournemouth Depot.

Below: 4VEP 3417 'Gordon Pettitt' and 4CIG 1497 at Bournemouth Depot.

Photo: The Author's Collection.

Training Days - South West Trains

As all of the trainers had worked extremely hard during the year, it was decided to close the Training Centre on 14th September 2007 and have a team day at The Great Cockcrow Railway at Lyne, near Chertsey in Surrey. The miniature railway is fully signalled with three signal boxes and one gate box to prototypical British signalling based on mid-1950's practice.

Nigel Trower who was a member of the railway group, organised the event and apart from incorporating a work element, we were also able to enjoy ourselves.

Above Top: Hardwick Central station.

Above: 'Driver' Dave Webb at the controls of U Class 1803.

Right: Cockcrow Hill Signalbox.

Opposite Page:

Top: 'Driver' David Timothy at the controls of 'Eureka'.

Middle: 'Signaller' Chris Lemon at the frame of Hardwick Central Signalbox (frame originally installed at Waterloo on the Waterloo & City Line).

Below: With red flag held steady, 'Handsignalman' Peter Connolly explains the rules.

Photos: The Author's Collection.

Training Days - South West Trains

From Left to Right: Dennis proving there's nothing in between, Nigel with his U Class and Tim in his element! A well deserved team day out on the Great Cockcrow Railway - September 2007.

Photos: The Author's Collection.

SOUTH WEST TRAINS
159

Training Days - South West Trains

The following week, David Timothy and myself returned to Petersfield to continue with our L9, L10 and A1 NVQ process and on the 10th October, I attended another SUG meeting, this time at Crewe. Some of the items discussed were as follows:

- Simulator sickness or 'motion imbalance'; crystalised ginger / wristbands given to students - perhaps improved graphics required
- Use of simulators for operational grades other than drivers
- Signaller's communications - importance of learning from them - the correct speech, etc.
- Member from Irish Rail asked the question - how do you measure whether simulators improve training practices?
- Debate on SPADS on simulators in a training environment or assessment environment
- Debate on adult learning (styles from Hugh Boyle - Southern RSSB).

It was decided to have a 'Works' Christmas party, so Chris Lemon and I organised this to take place at the Red Lion Hotel, Basingstoke on 14th December. Special awards were also given out that evening with an Award Shield for the most outstanding trainer.

Above: South West Trains Training Centre Outstanding Achievement Award Perpetual Shield.

Below: Guests of honour at the Christmas function were retired OTC South Side Trainers Mick Oakley and Fred Johnson with their respective wives.

Photos: The Author's Collection.

Above: Trainer Jez Morgan winner of the SWT Training Centre Outstanding Achievement Award Shield 2007 with Assistant Operations and Safety Training Managers Chris Lemon and Geoff Burch.

Below: Certificates of Appreciation were also awarded to Nigel Trower, Tim Reynolds and Peter Connolly.

Training Days - South West Trains

The Training Manager's post that Chris Lemon and I had been covering was advertised at the end of 2007 and Marc Sellis was the successful applicant. Marc hadn't come from a previous railway background and when he joined us on January 14th, Chris and I soon put him at ease ,showing him the ropes so to speak.

Quite a few changes were made to the Training Centre and I was kept busy during the year running Class 159, Class 455 and Class 73 courses.

It was then agreed that I could work a flexible 4-day week and invariably, I'd have the Friday off or the following Monday to make a long-weekend. Several other acting trainers were recruited and I had the job of being present on the interview panel.

Above: Changes at the Training Centre reflected on the Plasma screen and within the Welcome Pac

Left: Chris Lemon issuing instructions through a makeshift megaphone!

Left Below: Andy Nash examines the coupling bar on a Class 455.

Below: Pat Gray paddling up a shoe on a Class 455.

Below: Bottom: Class 455 contactors.

Photos: The Author's Collection.

A new position of 'Training Design Manager' had also been created and I was advised to apply.

This was not contested and meant that I had secured the position and would be given two other trainers to formulate

a Training Design team. The Class 455 fault cards issued to drivers was the first of my tasks.

The Customer Services team at White Rose Court, Woking were also going to merge with us and become 'Vocational Training' so I designed a similar welcome package for their display screen situated in their student's lounge. I also designed a welcome pack for students visiting either centre.

I was asked if I'd like to be the official photographer for the SWT Long Service & Retirement Presentations and it was also thought a good idea that students should receive a group photograph at the end of the course.

In September, we returned to the Great Cockcrow Railway for another Team Day and again had a great time.

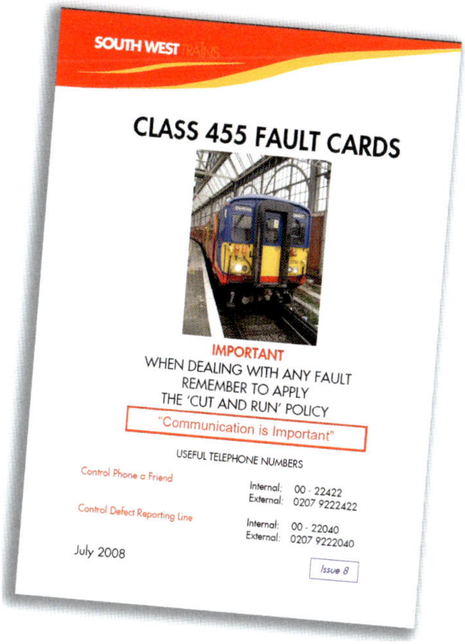

SOUTH WEST TRAINS

CLASS 455 FAULT CARDS

IMPORTANT
WHEN DEALING WITH ANY FAULT
REMEMBER TO APPLY
THE 'CUT AND RUN' POLICY

"Communication is Important"

USEFUL TELEPHONE NUMBERS

Control Phone a Friend	Internal:	00 - 22422
	External:	0207 9222422
Control Defect Reporting Line	Internal:	00 - 22040
	External:	0207 9222040

July 2008

Issue 8

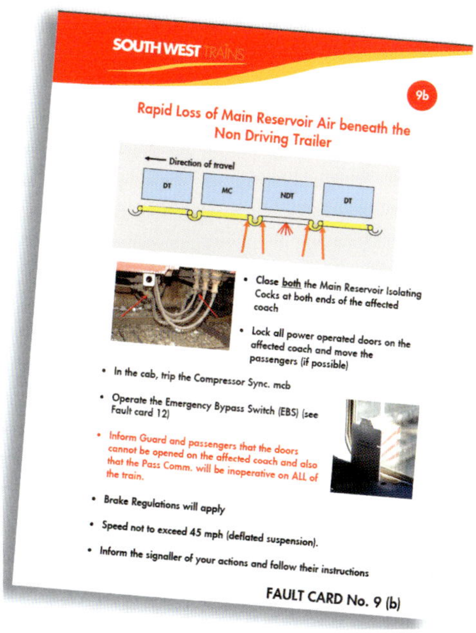

SOUTH WEST TRAINS

9b

Rapid Loss of Main Reservoir Air beneath the Non Driving Trailer

- Close both the Main Reservoir Isolating Cocks at both ends of the affected coach
- Lock all power operated doors on the affected coach and move the passengers (if possible)
- In the cab, trip the Compressor Sync. mcb
- Operate the Emergency Bypass Switch (EBS) (see Fault card 12)
- Inform Guard and passengers that the doors cannot be opened on the affected coach and also that the Pass Comm. will be inoperative on ALL of the train.
- Brake Regulations will apply
- Speed not to exceed 45 mph (deflated suspension).
- Inform the signaller of your actions and follow their instructions

FAULT CARD No. 9 (b)

Above Top Left: Standing Room only!

Photo: Matt Taylor.

Above Top and Left: Class 455 Fault Cards and just one of the faults covered in this comprehensive booklet.

Above: Les Sanders and Dave Webb discuss the Fault Card process.

Left: Les and Dave rectify the simulated fault.

Photos and Graphics: The Author's Collection.

Training Days - South West Trains

One of my tasks as Training Design Manager was to look at different ways to progress the learning process. Part of the driver's course included route learning where a trainee would be taught a particular route and asked questions about it at a later date.

Whilst learning the route (from the cab of a service train) the trainee would not only observe the route but would make notes of the various lineside features associated with it; these included signal positions, speed of line through points, crossings and junctions, and structures such as bridges, etc.

It was thought a good idea to produce a number of photographs of these features at different locations along the route. These photographs would then be shown to the trainee with the identification points removed, and the trainee would be asked to identify the location and lineside features associated with it.

In order to construct this exercise, my work colleagues Chris Lemon, Jez Morgan and I (Chris driving and Jez and I armed with our Nikon cameras) took a series of photographs from the cab of a Class 455 unit over various routes - some of the results are reproduced below and on the following page.

Above: Chris Lemon doing the driving on the Class 455.

Below: Approach to Hampton Court Junction on the Up Main Local - signal with green aspect to continue on the Up Local line. Lineside features include: (A) Vertical White Diamond sign (coasting board) (B) Permanent Speed Restriction indicator (C) Converging line from Guildford via Cobham (D) TPWS Grid (E) Horizontal White Diamond sign with black X signifies that the lineside telephone must not be used unless in an emergency (F) Signal Post Telephone - direct line to Signaller (G) Junction Indicators - (positions 4 & 5) (H) Overbridge leading to Hampton Court (I) Hampton Court Junction Substation (J) Track Circuits.

Photo: The Author's Collection.

Above: Approach to Waterloo Home Signal on the Up Main Slow line showing a signal displaying a yellow proceed aspect with Junction Indicator [3] to indicate that we have a clear route into platform 3 at Waterloo as far as the buffer stops.
Lineside features include: (A) Signal Gantry with other signals for different incoming lines (from left to right) (B) Windsor Reversible, (C) Up Windsor, (D) Up Main Relief, (E) Up Main Fast and (F) Up Main Slow (G) Position Light signals (H) Theatre Box Indicators (I) AWS Magnets (J) Track Circuits (K) Signal Number (in our case W2) (L) Waterloo SubStation.

Below: Just two pages from the Principles of Route Learning Assessment - do you know the answers?

Photos: The Author's Collection.

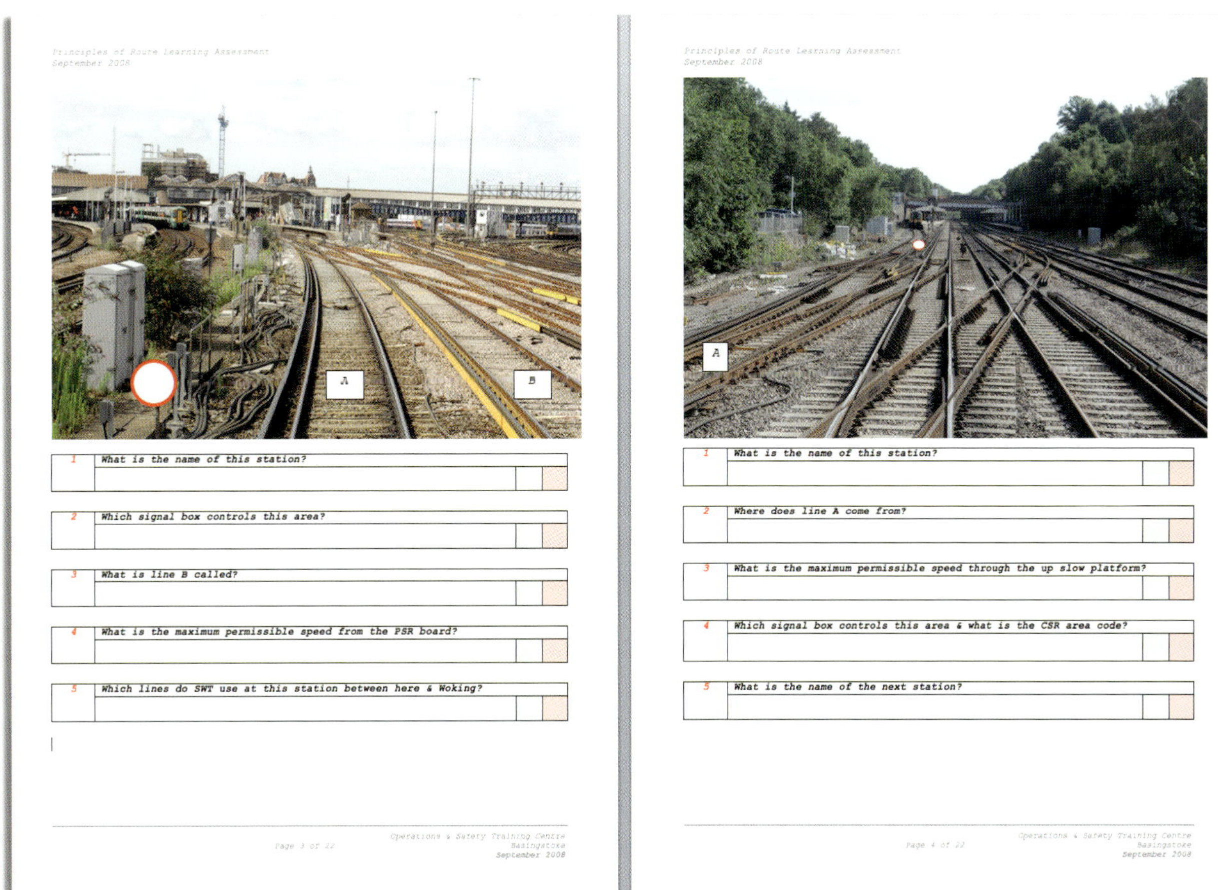

Principles of Route Learning Assessment
September 2008

1 What is the name of this station?

2 Which signal box controls this area?

3 What is line B called?

4 What is the maximum permissible speed from the PSR board?

5 Which lines do SWT use at this station between here & Woking?

Page 3 of 22
Operations & Safety Training Centre
Basingstoke
September 2008

Principles of Route Learning Assessment
September 2008

1 What is the name of this station?

2 Where does line A come from?

3 What is the maximum permissible speed through the up slow platform?

4 Which signal box controls this area & what is the CSR area code?

5 What is the name of the next station?

Page 4 of 22
Operations & Safety Training Centre
Basingstoke
September 2008

Training Days - South West Trains

Whilst visiting Salisbury Signalling Centre one day and looking at the model railway that they used as a training aid, it was decided to have one built for the Training Centre. This was duly sanctioned by Martin Peakall, Head of Operational Standards and was built and fitted by a Salisbury Signaller.

In January 2009, I performed my final Class 455 course and in February, because there was a slump in the economic climate, my job as Training Design Manager ceased to exist. Marc Sellis informed me that I still had a job as a trainer at the O&STC but I would have to return to working a 5-day week which I didn't relish. A voluntary severance package was also on offer and with some hesitation, I decided to take early retirement.

I'd enjoyed my time with South West Trains and working on the railway again and had made a lot of new friends.

Now in retirement, I've had time to write about my experiences and still keep in touch with friends and colleagues that I've had the pleasure of working with over the years. Hopefully in the future I'll probably be taking photographs of some of them again when they receive their Long Service or Retirement Awards!

Right and Below: The model layout built in 00 gauge with superb detail. A variety of incidents could be introduced to show students the implications.

Photos: The Author's Collection.

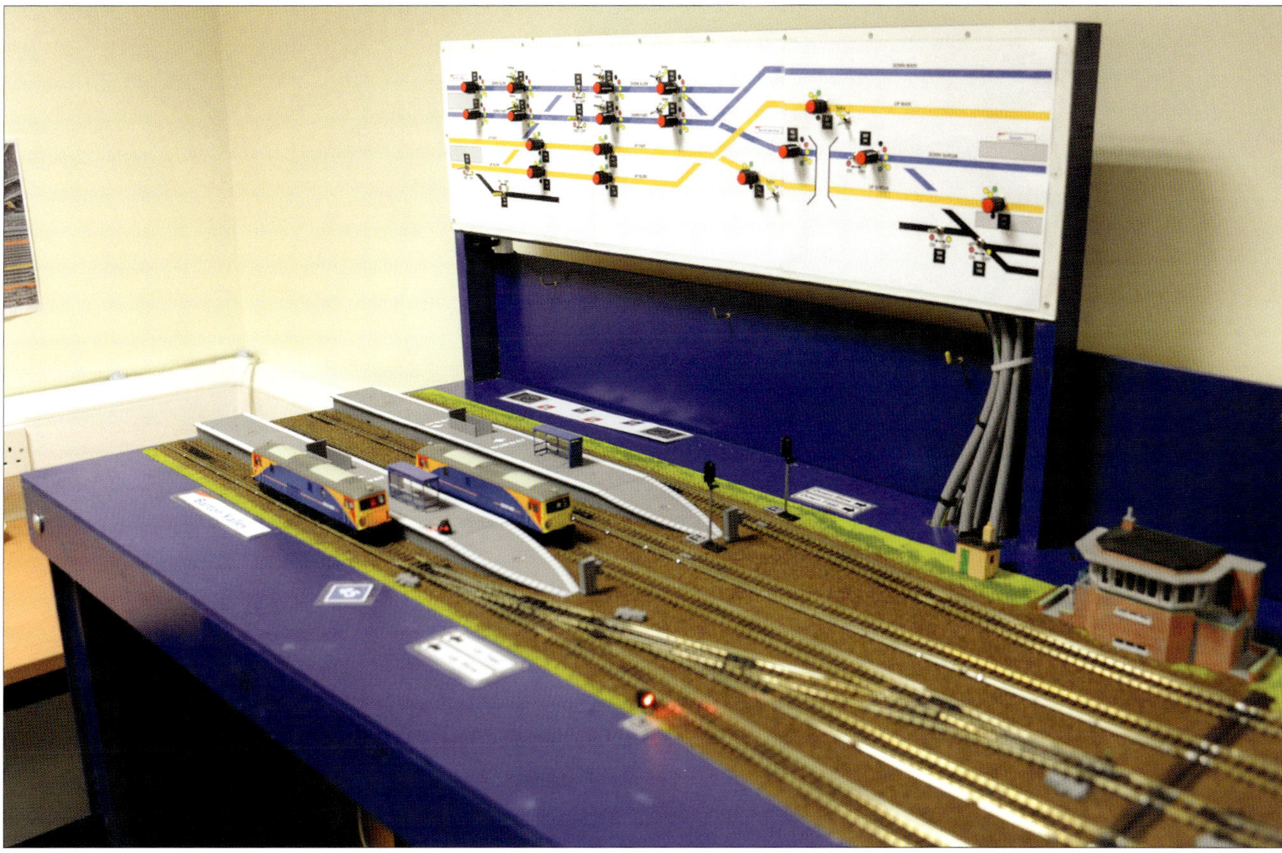

Above and Below: Two Class 73/2 locomotives in SWT liveries await signal clearance worked by the panel box. Full display of track circuits was also a feature.

Photos: The Author's Collection.

Training Days - South West Trains

Above: Claire James (Bournemouth Trainee Driver) receiving her 'award' from Trainers Dennis Birch and Chris Foot for achieving a 'perfect score' on the Final BDT Rules Assessment December 2008.

Below: Basic Driver Course BDT3 - December 2008 flanked by Trainers Dennis Birch and Chris Foot.

Photos: The Author's Collection.

Geoff Burch
Operations & Safety Training Centre
Spring Park House
Basingstoke
5th February 2009

Removal of Training Design Manager Post

Dear Marc,

Following on from our meeting yesterday, it is with regret to inform you of my decision not to accept the post of Operations Trainer that you kindly offered me.

I'd appreciate it if you would contact Andrew Welsby informing him of my final decision so that the Voluntary Redundancy process that was also offered to me can be set in motion.

I would also like to say what a pleasure it has been to work with you for the past year but feel that I wouldn't be happy staying in the training center under the present conditions imposed on us by this economic crisis.

Good luck in the future.

Yours faithfully

Geoff Burch

Above: My final letter to Marc informing him of my decision to take voluntary redundancy.

Left: Display of the posts that I held within SWT and other Rail Companies.

Photo: The Author's Collection.

SOUTH WEST TRAINS

28/02/2009

Ref: Mr Geoff Burch

To Whom It May Concern:

Mr Geoff Burch has been employed by South West Trains for the past three years, in that time his professionalism and wealth of experience has been invaluable to the organisation.

Geoff has worked in a number of important management positions including Operations Trainer, Operations & Safety Training Manager and Vocational Training Design Manager. He has approached all of his duties with a consistently high level of commitment and has always delivered excellent results. Geoff's experience and knowledge has meant he is seen as a subject matter expert and has always been willing to help and coach his colleagues. His expertise in e-learning has been a particular strength and his contribution to our e-learning capability has been dramatically enhanced thanks to his hard work.

I would happily re-employ Geoff and consider his departure a great loss to my team, his attitude to all aspects of his job is exemplary and his broad skills base means he has been able to work on a wide variety of projects from course design to Driver assessment.

Geoff is highly regarded by his colleagues and managers alike and is a well respected professional within the UK rail industry.

Yours faithfully

Marc Sellis
Vocational Training Manager
South West Trains

www.southwesttrains.co.uk

INVESTOR IN PEOPLE

Stagecoach South Western Trains Limited
Registered in England and Wales no. 5599788
Registered office: Friars Bridge Court
41-45 Blackfriars Road
London SE1 8NZ
DX 119558 Blackfriars 2
A part of Stagecoach Group plc

Above: A glowing reference from Marc Sellis, Vocational Training Manager, South West Trains on the Author's retirement.

Graphic: The Author's Collection.

Epilogue

I've designated this chapter of my book to photographs of any type of Electrical Multiple Unit (EMU), Diesel Electric Multiple Unit (DEMU) or locomotive that I've seen in my early life as a trainspotter and in my days of working on the railway that especially appealed to me.

The first shows two different types of electric locomotives that I saw at Battersea Wharf in October 1960 when I was travelling from Victoria to Clapham Junction after seeing the *'Golden Arrow'* leave Victoria (in those days steam-hauled by a gleaming Bulleid Pacific or BR Standard Class 7 'Britannia' locomotive).

I remember telling my school chums that I'd seen an blue electric locomotive with pantograph in the sidings at Battersea and they wouldn't believe me!

It wasn't until recently that I found out that E3056, the first of the AL5 Class was indeed at Battersea Wharf; standing alongside HA Class E5022 at an exhibition between 3rd and 6th October 1960. At the time, the British Transport Commission (BTC), in association with the British Electrical & Allied Manufacturers' Association and the Locomotive & Allied Manufacturers' Association of Great Britain, was staging an Electrification Conference at Battersea. No. E5022 was bound for the Southern Region and No. E3056 was destined for the LMR's newly electrified WCML service, both locomotives being products of Doncaster Works. E5022 had 2700hp which packed quite a punch for a small Bo-Bo locomotive and proved useful in both theatres of heavy freight and express passenger work.

Above: HA Class E5022 and AL5 Class E3056 that were both present at an exhibition at Battersea Wharf between 3rd and 6th October 1960.

Photo: Bob Hind Collection.

Below: British Railways Class 71 E5001 on display at the National Railway Museum, Shildon.
E5001 is an electric locomotive which could be powered either via a third rail or overhead wire. It was built in Doncaster by British Railways in January 1959. Class 71's were introduced for the Kent electrification scheme to haul freight and express passenger services and could reach 90mph.

Photo & Caption: John Simpkins.

Epilogue

Above: 'Warship' D822 'Hercules' heads through Woking with the down 'Atlantic Coast Express' (ACE) on Sunday 9th July 1967.

Photo: Bob Hind Collection.

Below: Class 74 (electro-diesel converted from HA Class 71 electric) E6109 drops back behind the signal on platform 10 at Waterloo in October 1971.

Photo: Stuart Ray.

Above: 4CEP 2317 leads the 12.23 Waterloo to Portsmouth Harbour service through a rain-lashed Worplesdon station on 13th December 2003. Being the station nearest to my home, I couldn't resist adding this photograph!

Photo: Martin Loader.

Below: Whoops! This slippery mishap between a Post Office vehicle and a 350hp shunter could have been a lot worse had the shunting locomotive not have been there!

Photo: The Author's Collection.

Epilogue

Above: 'Deltic' D9000 'Royal Scots Grey' at Woking Yard as a static display in May 1988 as part of the 'Woking 150' event.

Photo: Ian Docwra.

Below: Woking Driver Martin Peakall on a Class 37 at the same event in May 1988.

Photo: The Author's Collection.

Above: Framed by the Warren Truss Steel Bridge spanning the River Wey, two-tone green Brush Type 4 D1544 heads the 4O16 Leicester to Redhill parcels service on 1st August 1970. It has just left the London Waterloo to Portsmouth direct line at Shalford Junction near Guildford.

Photo: Gordon Edgar.

Below: Taking centre stage is DP1, the Deltic prototype at the NRM Shildon. The Deltic Prototype was built by the English Electric Company in Preston in 1955. The two 18-cylinder two-stroke engines that powered the Deltic began life as marine engines for naval patrol boats.

Photo & Caption: John Simpkins.

Epilogue

Above: *Network SouthEast liveried Class 47 No. 47707 'Holyrood' storms away from Woking with a morning Waterloo - Exeter service on 27th July 1991.*

Stabled on the up side in Hurdles Road siding are two Class 33's including 33057 and, appropriately for the location, Class 73/1 electro-diesel 73134 'Woking Homes 1885-1985'.

Photo: Gordon Edgar.

Epilogue

Above: Viewed from Ferry Lane Bridge, 4SUB 4106 heads towards Farncombe with the 11.23 Waterloo to Portsmouth & Southsea stopping service on 27th June 1969. This type of unit first appeared in 1941 and was put into service on the Victoria to Orpington line. Two motor brake second compartments sandwiched two trailer second compartment coaches, one of which had been designed as a composite. They were built with steel underframes and body panels, timber frames supporting the body panels and with a canvas roof.

This generation of 4SUBs had domed cab fronts and in that respect were similar to the 2HALS.
Woe betide any second-class passenger wanting to use the toilet on this long journey as this type of stock didn't possess one! It also didn't have any first-class accommodation.

Photo: John Scrace.

Epilogue

Above: Conceived by Oliver Bulleid for the Southern Railway's commuter route from London Charing Cross to Dartford, the two 4DD electric multiple units were the only double-deck trains to run on the main line railway network in Britain. I remember catching one of these trains from London Bridge to Hither Green for a 350hp diesel shunter course with Instructor Dave 'Spud' Tate in 1970. Here Unit No. 4902 prepares to leave Charing Cross with a Dartford via Bexleyheath service in July 1971.

Photo: Mike Morant Collection.

Below: Type 3 diesel-electric 'Crompton' D6524 heads towards Sturt Lane Junction's cleared home signal on its way to Waterloo with a passenger service on 22nd August 1964. The lower quadrant home and distant semaphore signals on the left of the gantry would allow trains onto the west spur to join the Ascot line at Frimley Junction.

Photo: David Christie.

Above: A murky morning as the 10.53 stopping service leaves Guildford from platforms 6 and 7 (up the Gulley) circa 1965. The train consists of 2x2HAL units, the leading unit being No. 2644. The headcode stencil 7 denotes the train is a stopping service to London Waterloo via Woking and will call at Worplesdon, Woking, West Byfleet, West Weybridge, Weybridge, Walton, Hersham, Esher, Surbiton and Waterloo.

Photo: Leigh Darnton.

Below: 12-Car Portsmouth Express headed by 4COR 3127 passes Peasmarsh Junction with a Waterloo - Portsmouth Harbour service on 20th June 1961 - just two months after I'd started work for British Railways. The branch line to Horsham can be seen to the right of the photograph - station stops being Bramley, Cranleigh, Baynards, Rudgwick, Slinfold, Christ's Hospital and Horsham.

Photo: Richard S Greenwood MBE.

Epilogue

Above: A Hampshire Diesel Electric Multiple Unit (DEMU) No. 1133 runs into Basingstoke on the Down Fast line to continue its journey from Reading to Southampton. This DEMU was a 3-car set and had similar cab controls to the 1957 4EPB stock and an English Electric 4-cylinder type 4SRKT 600hp engine similar to the one fitted to Class 73 locomotives. A fine array of semaphore signals for the up lines are displayed on a gantry at the London end of the platform.

Photo: Bob Hind Collection.

Below: Class 33/1's 33119 and 33106 kick up a stink as they propel a 4TC unit out of Basingstoke with the 12.12 Salisbury - Waterloo service on 17th May 1988.

Photo: Stuart Ray.

Above: The Western Region's Brown-Boveri A1A + A1A gas turbine locomotive No. 18000 propelling out of Paddington Station. I saw this locomotive at Reading on several occasions myself in the late 1950s and was nicknamed 'Kerosene Castle' on account of the aroma it always left in its wake.

Photo: Mike Morant Collection.

Below: Midland Pullman six-car diesel-electric unit at St. Pancras station on 15th June 1962. The train had two kitchens and a full meal service was provided at every seat.

Photo: Alex McClymont.

Epilogue

***Above:** Guildford station and town in the evening sunlight (looking in a southerly direction) taken from a balloon that my Dad and I were travelling in for his 70th birthday in 1988. Notice all of the trains shown with the exception of a Diesel Mechanical Multiple Unit (DMMU) forming a Redhill - Reading service on platform 8, are EMU 'slam-door', 1957 HAP and 1963 4VEP stock. The passometer (walkway) across the station which links Guildford Park Road is also receiving a facelift.*

Gone now from this aerial view is Guildford Panel Box (in the foreground) but most of the other features haven't altered except for platform 1 (down bay) that has now been lengthened to accommodate a 10-car train (2x 455 units + 1x 456 unit).

Photo: The Author's Collection.

Epilogue

Above: Class 47's (or remains thereof) and EMU coaching stock stacked up at Vic Berry's Scrapyard at Leicester on 26th August 1990. Class 47 No. 47113 had been withdrawn after an accident at Ripple Lane in 1988.

Photo: Stuart Ray.

Below: Talking of scrapyards - The Author with some of his fellow trainers from OTC South Side at a reunion in November 2012. Back row from left to right: The Author, Tim Morgan, Eric Harris, Derek Gane, Eric Christian and Bernie Byrne. Front row from left to right: Fred Johnson, Ken Norris, Don Ottignon, Cyril Sweet, Mick Oakley and John Rutter.

Photo: The Author's Collection.